AF736558

Divisions of Law

THE HISTORY AND THEORY OF INTERNATIONAL LAW

General Editors
NEHAL BHUTA
Chair in International Law, University of Edinburgh
FRANCESCA IURLARO
Max Planck Institute for Comparative and International Private Law, Hamburg
ANTHONY PAGDEN
Distinguished Professor, University of California Los Angeles
BENJAMIN STRAUMANN
ERC Professor of History, University of Zurich

In the past few decades, the understanding of the relationship between nations has undergone a radical transformation. The role of the traditional nation state is diminishing, along with many of the traditional vocabularies which were once used to describe what has been called, ever since Jeremy Bentham coined the phrase in 1780, "international law." The older boundaries between states are growing ever more fluid, new conceptions and new languages have emerged which are slowly coming to replace the image of a world of sovereign independent nation states which has dominated the study of international relations since the early nineteenth century. This redefinition of the international arena demands a new understanding of classical and contemporary questions in international and legal theory. It is the editors' conviction that the best way to achieve this is by bridging the traditional divide between international legal theory, intellectual history, and legal and political history. The aim of the series, therefore, is to provide a forum for historical studies, from classical antiquity to the twenty-first century, that are theoretically informed, and for philosophical work that is historically conscious, in the hope that a new vision of the rapidly evolving international world, its past and its possible future, may emerge.

PREVIOUSLY PUBLISHED IN THIS SERIES

The Unseen History of International Law
Mark Somos, Matthew Cleary, Pablo Dufour, Edward Jones Corredera, Emanuele Salerno

The New Haven School
American International Law
Rián Derrig

Socialism and International Law
The Cold War and Its Legacies
Raluca Grosescu, Ned Richardson-Little

Odious Debt
Bankruptcy, International Law, and the Making of Latin America
Edward Jones Corredera

A Century of Anarchy?
War, Normativity, and the Birth of Modern International Order
Hendrik Simon

The Individual in International Law
Anne Peters, Tom Sparks

Divisions of Law

Legal Science in the Iuris Universi Distributio *of Jean Bodin*

DANIEL LEE

Professor of Political Science and Law
University of California, Berkeley

OXFORD
UNIVERSITY PRESS

OXFORD
UNIVERSITY PRESS

Great Clarendon Street, Oxford, OX2 6DP,
United Kingdom

Oxford University Press is a department of the University of Oxford.
It furthers the University's objective of excellence in research, scholarship,
and education by publishing worldwide. Oxford is a registered trade mark of
Oxford University Press in the UK and in certain other countries.

© Daniel Lee 2026

The moral rights of the author have been asserted.

All rights reserved. No part of this publication may be reproduced, stored in a retrieval system, transmitted, used for text and data mining, or used for training artificial intelligence, in any form or by any means, without the prior permission in writing of Oxford University Press, or as expressly permitted by law, by licence or under terms agreed with the appropriate reprographics rights organization. Enquiries concerning reproduction outside the scope of the above should be sent to the Rights Department, Oxford University Press, at the address above.

You must not circulate this work in any other form
and you must impose this same condition on any acquirer.

Public sector information reproduced under Open Government Licence v3.0
(https://www.nationalarchives.gov.uk/doc/open-government-licence/)

Published in the United States of America by Oxford University Press
198 Madison Avenue, New York, NY 10016, United States of America.

British Library Cataloguing in Publication Data
Data available

Library of Congress Control Number: 2025946725

ISBN 9780198810483

DOI: 10.1093/9780191847806.001.0001

The manufacturer's authorised representative in the EU for product safety is
Oxford University Press España S.A. of Parque Empresarial San Fernando de Henares,
Avenida de Castilla, 2 – 28830 Madrid (www.oup.es/en or product.safety@oup.com).
OUP España S.A. also acts as importer into Spain of products made by the manufacturer.

Translation of *Iuris Universi Distributio* by Jason Aaron Brown

For Thomas

Contents

Preface and Acknowledgements

I originally encountered the *Iuris Universi Distributio* while I was preparing my study of Jean Bodin's theory of sovereignty, *The Right of Sovereignty*.[1] I instantly recognized its importance, both as an innovative work in sixteenth-century jurisprudence, as well as a valuable tool to decipher Bodin's technical legal vocabulary and doctrinal arsenal.

With this book, I invite readers, especially scholars of Jean Bodin and of the history of early modern jurisprudence, to study this unusual text and the circumstances of its origins. It is, I believe, a worthwhile academic enterprise for several reasons. The *Distributio* reveals, first of all, how much Bodin was committed to the project of laying down the foundations for a new modern legal science, a jurisprudence removed from the continuing stranglehold of classical Roman law. Partly inspired by the Ciceronian ideal of a *ius universum*, a universal "inter-national" legal system for all peoples, Bodin's work also belonged to the sixteenth-century reforms in legal pedagogy and the "internationalization" of jurisprudence.

For scholars of Jean Bodin, the *Distributio* is a vital source. Juridical concepts and doctrines were strategically interwoven into many of his published works, especially in Bodin's most important work of social and political theory, *Les Six Livres de la République*. The *Distributio* elucidates much of the legal reasoning employed in Bodin's political theory.

Perhaps the most notable feature of Bodin's *Distributio* is its original tabular form of presentation, as a "tableau du droit universel." As I will argue in Chapter 1, the *Distributio* is one of the most important examples of "legal Ramism," a style of academic jurisprudence that began to blossom in the sixteenth century, based on a logic of systematic "division" (*distributio*) applied to all the major academic fields of the early modern university. Bodin's original published version of the *Distributio*, from 1578, reveals him to be an especially visual thinker relying on a cartography of legal concepts.

What follows in this volume is a collection of papers studying various aspects of Bodin's *Distributio* and the broader context of early modern legal science. The book also includes the first full translation of Bodin's *Iuris Universi Distributio* in English, expertly prepared by Jason Aaron Brown.

* * *

[1] Daniel Lee, *The Right of Sovereignty: Jean Bodin on the Sovereign State and the Law of Nations* (Oxford: Oxford University Press, 2021).

I owe special thanks to Jason Aaron Brown who prepared an expertly crafted translation and conducted a careful comparative textual study of the 1578 and 1580 editions of the *Distributio*. His work constitutes a major scholarly accomplishment and an enormous service for scholars of Bodin and legal historians, and I am deeply grateful for his dedication to this project. This book would not have been possible without Jason's splendid textual work.

In recent years, numerous research assistants at Berkeley have supported this project at various stages, and I thankfully recognize their vital contributions to this project: Sybbil Nickerson and my undergraduate research assistants appointed through the Berkeley Undergraduate Research Apprentice Program (URAP), Solenne Bideau, Amy Guo, Nathan Martins, and Ria Utz.

Princeton University Library Special Collections was the only place in the Western Hemisphere that, to my knowledge, held the original 1578 print version of Bodin's *Distributio*. I am especially grateful to Stephen Ferguson and the Special Collections professional staff at Princeton for preparing digital images of the *Distributio* for my use during the Covid pandemic lockdowns. In the Covid aftermath, I was finally able to inspect the *Distributio* at Princeton in person in 2022, and I wish to thank Melissa Lane and the University Center for Human Values for making that research visit possible.

My academic home, the Charles & Louise Travers Department of Political Science and the Division of Social Sciences at Berkeley, made possible the completion of this project with a generous summer research grant, and I'd like to express my sincere gratitude to Susan Hyde, while in her capacity as Department Chair, and Serena Groen, Chief of Administration, for making that support possible.

Numerous colleagues have generously given their time to provide their expert advice on this project at various stages. I especially wish to acknowledge Cliff Ando, Daniela Cammack, Dominique Couzinet, Wolfgang Ernst, the late Julian Franklin, the late Ralph Giesey, Anthony Grafton, David Singh Grewal, Kinch Hoekstra, Ian Maclean, Diego Quaglioni, Richard Tuck, and the late Mario Turchetti.

The general editors for the Oxford History and Theory of International Law—Nehal Bhuta, Anthony Pagden, and Benjamin Straumann—have been ideal partners to work with, both for this title and for my previous title in this series. It is my pleasure, once again, to express my gratitude to them for their continuing support. I have also had the good fortune to work with an outstanding professional editorial team at Oxford University Press and wish to express my gratitude to the many editors involved with this title over the years, including especially during the most challenging years of the Covid-19 pandemic: Merel Alstein, Lisa Butts, Robert Cavooris, Eleanor Hanger, and Jacqueline Ridberg Larabee.

Bodin once described the family as a *communauté naturelle*, a natural association, *allies par amitié*. I am grateful for the blessings of my *communauté naturelle* and express my thanks to my family—Rebecca, Caleb, Elizabeth—as well as to my parents, Christopher and Sharon, for their continuing support over many years of my continuing research.

Series Editors' Preface

The name of Jean Bodin is not traditionally featured in the canon of legal scholarship as prominently as it is amongst the classics of political theory. One of the reasons for this disciplinary exile, as Daniel Lee puts it, is "the simple fact that he gave up" as a lawyer. While Bodin may have indeed failed to pursue a legal career, the legal implications of his theories are undeniable. Over years of research on such implications, Daniel Lee has successfully removed Bodin from his legal exile. Lee's extensive engagement with Bodin's legal theory is further witnessed by his monograph *The Right of Sovereignty*, published in 2021 in this very same series.

This book is the first English translation of Bodin's *Iuris Universi Distributio*, "A Division of Law as a Whole." It was published in 1578, two years after his most famous *Les Six Livres de la République* ("Six Books on the State"). Daniel Lee's three initial chapters serve as a robust introduction to the text, translated into English (elegantly and astutely) by Jason Aaron Brown. A thorough and informative Translator's Preface guides the reader through the editorial choices, syntactic difficulties, and semantic oscillations encountered in the translation process. An inherently visual and pedagogical project, Bodin's *Distributio* sets the foundations for a universal jurisprudence. According to a well-known intellectual tradition, deriving from Roman law and stretching all the way to contemporary studies of comparative international law, the law of nations has an essentially comparative flavor. The laws of the world can be derived by comparing and collecting the laws of the different peoples inhabiting it.

However, comparative method is easier said than done; collector's mania, in the hands of sixteenth-century jurists, easily falls victim to the tropes of their preferred literary genre, the legal commentary: exhausting accumulation and intergenerational hairsplitting. According to Lee, instead of following the traditional patterns of commenting on Justinian's civil law, "Bodin presented a deliberately heterodox system that instead reorganized the whole of jurisprudence according to the four major Aristotelian causes—formal, material, efficient, final." The title of this book itself, *Distributio*, refers to the rhetorical tradition of *inventio* and *dispositio*, that is, the idea that to organize knowledge *is* to advance knowledge. Here, organizing jurisprudence appears to be a holistic project, a retrieval of law's epistemic wholeness and integrity. However, Lee warns us, Bodin's appeal to this rhetorical tradition should not be interpreted as a homage to the humanistic tradition; quite on the contrary, as a critique of it. Thus, Bodin reduces jurisprudence to an Aristotelian architecture of causes. To interpret a wide array of heterogeneous legal sources, the jurist should look at the following criteria: what does the law look like (formal cause); what is its content (material); how does it operate (efficient), and ultimately, what is it for (final)? From this perspective, Lee's book reads as an innovative addition not only to the history of international law, but also to its intellectual connection to Aristotelianism and the rhetorical tradition.

A crucial concept of Bodin's universal theory of law is that of harmonic justice. Two are the traditional Aristotelian theories of justice: commutative justice, based on arithmetic proportion, and distributive justice, based on geometric proportion. Against this traditional dichotomy, which, if taken to the extremes, might lead to unreasonable consequences, Bodin proposes a third way called *la justice harmonique*, or harmonic justice. According to Lee, Bodin's harmonic justice is "a mixture or blend of commutative and distributive justice, inspired by the various forms of Pythagorean harmony emerging from the early modern theory of polyphonic music." In this respect, Lee quotes Gioseffo Zarlino's *Istitutioni harmoniche* (1558), one of the most important early modern treatises on harmony, in which Zarlino expounds the differences between the three types of proportions: arithmetic, geometric, and harmonic. In music theory, intervals are a form of order; think of the *diabolus in musica*, the dreaded tritone (a succession of three tonal intervals), regarded as diabolical by the Christian musical tradition. Conversely, harmony configures not only liturgy but social order as well. And, according to Bodin, jurisprudence should, too, cultivate a politics of harmony, based on a proportional harmonization of voices.

While recent studies on acoustic jurisprudence have rediscovered the aural, oratorical dimension of law, Bodin's text (and Lee's interpretative acumen) allow us to trace a textual genealogy of the idea of law as *nomos*, in the Ancient Greek sense of both "law" and "musical composition." While we might not necessarily be attracted by the promise of harmonization of all laws into a universal system—the postmodern ear being attuned to polyrhythmic dissonance, the language of "social harmony" being too often misused to silence less dominant voices—the promise of ordering reality through sound is a powerful one. Law is, ultimately, the words we speak to each other.

And speaking of sound: it is always precious to have a classic such as Bodin in translation. To have these words resonate, today, like echoes of justice past.

Francesca Iurlaro
Istanbul, September 2025

Table of Abbreviations

Works by Bodin

Colloquium	Jean Bodin, *Colloquium Heptaplomeres de Rerum Sublimium Arcanis Abditis*, ed. Ludovicus Noack (Paris: Typis Friderici Guilelmi Baerensprung, 1857).
De Republica	Jean Bodin, *De Republica Libri VI* (Paris: Jacques Du Puys, 1586).
Distributio	Jean Bodin, *Iuris Universi Distributio* (Paris: Jacques Du Puys, 1578).
Methodus	Jean Bodin, *Methodus ad Facilem Historiarum Cognitionem* (Paris: Apud Martinum Iuvenem, 1572). [Note there is a pagination error in this edition, page "141" is followed by page "242"]
Method	Jean Bodin, *Method for the Easy Comprehension of History*, trans. Beatrice Reynolds (New York: Columbia University Press, 1945).
République	Jean Bodin, *Les Six Livres de la République* (Paris: Jacques Du Puys, 1583).

Other works

Gaius	*Institutes of Gaius*, ed. Francis de Zulueta (Oxford: Clarendon Press, 1953).
Popular Sovereignty	Daniel Lee, *Popular Sovereignty in Early Modern Constitutional Thought* (Oxford: Oxford University Press, 2016).
Right of Sovereignty	Daniel Lee, *The Right of Sovereignty: Jean Bodin on the Sovereign State and the Law of Nations* (Oxford: Oxford University Press, 2021).

Roman and canon law

I have generally consulted two editions, a French and an Italian, of the *Corpus Iuris Civilis*: The Lyon 1558/1560 and the Venice *Editio Postrema* of 1569/1574, both of which would have been accessible to Bodin.

D.	*Digestum Vetus* [D.1.1.1–24.2.11] *Infortiatum* [D.24.3.1–38.17.10] *Digestum Novum* [D.39.1.1–50.17.211] *Pandectarum Iuris Civilis* (Lyon: Apud Hugonem à Porta [Hugues de la Parte], 1560). *Pandectarum, seu Digestorum Iuris Civilis*, Editio Postrema (Venice: Apud Nicolaum Bevilaqua, 1569).

C.	*Codex* [C.1.1.1–9.51.13] *Codicis Iustiniani* (Lyon: Apud Hugonem à Porta, 1560). *Codicis Dn.Iustiniani*, Editio Postrema (Venice: Apud Nicolaum Bevilaqua, 1574). *Codex* [C.10.1.1–12.64.1] *Volumen* (Lyon: Apud Hugonem à Porta, 1558).
Inst.	*Volumen* (Lyon: Apud Hugonem à Porta, 1558). *Institutiones Divi Caesaris Iustiniani*, Editio Postrema (Venice: Apud Nicolaum Bevilaqua, 1569).
Nov.	*Volumen* (Lyon: Apud Hugonem à Porta, 1558). *Novellae Constitutiones Divi Caesaris Iustiniani, Quae Authentica Vulga Appellant*, Editio Postrema (Venice: Apud Nicolaum Bevilaqua, 1569).
X.	Gregory IX, *Decretales* [*sive Liber Extra*] *D. Gregorii Papae IX* (Rome: In Aedibus Populi Romani, 1582).

Table of Figures

Editions and Translations

Jean Bodin, *Ivris Vniversi Distribvtio* (Paris: Jacques Du Puys, 1578).

Jean Bodin, *Juris Universi Distributio* (Köln: Apud Joannem Gymnicum, 1580).

Jan Kocin, *Nova Distribvtio Ivris Vniversi* (Prague: George Nigrinus, 1581).

Jean Bodin "Tableau du droit universel," in *Oeuvres Philosophiques de Jean Bodin*, ed. and trans. Pierre Mesnard (Paris: Presses Universitaires de France, 1951).

Jean Bodin, *Exposé du droit universel: Juris universi distributio*, trans. Lucien Jerphagnon, ed. Simone Goyard-Fabre (Paris: Presses Universitaires de France, 1985).

Jean Bodin, *Iuris Universi Distributio*, ed. Witold Wolodkiewicz (Naples: Jovene, 1985).

A. London Fell, *Origins of Legislative Sovereignty*, Vol. 3, *Bodin's Humanistic Legal System and Rejection of Medieval Political Theology* (Boston: Oelgeschlager, Gunn, and Hain, 1987).

Jean Bodin, *La Iuris Universi Distributio di Jean Bodin*, ed. Cecilia Pedrazza Gorlero (Rovereto: Edizioni Osiride, 1999).

Introduction: Dividing Law

Law as a Whole

The dedication of Jean Bodin's *Methodus*, his first major published work of historical scholarship, opens with a description of an earlier project he had just recently completed:

> Wise men should bring together and compare the legal framework of all states, or of the most famous states, and from them compile the best kind. To this objective I directed all my studies – all my thoughts. At the beginning I outlined in a table the form of law as a whole [*iuris universi formam*] … so that from the very sources we may trace the main types and divisions of types down to the lowest, yet in such a way that all members fit together. In this exercise, truly, I have appreciated the saying of Plato—nothing is more difficult or more nearly divine than to separate accurately. Next I have established postulates, on which the entire system rests as on the firmest foundation. Then I have added definitions. Afterward I laid down as briefly as possible precepts called "rules" according to the proposed form, as if to a norm. At one side I added, in brief notes, the interpreters of Roman law, so that from the same sources whence I have drawn, each man can take to his own satisfaction.[1]

This "form of the law as a whole in tabular representation" [*iuris universi formam… in tabula*] was a reference to a youthful work that Bodin had prepared during his time in the law faculty of the University of Toulouse as an aspiring law professor.

This was the work entitled *Iuris Universi Distributio* (for convenience, I shall hereafter refer to this work simply as the *Distributio*), which would only finally be published for the first time, nearly twenty years later in 1578, as an appendix to an early modern print edition of Azo's commentary on Justinian's *Code*.[2] From

[1] Jean Bodin, *Method for the Easy Comprehension of History*, trans. Beatrice Reynolds (New York: Columbia University Press, 1945), 2–3; Jean Bodin, *Methodus ad Facilem Historiarum Cognitionem* (Paris: Apud Martinum Iuvenem, 1572), sig.․∴.3ro. Bodin's reference to Plato is likely *Phaedrus* 266^{a}–266^{b}. Bodin would have been thirty-six years old when the *Methodus*, a work on comparative historical methodology, was first published.

[2] Azo, *Azonis ad singulas leges XII librorum Codicis Justinianei commentarius* (Paris: Apud Sebastianum Nivellium sub Ciconiis, via Iacobaea, 1577).

Divisions of Law. Daniel Lee, Oxford University Press. © Daniel Lee 2026. DOI: 10.1093/9780191847806.003.0001

Bodin's own writings, we know a good deal concerning the intended purposes of the work.

Its most remarkable feature was its grand visual presentation in tabular form. Indeed, during the French Enlightenment, this work was known as the "Tables du Droit"—the "tables of law."[3] Its succinct, economical presentation of law as a grand table, organized into conceptual divisions and subdivisions, was intended to function as a study guide for law students navigating the many topics of civil law for the first time. The original work was printed on six large folios and was probably intended to be posted up on a wall to function as a pedagogical instrument, an easily accessible reference for both teachers and students of civil law.

But Bodin's purposes in this work reached beyond pedagogy. The *Distributio* was nothing short of a preview for a system of universal jurisprudence, a visual illustration of the various parts that all complete legal systems must include. This was a far more ambitious vision than what he had been exposed to as a law student at Toulouse. Whereas the law schools of France, like the rest of early modern Europe, treated legal education and scholarship as the formal academic study of the *ius civile* (i.e., the "civil law" or *droit civil* based on classical Roman law), Bodin hoped for a reformed jurisprudence appropriate for a modern age that prioritized the *ius universum* (or *droit universel*), a Ciceronian aspiration for a universal system of law shared in common by all peoples and all nations. The *Iuris Universi Distributio* was Jean Bodin's attempt to help realize that vision in the jurisprudence of the sixteenth century.

Jean Bodin as a Jurist

This book presents a monographic study of Jean Bodin's legal science, as well as the first English translation of the *Iuris Universi Distributio*. Bodin (*ca.*1530–96) is not typically remembered in modern legal scholarship for his contributions to jurisprudence. His fame rests upon his work as a political theorist of the sovereign state, as an advocate of religious pluralism and toleration in the face of unspeakable violence fueled by zealotry, as a scholar of historical methodology, as a stern critic of monetary devaluation, as a pioneer in identifying and managing the social problem of witchcraft, and as a member (for a relatively limited period) of the royal government of the Valois monarchy. But he is not typically recognized as a jurist.

There are two reasons for this. Sixteenth-century France was a veritable golden age of jurisprudence and produced some of the most renowned jurists in all of Western legal history: François Le Douaren, Charles Du Moulin, François Baudouin, Jacques Cujas, André Tiraqueau, François Hotman, Hugues Doneau.

[3] Gilles Ménage, *Vitae Petri Aerodii, quaesitoris andegavensis, et Guillelmi Menagii, advocati regii andegavensis* (Paris: Apud Christophorum Journel, 1675), 142.

In this legal culture, Bodin very easily would have been overshadowed by his far more accomplished peers in law, exemplifying the "French school" of civil law, or the *mos gallicus ius docendi*.

The other reason why Bodin is not usually recognized as a jurist is the simple fact that he gave up. He tried to pursue a career as a legal scholar at Toulouse in the 1550s but ultimately failed. He then tried briefly in the 1560s to pursue a career as a practicing lawyer as an *avocat du roi* (a lower-ranking barrister) in the Parlement of Paris, before his patron, Guy Du Faur, Seigneur de Pibrac, positioned him elsewhere in various minor official roles in service to the Valois monarchy, just on the eve of the Massacre of St. Bartholomew.[4]

But I think it is a mistake to ignore Bodin's early work and contributions as an aspiring academic jurist. I aim to make a positive case for interpreting Bodin as a major contributor, not only to the legal culture of early modern France but also to the emerging modern aspiration for an "inter-national" legal science, for all peoples [*omnium populuorum*], and not just for the descendants and heirs of Justinian's Roman law. Such a study reinterpreting Bodin as a jurist will, I believe, be worthwhile for several reasons.

One reason is that Bodin's social and political theory was explicitly juridical. His most important work in this regard, *Les Six Livres de la République* (originally published in 1576), was the first systematic attempt to craft a theory of sovereignty, as an abstract unifying quality definitive of every independent state in history. The *République* was a work saturated with legal doctrine and citations to authorities that only a professional lawyer could produce or understand. This has presented a huge interpretive problem for modern readers of Bodin who may not be familiar with the legal arguments he is invoking nor with the sources from which he is pulling that analysis. Indeed, in some modern editions of Bodin's *République*, the extensive marginalia which signal the range of legal authorities in Roman and canon law are simply omitted.[5] Understanding the logic of Bodin's strategic legal reasoning will elucidate the sort of arguments he is trying to make about society and the state.[6]

[4] Howell Lloyd, *Jean Bodin, This Pre-eminent Man of France: An Intellectual Biography* (Oxford: Oxford University Press, 2017), 92–94.

[5] For example, the abridged edition of Bodin's *République* prepared by M. J. Tooley (Oxford: Blackwell, 1955) and by Julian Franklin, *On Sovereignty* (Cambridge: Cambridge University Press, 1992) both omit all the legal marginalia. The modern Italian edition prepared by Margherita Isnardi Parente and Diego Quaglioni, however, preserves the marginalia, converted into modern standard citations, in *I sei libri dello stato* (Turin: UTET, 1964–67). So too does the (incomplete) bilingual edition of the French and Latin texts prepared by Mario Turchetti, in *Les Six Livres de la République/De Republica Libri Six* (Paris: Classiques Garnier, 2013).

[6] I offer, as one example, Bodin's analysis of the position of magistrates, officers, and commissioners, discussed in *République* III, 2–3. Whereas commissioners held their power by way of a *precarium*, officers and commissioners held their public powers by way of an agreement, analogous to a Roman real contract such as a contract of *depositum* or of *commodatum*. See my "Office Is a Thing Borrowed: Jean Bodin on Offices and Seigneurial Government," *Political Theory* 41, no. 3 (2013): 409–40.

The other reason why I believe a study of Bodin as a jurist will prove valuable has less to do with Bodin, per se, and more to do with the academic legal culture of sixteenth-century Europe. To wit: Bodin's *Distributio* exemplifies the growing dissatisfaction among academic jurists during Bodin's lifetime with the continuing dependence upon classical Roman law, both for legal education as well as the legal reasoning of early modern courts.[7] Some were simply fed up with the strategic disfiguring of Roman legal texts performed by medieval lawyers and judges. Others—the legal humanists, discussed in Chapter 1—desired a proper restoration of the original Roman law texts to a pristine condition.

The more creative (and, arguably, more farsighted) lawyers of the sixteenth century, however, sought to move beyond the Roman law of Justinian entirely and toward a system of law that was proper, not only for ancient Romans but for all peoples of all ages. The aim was not so much *ius civile* (*droit civil*), but rather *ius universum* (*droit universel*)—the "law as a whole" or universal law.

At least, that was the ambition. Bodin's *Distributio* was one example of this effort, but it was not the only one, as we shall see in Chapter 1. Many academic lawyers of his and succeeding generations sought to construct a legal science beyond Roman law. Was this possible?

The Ideal of the *Ius Universum*

Bodin's proposed method was explicitly empirical and comparative.[8] If the goal was to construct a grand *ius universum*, it would be necessary to collect extensive raw data and inspect systematically the *ius omnium populorum*—the "law of all peoples."[9] This meant studying the legal practices and institutions, not only of the Romans, nor simply that of his native France, but of everyone.

Bodin's vision for a comparative jurisprudence was much more ambitious. He announced this vision in the opening dedication of the *Methodus*, where he unveiled his more unconventional legal sources for such a project:

[7] The reason for this dependence is easy to diagnose. The legal curriculum of the Continental European universities typically began with a year-long study of the *Institutes* of Justinian, a sixth-century work that functioned as the introductory textbook for first-year law students throughout the Middle Ages and the Renaissance. Bodin almost certainly began his legal studies at Toulouse with the *Institutes*, especially considering that Jacques Cujas was hired as a *hallebardier* when Bodin was a student at Toulouse, specifically for the purpose of lecturing on the *Institutes*.

[8] Simone Goyard-Fabre, "Commentaire philosophique de l'Exposé du Droit Universel," in Jean Bodin, *Exposé du droit universel: Juris universi distributio*, trans. Lucien Jerphangnon, ed. Simone Goyard-Fabre and René-Marie Rampelberg (Paris: Presses Universitaires de France, 1985), 167 cites Jean Moreau-Reibel's characterization of the *Distributio* as *la première recherche de droit public comparé est.* Jean Moreau-Reibel, *Jean Bodin et le droit public comparé dans ses rapports avec la philosophie de l'histoire* (Paris: Librairie Philosophique J. Vrin, 1933).

[9] The label *ius omnium populorum* is sometimes treated as equivalent to *ius gentium* as Gaius understood it in classical Roman law, the shared body of legal principles accessible to Romans and non-Roman peregrines alike.

> I collected and added the legislation [*leges*] of peoples who have been famous for military and civil disciplines ... Consideration is given to the decrees [*legibus*] of the Persians, the Greeks, and the Egyptians, no less than to the Romans. From the Pandects of the Hebrews, also, chiefly from the books of the Sanhedrin, I planned to take all the best things ... Not to be without the statutes [*leges*] of the Spanish and of the British and of all the more famous states of Italy and of Germany (for it would be endless to seek the more obscure), I trusted to be able to join them to our own at the same time. I wish that we might also possess the civil code of the Turks [*Turcarum iure civili*] ... All this material, then, approved and confirmed by the opinions of jurisconsults and historians, makes that branch of learning [i.e., jurisprudence] more famous and more worthy of honor than if it had depended upon the will of one people, the Romans – especially when our Roman material for the most part is found to be suppositions of the later Greeks.[10]

Not only, then, did Bodin look outward. Even within the boundaries of his own native France, Bodin recognized the heterogeneous and provincial character of early modern French law which also called for a comparative legal methodology. In this respect, Bodin was shaped by the pathbreaking, sometimes polemical, scholarship on the French *droit coutumier* and feudal law of his contemporaries such as Charles Du Moulin, Eguinaire Baron, Etienne Pasquier, and François Hotman.[11]

Bodin's advocacy of comparative empirical legal research, however, was not strictly academic. By studying many different legal sources and identifying salient patterns across legal traditions and contexts, Bodin thought it might be possible, in principle, to select the best and to rearrange them into a more logical pattern as the basis for a universal law for all peoples.

Such a grand project would require, however, as a preliminary step, something like a blueprint, what Bodin described in the preface to the *Distributio* "as a kind of ground-plan [ἰχνογραφίαν]," comparable to what "architects have been in the habit of making to be inspected and modeled, so that one may clearly grasp whether the edifice under construction will be long-enduring and useful." While Roman law has, for centuries, served as this ground-plan, Bodin has rejected its utility for the purpose of creating the *ius universum*.

But despite his outward disdain for Roman law, he cannot avoid it. Indeed, it provides the rudiments for organizing a prospective universal system of law.[12]

[10] *Method* 3–4; *Methodus* sig..∴.3vo–.∴.4ro.

[11] Donald Kelley, "De Origine Feudorum: The Beginnings of an Historical Problem," *Speculum: A Journal of Mediaeval Studies* 39, no. 2 (1964): 207–28; Donald Kelley, "The Rise of Legal History in the Renaissance," *History and Theory* 9, no. 2 (197): 174–94; Marie Seong-Hak Kim, "Civil Law and Civil War: Michel de l'Hôpital and the Ideals of Legal Unification in Sixteenth-Century France," *Law and History Review* 28, no. 3 (2010): 791–826.

[12] Bodin, of course, understands that, in the later centuries of Roman history, Roman law itself was no longer simply the *ius civile* exclusive to the Romans, but an "international" *ius gentium* inclusive of those peregrine peoples conquered by the Romans and subdued under its imperium.

The *Distributio* will be familiar to anyone who has already studied Roman law—especially in its substantive legal principles and the legal language lifted directly from Justinian.

What must be stressed at the outset is that Bodin does not take Roman law wholesale. Justinian's Roman law is the disfigured patient on which Bodin will perform reconstructive surgery. The intellectual challenge was to present the law in a more logical, rational form while preserving its substance. And the key to this strategy was proper division, or *distributio*.

Distributio: A "Right Division"

Jean Bodin's *Distributio* belongs to a genre of early modern legal scholarship that I will call, in Chapter 1, "Legal Ramism." Named after the French pedagogical reformer, logician, and philosopher, Pierre de la Ramée (Ramus), Ramism was a reform movement in the universities of the sixteenth century, targeting especially the traditional pedagogical methods of Scholastic Aristotelianism. Chapter 1 explores how this Ramist reform movement spilled over into the law faculties of early modern France and, eventually, beyond.

Since the twelfth century, formal legal education and scholarship in the universities of Continental Europe had centered primarily on the classical Roman law of Justinian, as well as the accumulated glosses, commentaries, and *consilia* of the Italian Bartolists. Law students of the European *ius commune* beginning their legal training, typically with a close study of Justinian's *Institutes*, were introduced to a bewildering set of distinctions in the law: *ius naturale*, *ius gentium*, *ius civile*; persons, things, actions; civil and praetorian remedies; delictal and contractual obligations; *ius civile* and *ius gentium* methods of conveying property ownership. And so forth. These distinctions were drilled into the unfashioned minds of legal novices (and, even today, law schools in the Civil Law world continue, to varying degrees, to follow this curricular pattern).

The University of Toulouse, Bodin's alma mater and one of the leading centers of legal education and scholarship in early modern France, was no exception. But Toulouse of the sixteenth century was a law faculty undergoing a period of rapid intellectual transformation, due to the complaint that Justinian's system was arbitrary and lacked a transparently logical order.

A new genre of academic scholarship thus began to appear in the sixteenth century. Inspired by the techniques of Ramism, these legal "systematists" sought to dismantle the form of Justinian's system and reconstruct the civil law according to a more logical, rational pattern, following Ramist (and ultimately Ciceronian) principles of *inventio* and *distributio*—discovery and division. These included academic lawyers such as Eguinaire Baron, François Connan, Hugues Doneau, and Jean Domat.

Jean Bodin's *Distributio* belonged to this genre and school of legal Ramism which reconstructed the whole of civil law, the *ius universum*, according to a "right division" [*in recta divisione*]. Instead of following the traditional patterns in Justinian's civil law, Bodin presented a deliberately heterodox system that instead reorganized the whole of jurisprudence according to the four major Aristotelian causes—formal, material, efficient, final.

The Formal Cause: The first *distribuenda* of jurisprudence in Bodin's system was the formal cause. Here, Bodin offers a typology of law (in the broad generic sense of *ius* or the French, *droit*). One of the most striking features of Bodin's system is his rejection of the classical tripartite division of Justinian (D.1.1.1) into natural law [*ius naturale*], the law of nations [*ius gentium*], and civil law [*ius civile*]. Instead, he classifies all law, first, according to the *summa divisio* distinguishing between *ius naturale* and *ius humanum*, in a "dichotomy" [διχοτομία]. The latter category of "human law" is, then, secondarily subdivided into *ius gentium* and *ius civile*.[13]

Not only does this typology indicate the influence of the Ciceronian project of "reducing the law into a science" [*ius in artem redigendo*], it shows conclusively that Bodin was not a legal positivist, à la John Austin, who treated all valid law simply as the legislative command of a sovereign. Of course, as Bodin emphasizes in his most important work on sovereignty, the *République*, sovereigns can make and unmake positive law—a broad category which includes legislation [*lex*], special privileges, and edicts enacted by authorized subordinate magistrates. This is, indeed, the essence of a sovereign's "absolute power."[14] But not all law is the product of human legislation. Some laws originate in the agreement of all peoples [*consensus omnium gentium*] and in natural reason [*ratio naturalis*]. These cannot be altered or abrogated simply by an arbitrary sovereign act of will.

One final notable feature of Bodin's typology is the division between public law and private law. While Justinian acknowledges this division too (Inst.1.1.4; D.1.1.1.2), civil law almost in its entirety concerns private law. To be sure, Ulpian famously defines and acknowledges public law as that area of law concerning "sacred matters, priests, and magistrates" [*in sacris, in sacerdotibus, in magistratibus*], all of which were regarded as public responsibilities of the Roman state. But as a matter of legal science, public law was a negligible area of law. Bodin, by contrast, regards *ius publicum* as that area which concerns the public advantage [*utilitatem*], including legislation, the creation of magistrates, matters of war and peace, and rewards and punishments. It is the raw material from which Bodin will craft his own theory of sovereignty.

[13] This is, incidentally, the same basic legal typology as in Grotius at *De Jure Belli ac Pacis Libri Tres* (Amsterdam: Iohannes Blaeu, 1646), 3–7 [I, 1, §§9–15]. While I am not claiming that Bodin was a source or a direct influence on Grotius, it is important to note that Grotius did not originally create this system. The one important difference is the absence of divine positive law in the *Distributio*.

[14] Lee, *Right of Sovereignty*, 151–63.

The Material Cause: The second *distribuenda*, the material cause of jurisprudence, concerns the substance of law, and Bodin identifies three principal material causes: persons, things, and the deeds [*facta*] of persons. Students of Roman law will likely find this arrangement familiar, as it is patterned after Gaius's *summa divisio*:

> **D.1.5.1:** *Omne autem ius quo utimur vel ad personas pertinent vel ad res vel ad actiones.*
>
> The whole of the law observed by us relates either to persons or to things or to actions.[15]

The resemblance, however, is superficial, for what Bodin offers in the *Distributio* is a complete reworking of the substantive areas of civil law that extends beyond the limited context of the Roman Empire.

One example is the discussion of the law of persons. Legal personality in classical Roman law was based on three principal constituent elements—*libertas* (whether one's status was free or slave), *civitas* (whether one was a Roman or peregrine), and *familia* (whether one's position within a family was *sui iuris* or *alieni iuris*). Bodin interpreted personality somewhat differently—constituted by sex, by status, and by dignity. The last of these three is the most original and reflects what Bodin likely saw as a historical limitation of Roman law—namely, that it is the fossilized legal artifact of an ancient slaveholding society. For France, whose people were "frank and free" and never, so it was thought, had endured the burden of slavery, Roman law was fundamentally limited. Bodin's solution was to introduce a category of personality *ex dignitate*, indicating the various ways in which social rank, class, and function positioned the members of a society hierarchically, without invoking slavery.[16]

The most notable feature of Bodin's material causes was his treatment of "deeds" [*facta*]. In general, the law of deeds captured what Justinian and Gaius both classically refer to as the law of obligations—both contractual and delictal. But, whereas obligations were regarded as a branch of the law of things [*res*] in the classical system of Gaius and Justinian, Bodin created a whole new category for these obligations and their related transactions, separate from "things." His synthetic approach illustrates the deliberate choices that Bodin made in mapping a new universal legal system.

One example, which will be discussed in Chapter 2, is the three-way division of agreements by bare consent, by verbal stipulation, and by "synallagmatic" bilateral obligation. Not only does he show the direct influence of other legal Ramists, especially François Connan, his system anticipates the transformation of the law of

[15] Gaius 1.8.
[16] Cf. Lee, *Right of Sovereignty*, 133–34.

contracts away from the "nominate" system of ancient law, toward a general system that acknowledges even "innominate" contracts as binding.

The Efficient Cause: The efficient cause is the third *distribuenda* of Bodin's *Distributio*, and it is perhaps the most technically complicated aspect of Bodin's jurisprudence. As Bodin explains, the *efficientes* concern the execution of the law in disputes litigated in court before a judge. While it includes what Gaius regarded as "actions" and "exceptions"—legal remedies pursued in court by means of a lawsuit and subsequent legal defenses—it is much broader than simply the study of formal actions and exceptions. It concerns the function of courts and of judges—as Cicero once famously put it, *leges loquentes*.[17]

A recurring distinction, and one of the most perplexing, in Bodin's corpus of theoretical writing appears under this heading—that is the distinction between *legis actio* and *officium iudicis*.[18] Whereas the latter refers to a judge's role in ensuring equity beyond the limits of the law, the former indicates everything a judge may legally be empowered to do in court, whether in contentious or voluntary exercises of jurisdiction. These include those functions requiring the authority of a court [*imperium*], the judicial decision-making role of a court [*iurisdictio*], and the enforcement role of a court [*executio*].

As we will see in Chapter 2, much of this discussion derives from the humanist legal scholarship of the sixteenth century that attempted to make sense of the relationship between these concepts. Bodin's discussion of *legis actio* was patterned after the humanist attempt to reconstruct the major stages of a trial.

One takeaway from this discussion is just how seriously Bodin took the rule of law. Far from the caricature of Bodin's sovereign ruling subjects according to absolute and arbitrary will, Bodin's sophisticated understanding of the elements of legal process indicates the function of courts, to insulate a sovereign's arbitrary will through the medium of law.

The Final Cause: The fourth and final *distribuenda* concerns the teleological aim of jurisprudence. It is the shortest part of the *Distributio*, but also the most theoretically illuminating aspect of Bodin's entire system because it touches upon a feature of Bodin's thought that is typically ignored—his theory of justice.

This brief closing section defines justice, following Ulpian (D.1.1.10.pr), as "the rendering to each his due" [*iustitia suum cuique tribuens*]. Classical ethics typically distinguished between two main types of justice—commutative and distributive—reflecting two correspondingly different ways of interpreting what is "due," either according to strict legal equality or according to proportionally meritorious equity.

[17] Cicero, *De Legibus*, trans. Clinton Walker Keyes, Loeb Classical Library 213 (Cambridge: Harvard University Press, 1928), 460 [III, i, §2].

[18] Cf. *Methodus* 263 [VI, s.v.: *Quid summum imperium*]; *République* 440.

The distinctive feature of this final section, however, is Bodin's thesis that justice can take one of three forms, what he calls the "three daughters of Themis." Each of these three forms of justice corresponds to three mathematical proportions—the arithmetic, the geometric, and the harmonic proportions. The goal of law should be, in Bodin's view, what he calls "harmonic justice," which becomes the mathematical foundation for his vision of the ideal form of state.

Structure of the Book

The book is organized into three chapters.

Chapter 1, on "Legal Science and Legal Ramism," opens with a study of the historical context of the *Distributio* and the rise of "legal Ramism" in sixteenth-century France. I argue that the *Distributio* should not be understood as a specimen of humanist legal scholarship, but rather as a critical reaction to humanism, by offering an attempt to transform civil law into a proper methodical science.

Chapter 2, "Divisions of Law," offers a close textual study of the first three parts of the *Distributio*, covering the formal, material, and efficient causes of jurisprudence.

Chapter 3, "Harmonic Justice," concludes with a study of Bodin's theory of justice. Bodin advised his readers that the concluding part of the *Distributio* on justice should be studied in conjunction with "the final chapter of Book VI of *De Republica*."[19] As I will show, Pythagorean music theory and early modern ideas of polyphony not only shaped Bodin's theory of justice, they also served as a metaphor to explain social harmony in law as well as in the form of government. Bodin's influence evidently endured into the seventeenth century—most notably, in the work of the mathematician and astronomer, Johannes Kepler, who wrote a critical response to Bodin's theory of harmonic justice in the *Harmonices mundi*. Perhaps the most enduring normative thesis of Bodin's work is the tie made between sovereignty and justice: Only a harmonically governed sovereign state can realize justice.

I will conclude this study in a short Epilogue with a word on how legal divisions and typologies contributed to transformations of early modern jurisprudence, with consequences beyond the legal profession and the origins of a genre of "universal jurisprudence."

Included in this volume is the first English translation of the *Distributio*, prepared by Jason Aaron Brown. Unlike earlier modern editions of the *Distributio*

[19] Howell Lloyd claims that this reference to *De Republica* VI appeared only in the 1580 version of the *Distributio*. Lloyd is incorrect. The same comment appears in a marginal note of the 1578 *Distributio* fol. F. Lloyd, *Jean Bodin*, 62.

which rely on the 1580 Köln edition published by Joannes Gymnicus (such as the 1985 French edition by Lucien Jerphagnon and Simon Goyard-Fabre), the present translation relies on the tabular arrangement of the 1578 Paris edition published by Bodin's publisher, Jacques Du Puys, to correct inaccuracies and, thus, preserve the logic of Bodin's intended order.

1
Legal Science and Legal Ramism

Introduction

Jean Bodin's *Iuris Universi Distributio* ("A Division of Law as a Whole") was first published in 1578 by his Parisian publisher, Jacques Du Puys, two years after the appearance in print of his most important work of political theory, *Les Six Livres de la République* ("Six Books on the State"). It belongs to a technical sixteenth-century legal literature that attempted to rearrange civil law and jurisprudence in a more systematic and accessible fashion for the lay reader.

However, even though it was published in 1578, Bodin most likely wrote the *Distributio* decades earlier, in the late 1550s, when he was an aspiring law professor teaching civil law in the University of Toulouse, Bodin's own alma mater. The unusual work represented, in the words of one commentator, a "stock-taking of his legal studies up to that date, a sketch of what had been accomplished [and] what remained to be done."[1]

Why did Bodin write the *Distributio*? My goal in this chapter will be to explore some of the intellectual context of the *Distributio*, in order to understand better his motivations for writing such a work. In summary, Bodin wanted to make a bold statement about the universality of jurisprudence and the conceptual structure of all historical legal systems, whether French, Roman, or otherwise. In part, the *Distributio* functioned as a criticism of the continuing dependence on Roman law in the universities. But it was also a demonstration of the pedagogical value of loosening Justinian's stranglehold on the early modern legal curriculum and habits of legal reasoning, so as to enable the creation of a new modern legal science.

This chapter will begin, first, with an investigation of the contextual background of Jean Bodin's legal study at Toulouse. Toulouse of the sixteenth century exemplified the crossroads of Western legal science, representing, on the one hand, the decline of the medieval jurisprudence championed by Bartolus of Sassoferrato

[1] John L. Brown, *The Methodus ad Facilem Historiarum Cognitionem of Jean Bodin: A Critical Study*, Ph.D. Dissertation (Washington, DC: The Catholic University of America Press, 1939), 25–6. Bodin's comment in the opening dedication of the *Methodus* confirms that the *Distributio* antedates the *Methodus*. Howell Lloyd, by contrast, has suggested that the work is, at least partly, a product of Bodin's years in Paris. Howell Lloyd, *Jean Bodin, This Pre-eminent Man of France: An Intellectual Biography* (Oxford: Oxford University Press, 2017), 56.

Divisions of Law. Daniel Lee, Oxford University Press. © Daniel Lee 2026. DOI: 10.1093/9780191847806.003.0002

(1313–57) and his pupils, and, on the other hand, the "French school," or *mos gallicus*, of humanist jurisprudence that would blossom in sixteenth-century France. The style of legal reasoning represented by these "Bartolists" will become the target of humanist jurists who would come to dominate the law faculties of the French universities, especially in the law faculty of the University of Bourges. The chapter will then recount Bodin's experience at Toulouse, both as student and as a teacher of law. It is very likely that his own personal frustrations in teaching civil law may have inspired him to write the *Distributio*, as an attempt to systematize the whole of civil law into a more orderly and accessible area of study for the student. Following the pedagogical methods of Pierre de la Ramée [Ramus], reducing a complex subject such as jurisprudence through *inventio* and *distributio*, Bodin presented in this work a Ramist *distributio* of law, a specimen of a growing legal literature that I propose calling "legal Ramism."

The Decline of Bartolist Legal Science

Jean Bodin studied civil law [*droit civil* or *droit écrit*; *ius civile*]—that is, Roman law—at the University of Toulouse, one of the preeminent law faculties and an international center for legal scholarship in *Ancien Régime* France. He likely arrived at Toulouse in 1550, after being released from the monastic vows he had taken in his youth with the Carmelite Order, and resided in Toulouse, on and off, for about a decade (with the exception of a possible voyage to Geneva and Lyon in 1552–53).[2]

Toulouse, like most universities in early modern Europe, focused on Roman law, the "learned law" that was the cornerstone of medieval legal science. Together with medieval canon law and feudal law, Roman law constituted the skeletal structure of the *ius commune*—that is, that body of law shared in common among all nations of Western Christendom.[3] Roman law was the standard point of entry into this venerable legal science. It was a legal science to which Bodin dedicated years of study at Toulouse.

A set of practical problems, however, faced both teachers and students of civil law. Their principal textbooks—the *Institutes*, *Digest* (or *Pandects*), *Code*, and *Novels* (or *Authentica*) of Justinian, altogether comprising what is now collectively

[2] Brown, *Methodus* 2. Bodin likely arrived in Toulouse in 1550, although one commentator has dated his arrival in 1548. Roger Chauviré, *Jean Bodin, auteur de la République* (Paris: Librairie Ancienne Honoré Champion, 1914), 20.

[3] The European *ius commune* must not be confused with English "Common Law." Civil and canon law, together, were simply known as the "Two Laws," and their practitioners, such as Baldus de Ubaldis, credentialed in both areas were degreed, J.U.D. (*juris utriusque doctor* or "doctor of both laws"). On the legal culture of the medieval *ius commune*, see especially the useful study of Manlio Bellomo, *The Common Legal Past of Europe, 1000–1800* (Washington, DC: The Catholic University of America Press, 1995).

called the *Corpus Iuris Civilis* ("the body of civil law")—were not only massively voluminous texts. They were also very ancient texts, fossilized archaic remnants of a long-dead, slaveholding civilization. Why would sixteenth-century French lawyers want to study a "dead law" like Roman law?

One answer might be constructed by way of analogy: Just as scholars of literature and rhetoric in the Renaissance benefited from the study of dead languages, such as classical Greek and Latin, so too did scholars of law believe they might similarly benefit from the study of a "dead law," like Roman law. Justinian's *Corpus* of civil law, thus, carried enormous pedagogical value for lawyers in training by gently forcing students to absorb the casuistry of the ancient jurisconsults and reason like a Roman praetor or judge in resolving cases as mundane as a property dispute or a commercial transaction involving a contract of sale. Roman law was, according to this view, not a "dead law." It was very much "alive" and a vibrant source of early modern jurisprudence accessible to courts, such as the Parlements of the *pays du droit écrit* in the South of France.

Jurists sometimes went even further in their veneration of Roman law, bestowing upon it the title of *ratio scripta* (i.e., the written embodiment of reason itself). Justinian's text, according to this view, was more than a historical artifact, a time-bound product of Roman-Byzantine jurists in the sixth-century court of the Emperor Justinian. Instead, Roman law itself was a window into timeless legal values and concepts, shaped by a universal reason accessible to all peoples, Roman or otherwise.

This attitude can be traced to the High Middle Ages, when Italian jurists, upon discovering an authentic surviving manuscript of Justinian's *Corpus Iuris Civilis* (now known as the *littera Florentina*) in the eleventh century, introduced scholars to a new style of legal reasoning, touched by *aequitas naturalis* (natural equity) itself.[4] These "Glossators" (so called because they recorded their legal reasoning in the form of marginal and interlinear "glosses" scattered throughout copies of Justinian's text) took the first steps in elevating the study of Roman law into a proper legal science.[5] Roman law was no longer simply a law for Romans. It gradually became a law shared in common among all peoples, or *gentes*, the fertile ground for a *ius commune*.

The Glossators, such as Azo, Accursius, and Odofredus, laid the groundwork for engineering a legal system based on the *Corpus Iuris Civilis*. Their many achievements include the principle *actiones a iure civili* and (particularly relevant for Bodin) the Glossatorial interpretation of *princeps legibus solutus* in conjunction

[4] D.2.14.1.pr: *Huius edicti aequitas naturalis est.*

[5] Kenneth Pennington has described this moment as the "Big Bang" of Western jurisprudence. Pennington, "The Big Bang: Roman Law in the Early Twelfth Century," *Rivista internazionale di diritto commune* 18 (2007): 43–70.

with the *Digna vox*, limiting the emperor's authority.[6] Collectively, the accumulated glosses were standardized as the *Glossa Ordinaria* and routinely included in volumes of Justinian's Roman law texts for academic study and interpretive guidance for practicing lawyers and judges.

These Glossators, however, were to be succeeded—and perhaps even overshadowed—by their fourteenth-century successors, the "Commentators" (so called because of their tendency to record their legal teachings in the form of topical "commentaries") or simply "Post-Glossators." In this effort, one name towers above all other practitioners of medieval jurisprudence—Bartolus of Sassoferrato (1313–57). So dominant was his influence over the medieval legal profession of the European *ius commune* that his later followers, such as Baldus de Ubaldis (1327–1400), Paul de Castro (d.1436), and Giasone del Maino (1435–1519), were dubbed "Bartolisti." Among lawyers, it became a common refrain: "*Nemo iuristi nisi Bartolisti*" ("No one is truly a jurist, unless they are Bartolists").

Bartolus died young—at forty-four years of age. Yet, during those years, he produced a vast body of work, while perched in the chair of civil law at Perugia, in the form, not of glosses, but of extensive commentaries on Justinian's lawbooks, topical treatises, and consilia (a specialized genre of legal opinions in medieval civil law), all of which would radically transform and creatively widen the possibilities of applying Roman law to legal problems arising in a post-Roman world.

Probably the most famous example of such Bartolist repurposing of Roman law concerned the legal doctrines governing the *imperium* (the supreme authority) of the Roman *princeps* (emperor), a topic of central importance for Bodin's own theory of sovereignty.[7] The *Digest*, at D.1.3.31, famously declared the emperor's immunity from laws of his own making: *Princeps legibus solutus est.* Bodin would later lean heavily on this principle of *legibus solutus* in developing his own theory of absolute power, and he did so by detaching the *legibus solutus* principle from its Roman imperial origins, so that it might become the core of a modern general theory of state sovereignty.[8]

Bartolus, for his part, observed that Ulpian assigned such legal immunity explicitly and exclusively to Roman emperors—the *principes.* That historical fact alone raised an important interpretive question concerning scope of application: Could anyone or anything else claim to be, like the Roman emperors of Antiquity, *legibus soluti*? The answer to this question ultimately depended on how strictly one read the Roman law text. The title of *Princeps* could be understood to mean, even in the

[6] *Glossa Ordinaria* ad D.1.1.5, in v.*obligationes*; ad D.1.3.31 in v.*princeps legibus*. Brian Tierney, "The Prince Is Not Bound by the Law: Accursius and the Origins of the Modern State," *Comparative Studies in Society and History* 5 (1963): 378–400.

[7] Bodin cited Bartolus and his most famous pupil, Baldus de Ubaldis, extensively as his most important authorities on interpreting D.1.3.31. Ralph Giesey, "Medieval Jurisprudence in Bodin's Concept of Sovereignty," in *Jean Bodin: Verhandlung der Internationalen Bodin Tagung in München*, ed. Horst Denzer (Munich: Verlag C.H. Beck, 1973), 174.

[8] Lee, *Right of Sovereignty*, 94–99.

Trecento in which Bartolus lived, a Roman emperor, a legal title claimed by the Holy Roman Emperor who, in practice, was an elected German king. The implication, however, was that no one else, besides a proper Roman emperor, could claim such an exclusive immunity.

Such a strict interpretive posture concerning who could lawfully claim the title and the immunities of the *Princeps* had potentially devastating consequences for nations starting to assert their own independence and something like Bodinian sovereignty.[9] Couldn't national monarchies, like the kings of France and England who recognized no superior, view their own kings also to be *legibus soluti*? Similarly, couldn't free cities and republics (i.e., "freed" from the authority of the Emperor or some other foreign power) like Perugia, Bartolus's home city, also enjoy immunities approximating the Roman *princeps*?

The answer for Bartolus was "Yes."[10] Bartolus was a vocal Guelph partisan of the civic culture of the Italian city-republics and their political independence from the pretensions of foreign powers, such as the Germanic emperor, who styled himself a Roman *princeps* and claimed a historical de jure title as King of Italy.[11] Independent republics like the great Italian cities, or *civitates*, such as Perugia, Florence, Lucca, Pisa, and Siena, all made their own laws and could be regarded as *legibus soluti*.

But the law of Justinian's *Digest* was very clear: Only a *princeps*—and nothing else—can be *legibus solutus*. So, how can a city, like Perugia, claim that immunity? Bartolus's simple solution, which has been described as the "crowning step" in Bartolus's political theory, involves an ingenious reinterpretation of *Princeps*: *Civitas sibi princeps est* ("A free city is a *princeps* unto itself.").[12] What makes a *civitas* a *sibi princeps* is its de facto independence to do the sort of things that a *princeps* can do in civil law—above all, to make new law and to exercise jurisdiction of final appeal. The latter provides one opportunity for Bartolus to make his point:

[9] The Duchy of Milan, under the rulership of the Visconti and the Sforza, presented an important case to test whether the Duke was a sovereign *princeps* or merely a subordinate of the Holy Roman Emperor. Numerous observers of Renaissance Italian politics such as Baldus, Machiavelli, and Bodin commented extensively on Milan, although they arrived at different conclusions. Bodin denied Milanese sovereignty, whereas Machiavelli did not hesitate to regard the new regime created by Francesco Sforza, precipitating the fall of the Golden Ambrosian Republic, as an independent state under the rule of a *principe nuovo*. Bodin, *République*, 213–14; *De Republica* 148–49 [I, 10]. On the case of Milan, see Jane Black, *Absolutism in Renaissance Milan: Plenitude of Power under the Visconti and the Sforza* (Oxford: Oxford University Press, 2009).

[10] Lee, *Popular Sovereignty*, 67–73.

[11] Bartolus explored these themes in his political tracts, *De tyranno*, *De regimine civitatis*, and *De Guelphis et Gebellinis*. These are collected in a modern critical edition by Diego Quaglioni, *Politica e diritto nel Trecento Italiano: Il De Tyranno di Bartolo da Sassoferrato* (Florence: L.S. Olschki, 1983).

[12] C. N. S. Woolf, *Bartolus of Sassoferrato: His Position in the History of Medieval Political Thought* (Cambridge: Cambridge University Press, 1913), 160; Joseph Canning, *Political Thought of Baldus de Ubaldis* (Cambridge: Cambridge University Press, 1987), 96. Bartolus of Sassoferrato, *In I^{am} Digesti Veteri Partem Commentaria* (Lyon, 1544), ad D.5.3.30; D.4.4.3; Bartlous of Sassoferrato, *Commentaria in II^{am} Digesti Novi Partem* (Lyon: Excudebat Petrus Fradin, 1555), ad D.48.19.4.

> If there is an appeal from the highest tribunal in the city, it will necessarily go to the city's superior. But supposing, as seems to be the case, that this city accepts and recognizes no superior? Then it must be its own superior [*sibi princeps*].[13]

It was precisely this palpable mismatch between the textual de jure formality and the observable de facto reality which opened new possibilities for Bartolus to use Roman law to introduce a creative jurisprudence for a post-Roman world.[14]

This Bartolist tradition of legal learning thrived in the universities and courts of the fifteenth century, a veritable golden age of European legal science. Its prophets were the leading jurists of the later Middle Ages, Baldus de Ubaldis, Paul de Castro, Alexander Tartagnus de Imola [Alexander Imolensis] (1424–77), and Giasone del Maino, authorities that Bodin will cite extensively as his own authorities in the *République*.[15]

But the dominance of Bartolist jurisprudence didn't last long. The Bartolism practiced in the universities and the law courts quickly became a target of active criticism starting in the closing decades of the fifteenth century. In part, this was due to increasing doubts that Roman law, the law of an ancient slaveholding civilization, could represent a universal *ratio scripta* for free peoples, as well as the realization that Roman law could no longer serve as a shared international *ius commune* among nations nurturing different legal customs and histories.

The more important reason for the decline of Bartolism, however, originated in the growing suspicion that lawyers and judges practicing a Bartolist style of jurisprudence routinely abused Roman law, mangling and twisting the texts into an unrecognizable form to suit their present juristic needs, especially in the practical context of litigation and pleading. The legal science practiced by Bartolists was not, in their view, really Roman law at all, but instead a monstrous abomination, using the classical law and legal language of Justinian.

A good illustration of this alleged abuse of Roman law was the Bartolist "tree of jurisdictions," which accompanied the *l.Ius dicentis* in the *Digest* (D.2.1.1), and would attract Bodin's attention, as we will see again later in Chapter 2.[16] Originally, in classical Roman law, this title dealt with the legal complexities arising from the appointment and authority of judges to hear and decide a legal dispute under the formulary system. The Roman formula involved a sort of legal division of labor. Litigants brought their case initially to the relevant magistrate—usually, one of the praetors—whose chief pre-trial function would be to draw up a document, called

[13] Reproduced from Magnus Ryan, "Bartolus of Sassoferrato and the Free Cities," *Transactions of the Royal Historical Society*. Sixth Series 10 (2000): 77, n.40, quoting Bartolus ad D.49.1.1.
[14] Quentin Skinner, *The Foundations of Modern Political Thought* (Cambridge: Cambridge University Press, 1978), 1:9–11.
[15] Giesey, "Medieval Jurisprudence in Bodin's Concept of Sovereignty," 174–77.
[16] Lee, *Popular Sovereignty*, 96–98.

the formula, summarizing, as joinder of issue [*litis contestatio*], the chief legal questions to be tried.[17]

However, the praetor did not personally hear or preside over the case. That function was typically delegated to a lay judge [*iudex*], a private person specifically appointed, by "nomination," and granted jurisdiction [*iurisdictio mandata*] to declare a verdict [*ius dicere*] according to the strict instructions in the praetorian formula. The main point in classical law is that such lay judges received, by delegation, only *iurisdictio*, but nothing more. Such judges never received the praetor's *imperium* which, by the law [*lex de imperio*] which originally appointed the praetor or magistrate to his office in the first place, is exclusive to him and not delegable to anyone else.[18] No private judge could ever wield such legal powers associated with praetorian *imperium*—above all, the *merum imperium* ("the pure authority") of life and death, the coercive "power of the sword" [*ius gladii*] to execute capital penalties.[19]

Medieval lawyers, reconstructing and glossing *Ius dicentis*, read these same passages in the *Digest* somewhat differently.[20] Instead of treating *imperium* and *iurisdictio* as details related to trial procedure and the constitution of Roman law courts, medieval jurists chose to reinterpret *imperium* and *iurisdictio* as generic concepts signifying different aspects of official public authority.

Confusingly, however, the latter—that is, official public authority—was also designated *iurisdictio*. This was because the word *iurisdictio* was understood to carry a double meaning. While it could mean, as the ancient Romans understood it, the judge's duty to pronounce a verdict [*ius dicere*] in a trial—his *officium ius dicentis*—the medieval Glossators observed that *iurisdictio* also signaled "*iuris-ditio*" which literally meant the "authority" [*ditio*] of law, or "legal authority."[21] In order to distinguish between these two meanings of *iurisdictio*, Glossators introduced a slightly more narrowly crafted terminology: Whereas *iurisdictio simplex* or *iurisdictio in specie sumpta* ("in the specific sense") indicated the appointed judge's function in declaring a verdict in a legal dispute, *iurisdictio in genere sumpta* ("in the generic sense") gestured toward the generic category of legal authority, *iuris-ditio*, which

17 The praetors held jurisdiction over most areas of civil law in Rome, although some legal disputes, particularly in commercial matters, came before the curule aediles whose charge was to oversee the public works and marketplace of Rome. Much of the Roman law of sale originates in the edicts of the aediles. In the provinces, jurisdiction belonged entirely to the provincial governors, from whom appeal could only be made to the Emperor.

18 This is the chief message of D.1.21.1.pr: *Quaecumque specialiter lege vel senatus consulto vel constitutione principum tribuuntur, mandata iurisdictione non transferuntur.*

19 D.2.1.3.

20 See especially chap. 1 of Myron Piper Gilmore, *Argument from Roman Law in Political Thought, 1200–1600* (Cambridge: Harvard University Press, 1941); Guido Rossi, "Deconstructing *Iurisdictio*: The Adventures of a Legal Category in the Hands of the Humanist Jurists," in *Reassessing Legal Humanism and Its Claims: Petere Fontes?*, ed. Paul J. du Plessis and John W. Cairns (Edinburgh: Edinburgh University Press, 2016), 62–63; Lee, *Popular Sovereignty*, 83–98.

21 This secondary meaning, *iuris-ditio*, can be traced to Azo's *Summa* on C.3.13.§1.

included authority of all ranks and kinds, including all those forms of authority designated in classical Roman law as *imperium*.[22]

This interpretive practice evidently antedated Bartolus. In the *Glossa Ordinaria* on D.2.1.3 (v.*mistum est*), Accursius states that *iurisdictio* shall be understood to be a generic category of authority. But that gloss also specifies that there are degrees of *iurisdictio*, as evinced by related texts in Justinian's *Digest* (chiefly from D.1.21.1.; 1.21.5.1; 2.1.3):

> There are four grades of *iurisdictio*. For some are *merum imperium*, others are *mixtum imperium*, others *coercitio modica*, and finally others remain in its own name and are simply called *iurisdictio*.

Bartolus inherited from his Glossatorial predecessors this typology of *iurisdictio*, but he went even further in specifying different ranks and degrees of authority. What emerged was the beginning of a general theory and legal taxonomy of public authority, while deceptively using a familiar classical vocabulary originating in the civil procedure of Roman courts.

This Bartolist typology was later called the "tree of jurisdictions," or *arbor iurisdictionum*. It was typically reproduced as a visual accompaniment to the *l.Ius dicentis* (D.2.1.1), originally designed by the Bartolist jurist, Giasone del Maino (see Figure 1.1).[23]

Under each of the "branches" of this tree, Bartolus further specified the various ranks of authority, ranging from the *merum imperium maximum* of the *princeps* to the *iurisdictio minima* of a local petty judge, or what he called a *iudex mercenarius*.

This creative Bartolist treatment of *iurisdictio* as a generic concept of legal authority became canonical in the law schools of the late Middle Ages. But like many other areas of Bartolist legal science, it would soon be contested by lawyers who observed the hermeneutic chasm separating Bartolists from their classical Roman forebears. As one sixteenth-century jurist would observe, there was no textual evidence whatsoever to justify Bartolus's treatment of *iurisdictio in genere sumpta* as a generic category designating legal authority of all kinds.[24] Although clothed in the fashion of Roman legal language, the Bartolist doctrine of *iurisdictio* was not Roman at all, but a reflection of the hierarchies of power characteristic of medieval Europe—free cities, princes, and emperors.

[22] Rossi, "Deconstructing *Iurisdictio*," 62. I commented earlier on this in Lee, *Popular Sovereignty*, 82, following Constantine Fasolt, *The Limits of History* (Chicago, IL: University of Chicago Press, 2004), 275, n.75, which observes Godefroy's exposure of the false etymology of *ius dicere* in *iurisditio*.

[23] A version of this can be observed on the cover illustration of Lee, *Popular Sovereignty*, reproduced from the *Arbor Iurisdictionum* in Bartolus of Sassoferrato, *In I^{am} Digesti Veteri Partem Commentaria* (Lyon, 1544), fol. 45ro.

[24] This was the thesis of Andrea Alciato, *Paradoxorum ad Pratum, Libri Sex* (Milan: Alexander Minutianus, 1518), fol. 17ro–17vo [II, vii].

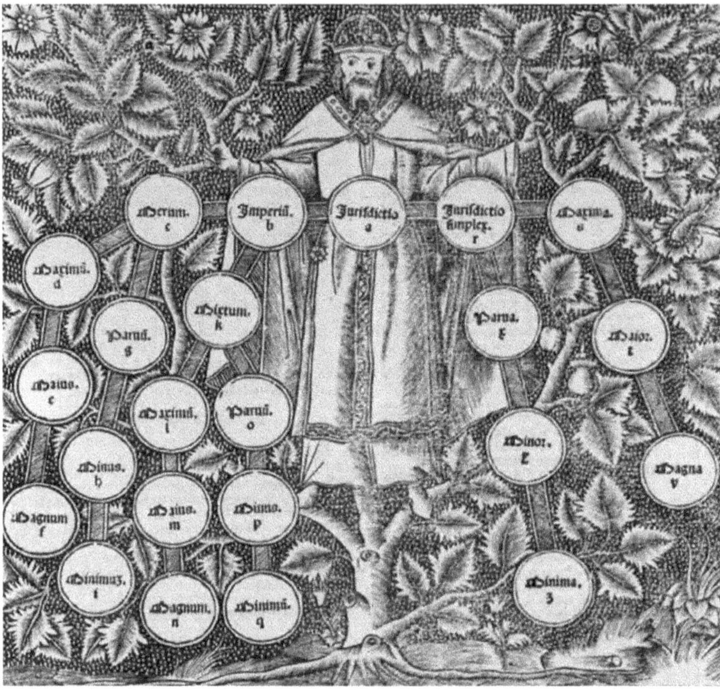

Figure 1.1 This is a detail from the 1544 print of the Tree of Jurisdictions in Bartolus's commentary on the *Digest*. The concept of jurisdiction is portrayed by the stem and trunk of the tree, while the various species of jurisdiction—*imperium* and *iurisdictio simplex*—are depicted as branches. Finer distinctions are portrayed as smaller branches.

These commentaries on *sibi princeps* and *iurisdictio* exemplified the Bartolist style of jurisprudence which, to later critics, appeared, at best, to be carelessness and, at worst, rampant and opportunistic abuse of Roman law. The most vocal among them, as we shall see, sought actively to introduce reform in how Roman law was taught, read, and interpreted, as well as to recover a "pristine" text of Justinian's lawbooks which, they believed, was corrupted over time. In reacting against Bartolus, Western legal science became, in effect, a textual science, and the champions of this textual science came to be known in modern scholarship as "legal humanists," so called because they were responsible for applying the philological and critical techniques of the *studia humanitatis*, a transformative methodology in early modern classical literature and Biblical scholarship, to the study of Roman legal texts.[25]

[25] The term "legal humanism" is a label invented in modern historical scholarship. It becomes prominent in the literature starting in the early twentieth century, possibly as an extension of the

Bodin's own attempt at outlining a legal science in the *Distributio* originates in response to the efforts of these legal humanists, whose headquarters was located in sixteenth-century France. What were the principal claims and ambitions of these French legal humanists?

The French School: The *Mos Gallicus*

Humanist jurisprudence was often called *mos gallicus ius docendi*—that is, the "French method of teaching law."[26] It was so called because this humanistic, philological approach to legal study, so fundamentally opposed to the Bartolist legal science championed in late medieval Italy—the *mos italicus*—was located chiefly (though not exclusively) in the France of Bodin's lifetime, and especially at the University of Bourges—an institution described by Donald Kelley as "the great centre of the French method."[27]

But, while France was recognized throughout sixteenth-century Europe for applying philological techniques of the *studia humanitatis* to the formal training of lawyers, the origins of this *mos gallicus* must be traced ultimately to Italy.[28] Indeed, the first legal humanists were not French lawyers, but Italian philologists, disillusioned by what they regarded as careless ahistorical and utilitarian exploitation of Roman law by Bartolist lawyers for the purpose of prevailing in courtroom litigation.[29] Encouraged by the scholarly achievements of humanist philologists in classical literature and especially in the area of Biblical scholarship in the context of the unfolding Reformation, advocates of the *studia humanitatis* expanded their scope

research on Renaissance humanism initiated by Jacob Burckhardt and the work of the Pandectists. Some early examples of the label "legal humanism" include David Baird Smith, "Roman Law and Political Theory," *Scottish Historical Review* 22 (1925): 249–77; Roger Latournerie, "L'humanisme juridique et l'acte de volonté," *Revue du droit public et de la science politique en France et à l'étranger* 64 (1948); Pierre Mesnard, "Introduction a la méthode de l'histoire de Jean Bodin," *Bibliothèque d'Humanisme et Renaissance* 12, no. 3 (1950): 318–23; Pierre Mesnard, "La Place de Cujas dans la querelle de l'humanisme juridique," *Revue historique de droit français et étranger* 27 (1950): 521–37; Domenico Maffei, *Gli inizi dell'umanesimo giuridico* (Milan: Giuffré, 1956). See, in general, Paul J. Du Plessis and John W. Cairns, eds., *Reassessing Legal Humanism and Its Claims: Petere Fontes?* (Edinburgh: Edinburgh University Press, 2016).

26 Donald Kelley, "Civil Science in the Renaissance: Jurisprudence in the French Manner," *History of European Ideas* 2 (1981): 261.

27 Kelley, "Civil Science in the Renaissance," 264. The University of Bourges was dissolved during the French Revolution. The humanistic style of academic jurisprudence, however, was not exclusive to France but also found adherents in Germany, the Low Countries, and in Spain.

28 On the Italian origins of legal humanism, see Domenico Maffei, *Gli inizi dell'umanesimo giuridico* (Milan: Giuffré, 1956).

29 Donald Kelley quotes a despairing remark by Petrarch: "The majority of our jurists ... caring little or nothing for the origins of law and the first fathers of jurisprudence, or anything except professional gain ... did not believe that knowledge of the arts and of literature would be of use." Donald Kelley, *Foundations of Modern Historical Scholarship: Language, Law, and History in the French Renaissance* (New York: Columbia University Press, 1970), 88.

of study to include Justinian's civil law. The first generation of Italian legal humanists included scholars whose work applied philological techniques to various parts of Justinianic texts, such as Angelo Poliziano (1454–94), Poliziano's friend and pupil Pietro Crinito (1475–1507), Giulio Pomponio Leto (1428–98), and Flavio Biondo (1392–1463).[30] Perhaps the most notable source of inspiration for this group of luminaries was Lorenzo Valla (*ca.*1406–57) and his "anti-Tribonianism," whose critical study of the Donation of Constantine not only showed conclusively that it was a forgery but demonstrated the efficacy of humanist scholarship in challenging dogmas—in this case, of papal plenitude of power.[31] What these humanists all shared in common was a growing suspicion that Bartolist practitioners of the civil law not only corrupted Justinian's text but perpetuated injustices in the interpretation and application of the law.

The emerging division among readers of Justinianic Roman law, between the more traditional Bartolist school of Italian Commentators and the novel humanistic school of philologists, was dramatized in a colorful dialogue, *De Corruptis Verbis Iuris Civilis*, written by Claudio Tolomei, a jurist, philologist, diplomat, and bishop of Curzola, known especially for the many letters written to numerous correspondents in sixteenth-century Europe.[32] Tolomei's dialogue positioned the Bartolist, Giasone del Maino (well-known for his reference works on civil law and for originating the tree of jurisdiction illustration), against the humanist, Poliziano, and revealed the emerging gap between Bartolists and humanists.

Most of these humanistic attempts at applying philological techniques to the critical study of Justinian's texts of civil law were literary efforts of textual scholarship. Their aim was not so much to reform the legal profession or the style of legal reasoning but, instead, the relatively more modest one of restoring a "pure" or pristine text of the *Corpus Iuris Civilis*—to "cleanse the Augean stables of law," as the task was described in Herculean terms.[33] For this reason, practicing lawyers generally regarded these Italian philologists as irrelevant "grammarians" and "antiquarians," whose work could not, or so it was thought, provide much practical value to practitioners of legal science in court. This anti-humanistic prejudice apparently had lasting effect among sixteenth-century lawyers. Alberico Gentili, the Italian-born Regius Professor of Civil Law at Oxford and one of the most prominent

[30] Kelley, *Foundations of Modern Historical Scholarship*, 39–50; Skinner, *Foundations of Modern Political Thought*, I: 201–4.

[31] Kelley, *Foundations of Modern Historical Scholarship*, 40. On this "anti-Tribonian" tradition, Kelley, in turn, recommends L. Palazzini Finetti, *Storia della ricercar delle interpolazione nel corpus iuris giustinianeo* (Milan, 1953).

[32] Claudio Tolomei, *De Corruptis Verbis Iuris Civilis Dialogus* (Siena: Simone Nardi, 1517).

[33] One humanist jurist, Hermann Vultejus, would simply describe the Accursian glosses as "the faeces of the latter centuries." Peter Garnsey, *Thinking About Property: From Antiquity to the Age of Revolution* (Cambridge: Cambridge University Press, 2009), 201, quoting from Vultejus on Inst.2.1 (1598).

anti-humanists, voiced his dissatisfaction with humanistic scholarship in a series of dialogues called *De Juris Interpretibus* (1582).[34]

Despite these methodological objections to legal humanism raised by practicing lawyers, its transformative influence on early modern jurisprudence, especially in the universities, was undeniable. Given the Italian origins of legal humanism, it was perhaps unsurprising that an Italian would establish the humanist legal movement in France, ultimately in the University of Bourges. That Italian was Andrea Alciato (1492–1550). But it is perhaps more of an irony that this Italian movement would eventually come to be known as the "French School," or the *mos gallicus*.

Alciato personified the humanistic spirit in jurisprudence. Even his name would be adopted by his later followers in France, who would be called the "Alciatei" in French academic jurisprudence. Alciato himself, however, originally was a product of the old Bartolist law curriculum still then in fashion in the Italian law faculties.[35] He entered the University of Pavia in 1508 to begin his formal legal education and then moved to Bologna in 1511 to continue his training.

Alciato then pursued a brief career as a practitioner pleading in the courts of Milan. It was there, as a practicing lawyer, that Alciato acknowledged the utilitarian value of the Bartolist legal science and learned to navigate through the relevant authoritative *consilia* literature to argue his cases before the courts. But the properly educated lawyer, he later counseled, must cautiously observe the precepts of the *studia humanitatis* in making use of the dead civil law of an ancient civilization. In this respect, Alciato's inspiration originated in Valla and Poliziano, who both envisioned a "systematic new approach to legal science" that broke decisively away from the Bartolist practice.[36]

Called to teach law in France, Alciato left Milan and his native Italy in 1518 to settle, first, in Avignon, and then, in 1529, at the university that would be hailed as the nerve center of the French School—the University of Bourges.[37]

Alciato's tenure as the Bourges chair of civil law lasted only four years. Yet, those four years were consequential for Western legal history. His work firmly established Bourges as the undisputed "home of the reformed jurisprudence," a reputation that would endure for the rest of the sixteenth century.[38]

One notable example of Alciato's legal scholarship concerns the Bartolist tree of jurisdictions, mentioned earlier. Bartolus was responsible for generations of

[34] Alberico Gentili, *De Iuris Interpretibus Dialogi Sex* (London: Apud Johannem Wolfium, 1582). However, he was not totally immune to humanist sensibilities in his treatment of the law of war. On this observation, see Christopher Warren, "Gentili, the Poets, and the Laws of War," in *The Roman Foundations of the Law of Nations: Alberico Gentili and the Justice of Empire*, ed. Benedict Kingsbury and Benjamin Straumann (Oxford: Oxford University Press, 2010), 146–62.

[35] Alciato was originally a pupil of two illustrious Bartolists at Pavia, Giasone del Maino and Filippo Decio [Decius].

[36] Skinner, *Foundations*, I: 204.

[37] Paul-Émile Viard, *André Alciato, 1492–1550* (Paris: Société anonyme du Recueil Sirey, 1926), 36, 40.

[38] Kelley, *Foundations of Modern Historical Scholarship*, 100.

lawyers becoming accustomed to viewing *iurisdictio* as a generic and broadly inclusive marker of legal authority of all ranks, including the highest authority of the *princeps*, the *merum imperium*. Alciato is widely credited for being the first to dismantle the Bartolist doctrine, by pointing out that *merum imperium* in civil law had nothing to do with the supreme authority of the *princeps*. Guido Rossi nicely summarizes the gist of Alciato's critique as follows:

> There is [according to Alciato] nothing in the sources to justify the idea of *iurisdictio* as a broad and all-encompassing genus. *Merum imperium* hardly entails a general, all-encompassing power. The sources speak of '*merum*' in the restrictive sense of '*solum*'—and not 'absolute' and 'unbounded,' as the civilians would have it. When *imperium* is *merum*, it has no *iurisdictio*. Deprived of any jurisdictional prerogative, *merum imperium* is just the *potestas animadvertendi in facinorosos homines* [D.2.1.3], that is, the power to inflict a punishment ... Correctly understood, *merum imperium* is but a magistrate's prerogative, not the supreme power reserved to the prince alone.[39]

Alciato's legacy in creating a humanistic *mos gallicus ius docendi* was ensured by his students, the "Alciatei." The void created by Alciato's departure from Bourges in 1532 was filled, first, by his immediate successor in the chair of civil law, Alciato's former pupil, François Le Douaren (Duarenus, 1509–59), a torchbearer of the legal humanist school at Bourges. The Alciatei also included other luminaries of French humanist jurisprudence, all tied to Bourges—Eguinaire Baron (*ca.*1495–1550), Jacques Cujas (1522–90), François Connan (1508–51), and François Hotman (1524–90). Particularly noteworthy is another alumnus of the Bourges law faculty, the Protestant Reformer, Jean Calvin (1509–64), who received his legal education at Bourges and was counted among the Alciatei before he established his own base of operations in Geneva.

While united by their common intellectual lineage traceable to Alciato's tutelage, the Alciatei themselves were, during this tumultuous period of the Reformation, characterized by a robust pluralism of views, which was partly confessional in nature. Legal humanists at Bourges numbered Catholic as well as Protestant Reformers, including Calvin himself.

It was only inevitable, then, that the humanist lawyers of Bourges should split into academic factions. One group, led by Le Douaren during his tenure as chair of civil law, included the leading humanist lawyers of the following generation, among them François Hotman (author of the stridently anti-royalist Monarchomach

[39] Rossi, "Deconstructing *Iurisdictio*," 64, citing Alciato, *Paradoxorum ad Pratum libri sex* (1518) fol. 17ro [II, 6]; fol. 17vo [II, 7]. Cf. Gilmore, *Argument From Roman Law in Political Thought*, 56; Lee, *Popular Sovereignty*, 98–108, which observes that Alciato, on the old debate between Azo and Lothair on the *merum imperium* of the emperor, favored Lothair's unorthodox position that the *merum imperium* is exclusive to the *princeps*.

tract, *Francogallia*) and Hugues Doneau (Hugo Donellus, 1527–92), creating, as Donald Kelley described it, a "crypto-Calvinist club."[40]

Another faction was led primarily by Eguinaire Baron, an accomplished jurist renowned for applying humanist techniques to produce a genuinely comparative legal science that reached beyond Roman law to study legal institutions and practices of French and feudal law.[41] Once a teacher of Jean Bodin at Angers (and, according to Donald Kelley, a vital inspiration for Bodin's own comparative historical study in the *Methodus*), Baron assembled another group of lawyers including François Baudouin (Balduinus, 1520–73) and Jacques Cujas, who would eventually, in 1575, succeed Le Douaren as the chair of civil law at Bourges.

But despite their internal differences, the Bourges law faculty emerged as the undisputed center of legal humanism, fundamentally reshaping the agenda of legal scholarship and education in many sixteenth-century law schools in France and beyond.

Toulouse

Not all French universities, to be sure, subscribed to the innovative legal humanism that engulfed the law faculty of Bourges. For example, the University of Orléans, which, due to its relative proximity to Paris, served as the unofficial law faculty for the University of Paris (the teaching of civil law was forbidden at the University of Paris by a thirteenth-century papal decretal), remained more conservative and Scholastic in its teaching style of civil law. Since the Middle Ages, Orléans had remained steadfastly committed to the teaching of civil law in the older tradition of the Bartolist legal science.

The same might be said of Toulouse.[42] Located in the South of France, in the *pays du droit écrit* (the French regions where aspects of Roman law, the *droit écrit*, were recognized by courts as valid law in force), Toulouse was the university where Jean Bodin would receive his formal training in civil law in the 1550s and where, for a brief time, Bodin would teach as a *hallebardier* (a sort of untenured adjunct lecturer).[43] Described as "cosmopolitan" in character, the University of Toulouse

[40] Kelley, *Foundations of Modern Historical Scholarship*, 101. On Hotman's anti-royalist popular sovereignty, see Lee, *Popular Sovereignty*, chap. 4.

[41] This was achieved in his most original work, *Institutionum civilium ab Justiniano Caesare editarum libri IV, bipartita commentario* (1546), a "bipartite commentary" [*commentaria bipertita*] which "accommodated civil law to French customs and legislation" [*accommodata huius tituli ad mores Galliarum et leges regias*]. Donald Kelley, at "Gaius Noster: Substructures of Western Social Thought," *American Historical Review* 84, no. 3 (1979): 632, observed that Baron was understudied in legal history: There is "no useful study of any sort" on Baron. This still seems to be the case in the twenty-first-century literature.

[42] Lloyd, *Jean Bodin*, 21–22.

[43] Pierre Mesnard, "Jean Bodin à Toulouse," *Bibliothèque d'Humanisme et Renaissance* 12 (1950): 43; Linton Stevens, "The Contribution of French Jurists to the Humanism of the Renaissance," *Studies in the Renaissance* 1 (1954): 98.

was an international "center of scholarship that attracted students from all over Europe," including Navarre, Spain, and Germany.[44] Its law faculty, in particular, included luminaries such as Jean de Coras and Arnaud Du Ferrier and was known all over France and hailed as a "temple of civil learning" [*in hoc civilis sapientiae templo*].[45] It would also produce some of the most famous jurists of the sixteenth century, including even humanists, such as Jacques Cujas and Hugues Doneau [Donellus].

While not entirely immune from the humanistic novelties developing in the law faculty of Bourges, Toulouse remained steadfastly, as Pierre Mesnard once put it, "*solide bastion d'orthodoxie*."[46] Because of its historical connection to a more conservative style of teaching civil law, Toulouse was "not hospitable to the new theories of jurisprudence which had spread from Italy to France and which [Alciato] had introduced at the University of Bourges," a point demonstrated by the academic drama surrounding the potential appointment of Jacques Cujas, denounced as a mere "grammarian," to the Toulouse chair of civil law in 1554.[47]

Cujas's work on Roman law was, to some, an act of academic iconoclasm. His close reading and philological reconstruction of corrupted or obscure Roman legal texts—the most important of which was his *Observationum et Emendationum Libri XVII* (a work still actively consulted as an authority in modern legal scholarship)—threatened to undermine centuries of accumulated Glossatorial and Bartolist interpretive conventions. It is not surprising that he would have made enemies, including at Toulouse.

Bodin's time at Toulouse overlapped for some years with that of Cujas. A Protestant native of Toulouse, Cujas studied law at Toulouse under the tutelage of Arnaud Du Ferrier, whose teaching, Cujas would later claim in a 1556 speech delivered at Bourges, he followed exclusively.[48] After a period of independent and methodical study of ancient sources and languages, he returned to the faculty of law at Toulouse in 1547 to teach a *cours libre* on Justinian's *Institutes* as a *hallebardier*. Given his rising star power as a leading French philologist of Roman law in France and his personal connection to Toulouse, Cujas naturally sought a permanent professorial chair in civil law at Toulouse.

He had his chance in 1554 when a vacancy was announced.[49] An arrêt of the Parlement of Toulouse, dated February 17, 1554, revealed that five candidates

[44] Brown, *Methodus*, 1. Mesnard, "Jean Bodin à Toulouse," 39. Alban Cabos, *Guy Du Faur de Pibrac: Un Magistrat Poète au XVIe Siècle, 1529–1584* (Paris: Édouard Champion, 1922), 33.

[45] Jean Bodin, *Oratio de Instituenda in Republica Iuventute ad Senatum Populumque Tolosatem* (Toulouse: Ex Officina Petri Putei, 1559), fol. 30vo, quoted in Lloyd, *Jean Bodin*, 46. Deloume, "Tableau des Professeurs de la Faculté de Droit de Toulouse," *Revue des Pyrénées et de la France Méridionale* III (1891): 126.

[46] Mesnard, "Jean Bodin à Toulouse," 34.

[47] Marcel Fournier, *Histoire de la Science du Droit en France* (Paris: Librairie du Recueil Général des Lois et des Arrêts et du Journal du Palais, 1892), 3:247.

[48] Xavier Prévost, "Jacques Cujas (1522–1590)," in *Great Christian Jurists in French History*, ed. Olivier Descamps and Rafael Domingo (Cambridge: Cambridge University Press, 2019), 136.

[49] Brown, *Methodus*, 4–5.

presented themselves for appointment to the chair, of which the three most serious candidates were Jacques Cujas, Étienne Forcadel, and Martin Rossel.[50]

The candidate ultimately securing the appointment to the Toulouse chair of civil law, with some interference from the Parlement of Toulouse, was Étienne Forcadel, reportedly a mediocre jurist by comparison and described variously as a "Bartolist opposed to the new methods" yet also "a humanist in the style of [Jean de] Boyssonné and [Pierre] Bunel."[51] Having received an outside offer from the University of Cahors for a professorial appointment, Cujas finally left Toulouse permanently in November 1554.[52]

Perhaps the most intriguing aspect of this appointments process was the suspicion that Bodin, a student in his twenties at that time, somehow played the pivotal role in steering the appointment to the chair of civil law, the most senior academic appointment in law at Toulouse, away from Cujas, arguably the most accomplished French legal humanist of the generation after Alciato. As Pierre Mesnard concludes, Bodin's culpability in this entire affair is simply myth.[53]

The myth begins with an alleged personal quarrel between Bodin and Cujas. We don't know what the substance or origin of this quarrel could have been.[54] It has, however, led commentators to view the two as personal rivals. This is the allegation leveled against Bodin by Alexander Scott and E. Merille. Merille (1579–1647), in particular, accused Bodin of sinking Cujas's candidacy for the chair of civil law and actively plotting foul play and even a "cabal" against him.[55]

While it is true that Bodin later, after his own departure from Toulouse, expressed principled objections to the narrowness of Cujas's philological method, demonstrated above all in his groundbreaking philological work, *Observationum et Emendationum*, Bodin's overall attitude toward Cujas was more likely one of "emulation and admiration rather than of hostility."[56]

[50] Brown, *Methodus*, 4–5. Mesnard, "Jean Bodin à Toulouse," 44, locates his source in a compilation reportedly by Deloume, "Tableau des Professeurs de la Faculté de Droit de Toulouse," *Revue des Pyrénées et de la France Méridionale* III (1891): 126–27.

[51] Martin Rossel nominates Etienne Forcadel. There is some disagreement in the literature whether Forcadel was a Bartolist. Brown, *Methodus*, 5, characterizes Forcadel as a Bartolist, whereas Mesnard, at "Jean Bodin à Toulouse," 48–9, observes Forcadel's humanistic tendencies, particularly in his 1549 work, *Sphaera Legalis*. It needn't, however, be a binary interpretive choice. Disagreement also extends to Forcadel's reputation. Wim Decock describes him as a "top-notch professor of law" at Toulouse. Wim Decock, *Theologians and Contract Law: The Moral Transformation of the Ius Commune (ca.1500–1650)* (Leiden: Brill, 2013), 107.

[52] Lloyd, *Jean Bodin*, 20–24; Mesnard, "Jean Bodin à Toulouse," 46–47. See also Pierre Mesnard, "Un rival heureux de Cujas et de Bodin: Étienne Forcadel," *Zeitschrift der Savigny-Stiftung für Rechtsgeschichte: romantische Abteilung* 67 (1950): 440–58.

[53] Mesnard, "Jean Bodin à Toulouse," 44–51.

[54] Alexandra Gottely et al., eds., *Jacques Cujas, la fabrique d'un grand juriste* (Paris: Collège de France, 2024).

[55] E. Merille, *Dissertatio in libros tres ex Cujacio* in *Cujacii Opera Omnia*, ed. C. J. Fabroto (Naples, 1758), 3:791. Mesnard, "Jean Bodin à Toulouse," 44–45. Brown, *Methodus*, 8, comments that it was more likely that Bodin was "a disciple rather than a rival of Cujas." Paul Lawrence Rose, *Bodin and the Great God of Nature: The Moral and Religious Universe of a Judaiser* (Geneva: Droz, 1980), 21–22.

[56] Brown, *Methodus*, 9 cf. 8: "Moreau-Reibel considers the whole Cujas-Bodin affair a clash of methods rather than of personalities." Bodin cites Cujas on several occasions, sometimes critically

Cujas's departure and Forcadel's eventual formal appointment into the chair of civil law, reportedly on September 7, 1556, ensured that Toulouse would avoid, or at least forestall, following the humanist path of jurisprudence that the Alciatei pioneered in Bourges. It was in this environment, wary of the philological methods that Cujas and the "grammarians" represented, that Bodin received his formal legal education and took his first step in the field of legal scholarship.

Bodin's principal teacher in civil law at Toulouse was Jean de Boyssoné. He likely aspired to an academic teaching career in law and, like Cujas, taught a *cours libre* on Roman law for a brief period, also as a *hallebardier*. In this teaching role, Bodin was expected to prepare lectures on jurisprudence for his students, most likely following the titles of Justinian's *Institutes*. These lectures were intended perhaps as auditions or "job talks" for a possible tenured teaching appointment in the law faculty.[57] Indeed, according to one later source, Bodin's lectures were received "with great applause" [*grand applaudissement*].[58]

Ultimately, he failed on this version of the tenure track, or perhaps he was simply disillusioned by the medieval dreariness of life as a legal academic. As a result, Bodin decided to leave Toulouse, and its cloistered life of the university academic, and moved to Paris sometime around 1560, where he would pursue instead a legal practice, initially as an *avocat du roi* in the *chambre de consultation* in the Parlement of Paris, the supreme court of *ancien régime* France, under the patronage of Guy Du Faur, the Seigneur de Pibrac (the dedicatee of his most important work, the *République*).[59]

But he would not leave Toulouse before he wrote several short technical treatises on special topics in jurisprudence, early drafts for his later work in jurisprudence and political theory. These included essays on topics that Bodin would later reference retrospectively in both the *Methodus* and the *République*—*De Decretis*

(e.g., *République* 403, where he alleges that Cujas confuses *infamia* and *ignominia*) and sometimes approvingly (e.g., *République* 373 on the definition of *magistrat* and *officier*; *République* 463, citing Cujas's *Observationum et Emendationum Libri XVII* (Cologne: Apud Ioannem Gymnicum, 1578), 1–2 [I, 1], suggesting the removal of the text, "ex quo provinciam ingressus est," from l.2.ff. *De officio proconsulis* = D.1.16.2). Cf. Brown, *Methodus*, 24 which indicates an interpretive dispute on the *legis actio* between Bodin and Cujas. The dispute is recorded in Alexander Scott, *Tractatus de Controversis Jacobi Cujacii Sententiis et Singularibus Contra J. Bodinum* in Dominicus Albanensis, *Promptuarium Universorum Operum Jacobi Cujacii* (Naples, 1763), 3:Part 2, cols. 15–17.

[57] Brown, *Methodus*, 11; P. F. Girard, "La Jeunesse de Cujas (Toulouse, 1522–1554)," *Nouvelle revue historique de droit* 40 (1916): 500. See also Lloyd, *Jean Bodin*, 23, citing Cesare Vasoli, *Armonia e giustizia: studi sulle idee filosofiche di Jean Bodin* (Florence: Olschki, 2008), 16.

[58] Ménage, *Vitae Petri Aerodii*, 140.

[59] Bodin swears the oath in 1562. Lloyd, *Jean Bodin*, 92–93. Bodin's patron, Guy Du Faur, Seigneur de Pibrac, would be appointed *avocat-général* in 1565 to represent royal interests before the Parlement. It was through Bodin's connection to Du Faur, the Seigneur de Pibrac, that Bodin would obtain temporary appointments as the assistant to the *procureur du roi* (1567) and commissioner to oversee the reform of the forests of Normandy (1570).

et Iudiciis, *De Imperio*, *De Iure Imperio* [sic], *De Iurisdictione*, and *De Legis Actionibus*.[60] We can reasonably conjecture that these essays were most likely intended to be lecture notes for Bodin's *cours libre* on civil law, with particular focus on the public law of the state, an area of jurisprudence traditionally overlooked in the university law curriculum.[61] (We unfortunately can't verify this point because Bodin, at his deathbed, insisted in his will that they be burnt.)[62]

We do, however, have access to the scholarly results of these early drafts, scattered throughout Bodin's later works, such as the *Methodus*, the *République*, and the *De la Demonomanie des Sorciers*. The *République*, for example, which was ostensibly intended to present a general theory of state, develops a public law jurisprudence in explaining the legal functions and exercise of the state's sovereignty. In explaining the substance of sovereignty, Bodin felt compelled to return to the medieval jurisprudence on *iurisdictio* and *imperium*, ultimately rejecting and revising the conventional Bartolist teaching on *merum imperium*, by arguing instead that the rights and prerogatives constitutive of sovereignty (such as the right to make and unmake legislation, the right to declare war and conclude peace, and the right of pardon) belong to a category *sui generis*, what he calls *summum imperium* (literally, the "highest" authority)—or, in another word, *souveraineté*. This *summum imperium* was exclusive to sovereigns and could not be shared, either with inferior magistrates, who held a share of *imperium*, or with subjects.

By far the most important result of these early tracts on jurisprudence was the *Iuris Universi Distributio*—'A Division of the Law as a Whole'—the principal subject of this study and the fruit of Bodin's early work as an academic lawyer.

[60] Bodin's references to these papers are scattered and mentioned *passim* throughout his writings. *De Decretis* appears in *Methodus* 249. *De Imperio* is mentioned at *Methodus* 255, 267. *De Iure Imperio* [sic] appears at *Methodus* 262 and refers readers to "in cap.de iure maiestatis." The title "*De iure maiestatis*" was the title for Bodin's chapter on sovereignty in the Latin *De Republica* I, 8, suggesting that *De Iure Imperio* [sic] may have been an early working title for the *République* (or perhaps for Book I). The closing paragraph of *République* (1583), 251 [I, 10], which deals with the *vrayes marques de souveraineté*, refers readers to his *livre de Imperio*, which may have been one of these unpublished papers. Jean Moreau-Reibel, *Jean Bodin et le droit public comparé dans ses rapports avec la philosophie de l'histoire* (Paris: Librairie Philosophique J. Vrin, 1933), 207–8, n.1, has suggested, following a thesis in Sir Frederick Pollock's *History of the Science of Politics*, the possible influence of these tracts on the English Civilian, Sir Thomas Smith, author of *De Republica Anglorum*, during his stay in Toulouse in 1564–65.

[61] Moreau-Reibel, *Jean Bodin et le droit public compare*, 24. Gilmore, *Argument from Roman Law in Political Thought*, 94, conjectures the origin of these tracts to the period from 1559 to 1566.

[62] Gilles Ménage claims to have examined Bodin's will, with the order that these unpublished manuscripts were to be burnt. Pierre Bayle, *Dictionnaire historique et critique* (Basel: Jean Louis Brandmuller, 1741), 1:589 [s.v.: Bodin], citing Ménage, *Remarques sur la Vie de P. Ayrault*, 142, 143: "Il ordonna par son Testament, dont j'ay vu l'Original, que ses Livres *de Imperio, & Jurisdictione, & Legis actionibus, & Decretis, & Judiciis*, seroient brulez."

Distributio

The main interpretive question we must ask about Bodin's *Distributio* was whether he, too, subscribed to the humanist *mos gallicus* and practiced a form of humanist jurisprudence in the *Distributio*. This has been a disputed point for some time in the scholarship on Bodin's legal thought. Myron Piper Gilmore, for example, in his influential study on Roman law in early modern political thought, claimed that "the distinctions and arguments of the humanist lawyers of all schools were useful to him [Bodin] and it is not doubtful that he found a constant inspiration in their writings."[63] Ralph Giesey, by contrast, forcefully argued that Bodin's legal thought was straightforwardly shaped by the habits and techniques of Bartolist medieval jurisprudence.[64]

Both interpretive positions, in my view, miss the mark. Bodin was neither a legal humanist nor a Bartolist in any recognizably conventional sense. He self-consciously distanced himself from the *mores ius docendi* of both the Bartolist Italians and the Alciatei French. Instead, Bodin was actively engaged in his own juridical project in the *Distributio*, which revealed not only his revulsion toward the antiquarian humanistic veneration, even fetishizing, of the Roman law of Justinian but also his deep skepticism of the Bartolist credo that a universal legal science can be extracted and successfully built upon classical Roman law. Bodin felt the science of jurisprudence needed to move beyond Roman law, a move which many of his humanist contemporaries, still clinging to the notion that Roman law was the textual embodiment of *ratio scripta* and *vera philosophia*, were not yet ready or willing to make.[65] Bodin's *Distributio* is the most compelling evidence of this vision.

The *Iuris Universi Distributio* was first published as a series of tables printed continuously in six large folios by Bodin's Parisian publisher, Jacques Du Puys, in 1578, two years after the first publication of his most important work of political theory, *Les Six Livres de la République*.[66] It seems they were intended to be posted as one large diagram providing a grand conceptual cartography of civil law for students of jurisprudence. Its original conception, however, must be located decades

[63] Gilmore, *Argument from Roman Law in Political Thought*, 99.

[64] Giesey, "Medieval Jurisprudence in Bodin's Concept of Sovereignty," especially 172–80.

[65] Cf. Ian Maclean, *Interpretation and Meaning in the Renaissance: The Case of Law* (Cambridge: Cambridge University Press, 1992), 26–27.

[66] Two later editions of the *Distributio* appeared in Bodin's lifetime. In 1580, a prose version of the *Distributio* was published in Germany, *Iuris Universi Distributio* (Cologne: Ioannes Gymnicus, 1580), the textual basis for the modern French translations by Pierre Mesnard in *Oeuvres Philosophiques de Jean Bodin* (Paris: Presses Universitaires de France, 1951) and *Exposé du Droit Universel*, trans. Lucien Jerphagnon, ed. Simone Goyard-Fabre and René-Marie Rampelberg (Paris: Presses Universitaires de France, 1985). A third, possibly unauthorized, version of the *Distributio* in dialogue form was published by Jan Kocin as the *Nova Distributio Iuris Universi* (Prague: George Nigrinus, 1581), which was the subject of a study by Cecilia Pedrazza Gorlero, *La Iuris Universi Distributio di Jean Bodin* (Rovereto, Italy: Edizioni Osiride, 1999).

earlier. As John Brown concluded many years ago, the *Distributio* was "largely a product of the Toulouse years," developed while Bodin was still actively preparing and delivering his law lectures.[67]

Bodin laid out his purposes for writing the *Distributio* in the opening dedication (*Distributio* fol. A). He openly sympathized with the first-year law student in civil law who was faced with the burdensome task of studying a subject whose writings were "scattered and piecemeal in an infinite multitude of books and forensic literature." Bodin envisioned the *Distributio* as a solution to this problem, a convenient one-stop-shop in which the fundamentals of jurisprudence could be "collected into one body." But he distinguished his work with a further purpose, to stress the internal logical unity of jurisprudence, as a whole [*universum*], made up of interconnected parts:

> The different elements [of law], being linked one to another, and all fitted together and composed among themselves, may be taken in at a single glance and exhibit the form of an entire body. It is prepared such that the last things respond to the first, the middle to either, and each to all, and anyone can readily recognize what is antecedent and what is consequent.

The ultimate goal of the work, then, was pedagogical, whereby the student of law could follow a "method common not only to the teaching of the arts but also to all sciences."[68]

But the *Distributio* was more than just a pedagogical work. As Bodin explained, it was also intended to be an initial trial run, or as he put it, "a ἰχνογραφίαν ('ground-plan') of a future work, such a thing as architects have been in the habit of making to be inspected and modeled, so that one may clearly grasp whether the edifice under construction will be long-enduring and useful." Although Bodin never completed that work, we have the basic elements of his design.

Organized into four main parts, each part corresponding to an Aristotelian cause of law and legality, the *Distributio* was nothing short of an attempt to provide a visual mapping of the vital features of an independent legal system—whether Roman, French, or otherwise.[69] In this respect, the *Distributio* was not simply a

[67] Brown, *Methodus*, 25; Lloyd, *Jean Bodin*, 56. Diego Quaglioni, "L'Éducation du juriste face au pouvoir: la 'methodus' de Matteo Gribaldi Mofa," *Science politique et droit publique dans les facultés européennes, XIIIe–XVIIIe siècles*, ed. J. Krynen and Michael Stolleis (Frankfurt am Main: Klostermann, 2007), 347–57, suggests that Matteo Gribaldi Mofa's 1558 work, *De methode ac ratione studi*, may have been one possible inspiration for Bodin.

[68] Bodin's pedagogical approach resembles, to some degree, the *Paratitla*, summaries of the titles making up the *Code* and *Digest*, composed by Cujas and Hotman's *Partitiones Iuris Civilis Elementariae* (Basel: Apud Nicolaum Episcopium Iuniorem, 1561).

[69] In substance, however, the *Distributio* offered an analysis of the *droit écrit* recognized in the Parlements of the *pays du droit écrit* in the South of France—that is, the "Vulgar" Roman law as it was assimilated, over many centuries, into French civil law provinces and, later, would become the target of François Hotman's Germanic "Antitribonianism."

work intended to aid the study of *ius civile* (or Roman law) alone, but instead the systematic study of all historical legal systems, a juristic universality which Bodin captured by that fraught term, *ius gentium*.[70] It is Bodin's contribution to what might, in modern legal scholarship, be called general jurisprudence—*science du droit, allgemeine Rechtslehre*, or *Rechtswissenschaft*.

The title of the work, *Iuris Universi Distributio* ("a division of the law as a whole") is particularly noteworthy, laden with Ciceronian rhetorical and juridical meaning. *Distributio*, which can mean "division," "classification," "collocation," or "arrangement" into a logical order of some kind, specifically signaled the Ciceronian rhetorical concept of *dispositio*, introduced in *De Inventione* as the *rerum inventarum in ordinem distributio* ("the division or arrangement of items discovered into their proper order").[71] Such *distributio*, or arrangement, follows an initial stage of *inventio* ("discovery"), whereby an orator gathers and "discovers" [*invenire*] the facts and arguments relevant to the case he is preparing to present before a law court. But in Cicero's rhetorical theory, these tasks—*inventio* and *dispositio*—are intended to be only preliminary and preparatory stages of oratory which ultimately conclude in the public performative "delivery" [*pronuntiatio*] of the lawyer's eloquence.[72] Bodin's own *Distributio*, too, while focused on division and orderly arrangement of legal concepts, was a preparatory, classificatory work for that grander project on legal science yet to come.

The other observation about the title concerns the object (or, rather, the *res inventa*) of Bodin's *distributio*—that is, the *ius universum*. That latter term is also of Ciceronian origin, which can be located in *De Legibus* I, where Cicero distinguishes the *ius universum* (Bodin's *droit universel*) from "the law of eaves and house-walls" [*de stillicidiorum ac de parietum iure*] and other mundane areas of law characteristic of Roman law.[73] Bodin will later declare this to be a chief object of his studies in the *Methodus*, the goal of which was "to establish the *ius universum*" [*de universo iure statuere*], not exclusively from the study of the laws

[70] *Ius gentium* is typically translated into English as "the law of nations" and has been regarded, in modern scholarship, as interchangeable with the term "international law" owing largely to Jeremy Bentham, who coined the latter term. In classical law, however, *ius gentium* was that body of law observed in common by all peoples [*gentes*; Gaius prefers to say *omnes populi*], and not simply Romans. This not only justified Roman courts with jurisdiction over peregrines (or foreigners) to adopt *ius gentium* rules, especially in areas arising from international commerce and war, it also led Gaius famously, in a Stoic voice, to describe *ius gentium* as an expression of "natural reason." D.1.1.9.

[71] Cicero, *Cicero: In Twenty-Eight Volumes* (Cambridge: Harvard University Press, 1968), 2:18 [I, vii, §9]; cf. διαίρεσις. Cf. Quintilian, *The Orator's Education: Institutio Oratoria*, trans. Donald A. Russell, Loeb Classical Library 126 (Cambridge: Harvard University Press, 2001), 3:152 [VII, i, §2]: *dispositio utilis rerum ac partium in locos distributio*. Cf. *Divisio rerum plurium in singulas*. See also Quentin Skinner, *Forensic Shakespeare* (Oxford: Oxford University Press, 2014), 13–14; Peter Stacey, *The State in Machiavelli* (Cambridge: Cambridge University Press, forthcoming), chap. 1.

[72] Delivery, or *pronuntiatio* (*ex rerum et verborum dignitate vocis et corporis moderatio*), is the final part of the art of rhetoric, as Cicero lists them. *De Inventione* 20 [I, vii, §9].

[73] Cicero, *De Legibus*, 312–13 [I, iv, §14]. Cf. James Gordley, "Ius Civile: The Roman Jurists," in *The Jurists: A Critical History* (Oxford: Oxford University Press, 2013).

of "just one state" [*singularis cuiusdam civitatis*]—by which he means Roman law [*ex Romanis legibus*]. Instead, as we have seen earlier, the *ius universum* must be sought through a thoroughly comparative examination of "all the laws of all states, or those of the more famous states, collected together" and "from them extract the best kind" [*omnibus omnium aut magis illustrium rerumpublicarum legibus in unum collectis ... optimum genus ex iis conflarent*].[74]

Legal Ramism

Surely the most notable feature of the original 1578 *editio princeps* of Bodin's *Distributio* is a visible one. This tabular presentation, especially popular during the academic reforms of the sixteenth century, was the most distinctive feature of that style known generally as "Ramism," named after the French Protestant humanist logician and academic reformer, Pierre de la Ramée (Petrus Ramus, 1515–72).[75]

Murdered in the violence of the St. Bartholomew's Massacre, a climactic moment of the French Wars of Religion, Ramus attained a reputation as a humanist educator and also for his vocal hostility against the Scholastic academic habits that, in his view, needlessly placed obstacles which made learning in the liberal arts inaccessible to new students. Given his own humble origin, Ramus was perhaps the first in early modern France to advocate for accessibility and inclusion in higher education, a goal that would eventually shape his own pedagogical efforts to reform the university curriculum and restructure it according to the precepts of disputation that prioritized *inventio* and *dispositio*.

Ramus was licensed to teach in the liberal arts at the age of twenty-one, with the award of the Master of Arts from the University of Paris in 1536. He initially taught Aristotle's logic at two of the medieval academic foundations of the University of Paris, the Collège du Mans and the Collège de l'Ave Maria. He apparently disliked the Scholastic Aristotelianism so much that Aristotelian logic became the target of his first major critical work, the *Aristotelicae animadversiones* (1543), a heterodox work that would eventually cost him his teaching job and would later be banned by Francis I.

Ramus's patron, Charles de Lorraine (who would be made Cardinal by Pope Paul III in 1547, three years after Ramus was fired), eventually arranged to remove the ban by persuading Francis's son, the newly enthroned king, Henri II, to do so. The Cardinal was also instrumental in Ramus's eventual appointment in 1551 as

[74] *Methodus* sig.∴3ro-3vo. Among the sources cited here are the Persians, the Greeks, the Egyptians, and the Hebrews from the books of the Sanhedrin. This is, however, an unusual statement, considering how much the *Distributio* ultimately belongs to the tradition of legal scholarship and teaching of Roman law.

[75] On Ramus in general, see Walter Ong, *Ramus, Method, and the Decay of Dialogue* (Chicago, IL: University of Chicago Press, 1958).

"royal" or *regius professor* in eloquence at the newly established humanist Collège de France.

But even before this royal appointment, the Cardinal de Lorraine managed to find a new teaching position for Ramus in 1547—though not in logic, but in mathematics—at the Collège de Presles, an academic foundation in Paris to which Ramus would be attached for much of the rest of his life and, eventually, would serve as its head.[76] At the Collège de Presles, Ramus offered lectures to throngs of students in Paris, looking for an alternative to the unfashionable Scholasticism that continued to dominate the academic life of Paris.

It is very likely that Bodin attended these public lectures delivered by Ramus. While there is no direct surviving evidence for Bodin's attendance at Ramus's lectures, the Canadian scholar of Bodin, Kenneth McRae, once observed that the Carmelite monastery in Paris, where Bodin resided as a teenaged novitiate, was not only on the Rue des Carmes in the present-day 5e arrondissement Latin Quarter of Paris but situated directly opposite the Collège de Presles, where Ramus delivered his lectures to "unprecedented numbers of students."[77] We may reasonably conjecture that the young Bodin was among these many Parisian students who attended Ramus's public lectures. But not only did he probably attend, Bodin evidently adopted some of the fashionable Ramist methods in his own work.[78] The *Distributio* serves as evidence corroborating this Ramist influence.

Bodin was, of course, not alone in absorbing the influence of Ramism. Indeed, by the time Bodin likely started writing his legal tracts and preparing the *Distributio* during his Toulouse years in the 1550s, a generation of reform-minded academic lawyers in the early sixteenth century had already started applying the precepts of Ramism to legal education, so as to reform the study of civil law into a proper technical science—or, as Cicero put it, *ius civile in artem redigendo*.[79] The nineteenth-century German jurist and leader of the Historical School of Roman law, Friedrich Carl von Savigny, would later label these reformers *die Systematiker* ("systematists"

[76] He would ultimately die in the Collège as well. During the hysterical violence of the Massacre of St. Bartholomew, Ramus was killed in his private study at the Collège de Presles.

[77] Kenneth D. McRae, "Ramist Tendencies in the Thought of Jean Bodin," *Journal of the History of Ideas* 16, no. 1/4 (1955): 309. A subsequent study offers evidence claiming to corroborate McRae's hypothesis in a quarto volume now held in the Bodleian Library, Byw.T 4.25., which bears Bodin's signature and contains extensive notes on a humanist work closely associated with Ramus, the *Rhetorica* of Omer Talon, a colleague of Ramus at the Collège de l'Ave Maria. Giles Barber, "Haec a Johanne Bodin Lecta," *Bibliothèque d'Humanisme et Renaissance* 25, no. 2 (1963): 362–65.

[78] Barber, "Haec a Johanne Bodin Lecta," 362–65, further indicates Bodin's attachment to Ramism, by virtue of Bodin's handwritten notes on his personal copy of the Ramist *Rhetorica*, a work authored by Ramus's friend and colleague at the Collège de l'Ave Maria, Omer Talon. McRae has persuasively argued the influence of the Ramist method was not limited to the *Distributio*. It also can be detected in the *Methodus*, the *République*, as well as his translation of Oppian.

[79] Nor was the influence of Ramism in the "higher" learned professional faculties of universities limited to law. The work of Ramist theologians played a critical role in accelerating the pace of the Protestant Reformation. See, in general, Ong's *Ramus, Method, and the Decay of Dialogue*.

or "systematisers") for their attempts to redesign the whole structure of civil law into a more a logical, orderly system.[80]

I propose, instead, a different label (inspired by the work of the nineteenth-century German legal historian, Roderich von Stintzing)—"legal Ramism"—a label that reinforces the pedagogical values and rhetorical techniques of Ramism in early modern legal education.[81] The utility of this label, in my view, is that it fundamentally differentiates the programmatic aims of legal Ramism from those of legal humanism. While similar in some respects, especially in their hostility to Bartolist legal science, the key difference between Ramism and humanism lies in their differing attitudes to Justinian's legal text. Legal Ramists, while certainly beneficiaries of the textual scholarship produced by the humanist *mos gallicus* jurisprudence, nevertheless refused to treat the *Corpus Iuris Civilis* as sacrosanct, but actively reimagined the organization of civil law as a rational logical system, following the precepts of Ciceronian rhetoric and Ramism, and thereby moving far beyond the classical precedents inherited from Scaevola, Gaius, and Justinian.[82]

Among the legal Ramists were leading academic jurists of Bourges, La Douaren, Connan, Baron, and Doneau. What these systematists of law envisioned was a total reordering of Roman law into an updated architectonic system they regarded as more logical, more transparent and accessible for law students than Justinian's haphazard and chaotic system that routinely jumped from one legal topic to another, without any clear reason in the text for the transition.[83] This is how Ramists separated themselves from humanists: Legal Ramists routinely justified their approach by pointing to the pedagogical value of their method, which sought to organize the study of law as a journey from more general concepts to the more specific details and rules of law. In doing so, they envisioned the possibilities of transforming civil law into a proper science, rather than a textual exercise in casuistry focusing on Justinian.

In this Ramist spirit, the most daring academic lawyers, who attempted to illustrate the interconnected and systematic quality of jurisprudence, sought to display the civil law visually in a tabular form, indicating how major concepts of law might be subdivided into more minute legal categories and surgically reconstructed into

[80] Friedrich Karl Von Savigny, *Das Recht des Besitzes: Eine Civilistische Abhandlung* (Vienna: Druck und Verlag von Carl Gerolds Sohn, 1865), 10. Cf. Julian Franklin, *Jean Bodin and the Sixteenth-Century Revolution in the Methodology of Law and History* (New York: Columbia University Press, 1963), 27–35.

[81] Roderich von Stintzing, *Geschichte der Deutschen Rechtswissenschaft* (Munich: Drud und Berlag von R. Didenbourg, 1880), 1:145–50. The most important figure in this school of Ramist lawyers was Doneau [Donellus].

[82] Kelley, "Gaius Noster," 629–35.

[83] V. Piano Mortari, "La sistematica come ideale unamistico dell'opera di Francesco Connano," in *La storia del diritto nel quandro della scienza storiche* (Florence: L.S. Olschki, 1966), 526–28; "La scienza del diritto in François Baudouin," *Diritto, Logica, Metodo nel secolo XVI* (1978): 407–28; Alberto Ribeiro de Barros, "Bodin et la Projet d'Une Science du Droit: La *Juris Universi Distributio*," *Nouvelle Revue du XVI*[e] *Siècle* 21, no. 2 (2003): 65–66.

a more logical and orderly form. Some examples of this early modern genre of "legal systematization" (as Laurens Winkels described it) would include Johann Apel (1486–1536), Johann Thomas Freigius (1543–83), Matthew Wesenbeck (Wesenbecius, 1531–86), Hugues Doneau (Donellus, 1527–91), Pierre Grégoire (1540–97), and Rudolf Göckel (Goclenius, 1547–1628).[84] Bodin, the theorist of law, belongs to this group.

While legal humanists preserved the textual integrity of this classical law in historical context, legal Ramists, by contrast, attempted to update its formal presentation, following the Ramist (and ultimately, Ciceronian) pedagogical principle that complex systems should be developed chiefly through *inventio* and *distributio*. The overwhelming result in this legal-Ramist literature is a dichotomous arrangement (*distributio*), bisecting complex legal subjects into smaller species through ongoing bipartition. As we will see in the following chapters, this is precisely how Bodin approaches his own analysis of the concept of law [*ius*]: by breaking down the genus of *ius* into the two main species of "natural law" [*ius naturale*] and "human law" [*ius humanum*], dutifully following the Ramist fashion of methodical analysis.[85]

Observe the iconoclasm represented by legal Ramism. Justinianic Roman law wasn't organized by bipartition, but instead by tripartition.[86] Classical Roman jurists loved tripartitions as an organizing principle. Ulpian exemplified this love in his tripartite *divisio iuris* (D.1.1.1: *ius naturale*; *ius gentium*; *ius civile*), the tripartite *praecepta iuris* (D.1.1.10.1: *honeste vivere, alterum non laedere, suum cuique tribuere*), and in his outline of the triple functions of law (D.1.3.41: *Totum ius consistit aut in adquirendo aut in conservando aut in minuendo*). Probably the most famous tripartition of all in Roman law was Gaius's statement concerning the content of civil law in the opening of his *Institutes* 1.8: *Omne autem ius, quo utimur, vel ad personas pertinent vel ad res vel ad actiones* (D.1.5.1: "The whole of the law observed by us relates either to persons or to things or to actions").[87]

[84] Laurens Winkel, "Rights II," in *Cambridge Companion to Hugo Grotius*, ed. Randall Lesaffer and Janne Nijman (Cambridge: Cambridge University Press, 2021), 266, extends the reach of this early modern genre of legal systematization to Grotius's treatise of Roman–Dutch law. Cf. Robert Feenstra, "La systématique du droit dans l'oeuvre de Grotius," in *La sistematica giuridica: Storia, teoria e problemi attuali*, ed. Luciana Buccellato (Rome: Istituto della Enciclopedia Italiana, 1991). Johann Apel, *Methodica Dialectices Ratio, ad Iurisprudentiam Adcommodata* (Nuremberg: Apud Fridericum Peypus, 1535); Johann Thomas Freigius, *Partitiones Iuris Utriusque* (Basel: Ex Officina Sixti Henrricpetri, 1571); Hugues Doneau, *Commentarii de Jure Civili* (Lyon: Antonii Pillehotte, 1619); Pierre Grégoire, *Syntagma Iuris Universi* (Frankfurt am Main: Peter Fischer, 1599); Rudolf Göckel, *Lexicon Philosophicum* (Frankfurt: Matthias Becker, 1613). Freigius was Ramus's biographer and knew him in Basel. Thanks to Ian Maclean for the reference to Göckel.

[85] *Distributio* fol. A; *The Right of Sovereignty* 171–72. Cf. Freigius, *Partitiones Iuris Utriusque* fol. 2ro.

[86] D.1.1.1.2: *Privatum ius tripertitum est.* On this point, see Kelley, "Gaius Noster," 622–25, who attributes this "trichotomizing" in modern academic jurisprudence to von Savigny. Kelly reminds us that the young Marx originally adopted some of these *trichotomisch* habits, not from Hegel but from von Savigny. Henry Goudy, *Trichotomy in Roman Law* (Oxford: Clarendon Press, 1912), 20–22 identifies nineteen further trichotomies in Roman private law, most of which originate with Ulpian.

[87] "Things" is the typical English translation for the Latin, *res*. A better translation, in my view, that captures what the jurists intended might be "assets"—any fungible thing, whether corporeal or

Legal Ramists, who sought to introduce order to the apparent chaos in the organization of Justinian's texts, confronted these tripartitions and faced the practical challenge of rearranging, even forcing, them into simpler bipartitions, for the sake of pedagogical method and clarity. We can observe this immediately in how some legal Ramists attempted to reorganize Gaius's tripartite division of persons-things-actions into a bipartite scheme. Their radical solution, in effect, involved the elimination of actions entirely.[88]

Perhaps the most notable example of the Ramist reordering of civil law was to be found in the *Commentariorum Iuris Civilis* of François Connan (1508–51). Once a friend and classmate of Calvin at Bourges, Connan achieved distinction as one of the most original and even daring systematizers of civil law in a decidedly Ramist fashion.

Commenting on Gaius, Connan responded that Gaius's third category of "action" was entirely superfluous. It was, in Connan's view, sufficient to organize the whole of civil law according to a "bipartite division" [*bipartitam divisionem*] organized simply on the two principal juridical categories of "persons" [*personas*] and "things" [*res*]. Under these two basic categories could jurists, then, locate all "forensic actions" [*actiones forenses*]—that is, actions *in personam* (concerning obligations) and actions *in rem* (concerning property).[89] It represented a stark departure from the traditional curricular structure that lawyers on the Continent had studied for centuries, even at Toulouse.

* * *

Bodin, author of the *Distributio*, belongs to this early modern school of legal Ramism. It was a gateway into the modern schools of elegant jurisprudence, the *usus modernus pandectarum*, the modern natural law school, and modern codification movements.[90]

incorporeal, carrying a money value that could potentially be the object of litigation in court, including assets that you own, *in rem*, as property, and debts that are owed, *in personam*, as obligations.

[88] I argue, elsewhere, that, with the elimination of actions, legal Ramists made it possible to prioritize legal rights, in the place of actions. Rights *in rem*, or "real actions" [*jus reale*], take the place of *in rem actio*; rights *in personam*, or "personal actions" [*jus personale*], take the place of *in personam actio*. Rights and remedies thus begin to be decoupled, and it becomes possible to treat rights separately from litigation.

Some critics of Gaius and Justinian responded by enlarging Gaius's tripartition of civil law. Sebastian Derrer, *Iurisprudentia* I (Lyon, 1540), 53–54 [VIII, §§4–5], for example, organized his system around four items falling under the heading of *iuris obiectum*: *persona*, *res*, *commercium*, *persecutio* (*actio* as a label is eliminated). Freigius, *Partitiones Iuris Utriusque*, fol. 4vo, organized the major topics as *persona*, *res*, *actiones et exceptiones*, and *iudicia*.

[89] François Connan, *Commentariorum Iuris Civilis Libri X* (Basel: Apud N. Episcopium, 1562), 109 [II, 1, §1].

[90] For this trajectory in modern legal history, see Peter Stein, *Roman Law in European History* (Cambridge: Cambridge University Press, 1999); Randall Lesaffer, *European Legal History: A Cultural and Political Perspective* (Cambridge: Cambridge University Press, 2009).

We can observe, in particular, the influence of systematizers, such as Baron and Connan, on Bodin, who evidently thought highly of their systematic Ramist method.[91] As we shall see in later chapters, Bodin even credited Connan, by name, with rejecting the excessively narrow understanding of the word *actio*, adopted by Gaius and Justinian as an all-encompassing label for suit or legal remedy, and with developing an innovation in contract law that Bodin would follow in his own re-organization of contractual obligations.[92]

In the following chapters, we will examine more closely the details of the relatively sparse *Distributio* text and the interpretive choices that Bodin needed to make in reorganizing the substance of civil law as a system deserving of its own legal science. As we reconstruct some aspects of Bodin's legal reasoning, we will begin to see why Bodin's work exemplifies, as Michel Villey put it, the *cohérence du système* vital to legal Ramism and, more generally, modern legal science.[93]

[91] Bodin names Connan in the opening dedication of the *Methodus* fol.*4vo, alongside Du Faur, Bohier, Baron, Tiraqueau, and others, for "useful" [*utilitates*] lessons in civil life. Bodin also cites Connan as an authority in *République* 103; 218; 369, particularly on the legislative powers of the Roman senate via senatusconsulta.

[92] Connan on D.50.16.19.

[93] Michel Villey, "La Justice Harmonique selon Bodin," in *Verhandlungen der Internationalen Bodin Tagung in München*, ed. Horst Denzer (Munich: Verlag C.H. Beck, 1973), 301.

2
Divisions of Law

Introduction

The task of organizing and reducing the whole of civil law into an orderly, rational system is ultimately a task of efficient division. The challenge for the jurist is deciding how to make those divisions most effectively and where to distribute the various principles of civil law. Legal Ramists, such as Baron, Connan, Doneau, and Domat, who attempted to devise their own systems of civil law, each addressed this challenge in their own way.[1]

This chapter will explore how Jean Bodin, another legal Ramist, approached the practical task of organizing and dividing a body of law and reconstructing it into a rational system. Studying the details of the *Distributio* offers valuable insights into Bodin's interpretive choices resulting in the divisions of law presented in this work. It also reveals the authorities he consulted in ancient philosophy and rhetoric concerning the principles of division in Plato, Aristotle, and Cicero.

This chapter opens by focusing on Bodin's general theory of law—"law as a whole" [*ius universum*; *droit universel*]. Taking his inspiration from Cicero, Bodin declares that a proper legal science must be general in scope. It cannot, therefore, be a science based solely on the legal system of any one [*singuli*] historical state—even Rome. Instead, a proper jurisprudence, Bodin argues, must be based on the legal experience and practices of many different nations and peoples throughout history—a *ius gentium* (or as he sometimes phrases it, a *ius omnium populorum*).

The study of law is divided into four parts—or, following an Aristotelian approach, four "causes." This chapter will cover three of those causes. The first, the *forma* of jurisprudence, concerns two principal divisions of law—natural law vs. human law; public law vs. private law. The second cause, the *materia* of jurisprudence, addresses the substance of law—persons; things; deeds [*facta*], a deliberate critical response to Gaius who states that civil law concerns persons, things, and actions. It is under this category that Bodin reveals the influence of legal Ramism on his typology of contractual obligations. The third, the *efficiens* of jurisprudence, was the most complex area of the *Distributio* and concerns legal process. It is divided into two main areas—*legis actio* and *officium iudicis*. The bulk of this section,

[1] The work of the legal Ramists anticipated the later "elegant jurisprudence" of Roman-Dutch and French civil lawyers such as Grotius, Arnold Vinnius, Johannes Voet, Jean Domat, and Robert Joseph Pothier.

Divisions of Law. Daniel Lee, Oxford University Press. © Daniel Lee 2026. DOI: 10.1093/9780191847806.003.0003

as we shall see, concerns the "forensic" aspects of the law—in other words, what happens in court under the legal authority, or *imperium*, of a judge. The chapter concludes with a note on the ultimate purpose of this division, a topic that will be treated separately in Chapter 3.

Ius Universum: The Law as a Whole

The first order of business in Bodin's *Distributio* concerned the concept of "law itself" [*ius ipsum*], even before addressing the question of logical division.[2] The *Distributio* can be seen, in part, as Bodin's first attempt at providing the fundamentals of legal theory.

For this purpose, Bodin supplied a term to capture this broad concept of law. This was, we have already seen, *ius universum*, which might best be translated into modern English as "the law as a whole."[3] The label is actually Ciceronian in origin and can be located in the opening passages of Cicero's own treatise on law, *De Legibus*.[4] There, Cicero observes that professional Roman lawyers were rather limited in their expertise to "civil law" only—that is, the *ius civile* of Rome.[5] This civil law included the positive legislation encoded in the XII Tables promulgated by the Decemvirate, as well as the accumulated body of positive legislation in the form of statutes [*leges*], senatusconsulta, edicts, imperial decrees [*constitutiones principum*], custom, and the *responsa* of jurists. As a result, Roman jurisprudence, despite its claim to be a universal *ratio scripta*, or "written reason," effectively concerned only "trivial" [*exiguum*] legal matters, such as "eaves and house-walls" [*de stillicidiorum ac de parietum iure*] and the wording of "formulas for contracts and court procedure" [*stipulationum et iudiciorum formulas*]. What these civil lawyers neglected to study, in Cicero's view, was the *ius universum*, of which civil law was "confined to a small and narrow corner" [*in parvum quendam et angustum locum*].[6]

[2] *Distributio* fol. A: *Forma* [*iurisprudentiae*], *quae huic arti vim & essentiam tribuit, nihil est aliud quam ius ipsum, sine quo iurisprudentia nulla sit.*

[3] Pierre Mesnard, Lucien Jerphagnon, and Simone Goyard-Fabre have chosen to render *ius universum* into French as *droit universel*. However, I don't believe "universal law" (which was Beatrice Reynolds's preferred rendering in her translation of the *Methodus* at 2) captures the Ramist flavor of law as an undifferentiated whole. *Ius universum* signifies the systematic wholeness of a legal system, as opposed to the individual peculiarities located in a specific *ius singulare* or *ius proprium*.

[4] Cicero, *De Legibus*, trans. Clinton Walker Keyes, Loeb Classical Library 213 (Cambridge: Harvard University Press, 1928), 312; 314 [I, iv, §14; I, v, §17] and, indirectly, in *De Oratore* I–II, trans. E. W. Sutton and Harris Rackham, Loeb Classical Library 348 (Cambridge: Harvard University Press, 1948), 300–01 [II, xxxiii, §142], which references a now-lost work, *De iure civili in artem redigendo*.

[5] The opening title of the *Digest* presents two famous accounts of the principal sources of Roman private law. Justinian (D.1.1.1.2) identifies three, *ius naturale*, *ius gentium*, and *ius civile*, while Gaius (D.1.1.9) specifies two, the *ius gentium* and the *ius proprium ipsius civitatis*.

[6] Cicero, *De Legibus*, 314–15 [I, v, §17]. It should be noted that civil lawyers generally view *De Legibus* as a "vacuous" and "so utterly worthless a work," especially when compared to the work of

From Cicero, then, Bodin derives the first interpretive division framing the whole work. To wit: This *Distributio* is not intended to be an analysis of the trifles of civil law—that is, of *ius civile* (or *droit civil*). Instead, it is intended to be an analysis of "universal law" (*droit universel*) or "law as a whole," a general jurisprudence.[7] Bodin's deliberate focus on the *ius universum*, then, sets his *Distributio* far apart from other specimens of early modern legal Ramism, where the purpose was more modest in scope, to reorganize and systematize Justinian's civil law in what was thought to be a more orderly and logical fashion.

Bodin is quite explicit in expressing the low regard in which he holds classical Roman law, despite his frequent use of Roman law as his preferred legal authority. Justinian's civil law, Bodin states, is nothing but the law belonging only to one particular state [*unius civitatis proprium*] and, for this reason, civil law, whether Roman or otherwise, cannot possibly be the basis for a genuine legal science [*in artem non cadit*], deserving the title of a genuine *ius gentium*, shared and observed by all peoples.[8]

Dethroning Roman law from the privileged position that it traditionally enjoyed for centuries was an astoundingly audacious move.[9] As Bodin would later comment in the dedication to the *Methodus*, it is "absurd" what professional civil lawyers of his day have attempted: to "establish a universal law" from the legal system of "just one state"—that is, Rome [*ex Romanis legibus*].[10] If the goal is to establish *ius universum*, proper method demands a thoroughly comparative examination of "all the laws of all states, or those of the more famous states, collected together" and "from them extract the best kind" [*omnibus omnium aut magis illustrium rerumpublicarum legibus in unum collectis ... optimum genus ex iis conflarent*].[11] Bodin's vision of *ius universum* might even be described as early modern legal "meta-data," to reconstruct and extract recurring patterns of law across different historical legal systems.[12]

What legal science required, instead, was an aggregate *ius universum*, amassed together from empirical observation of the legal practices and rules of many states

Scaevola, Gaius, and Sabinus. Kelley, "Gaius Noster," 620, 622, citing Fritz Schulz, *History of Roman Legal Science* (Oxford: Oxford University Press, 1953), 94.

[7] A comparison may be attempted with Bodin's later work on natural philosophy, the *Universae Naturae Theatrum*, where the whole totality of nature can be divided into more specific "accidents."

[8] *Distributio* fol. A.

[9] In practice, though, the substance of the *Distributio* included material from the French *droit civil* which, in turn, was historically shaped by Roman law.

[10] *Methodus* sig..·.3ro. This is, however, an unusual statement, considering how much the *Distributio* ultimately belongs to the tradition of legal scholarship and teaching of Roman law.

[11] *Methodus* sig..·.3ro–3vo. Among the sources cited here are the Persians, the Greeks, the Egyptians, and the Hebrews from the books of the Sanhedrin.

[12] Bodin's interest in comparative legal research was clearly inspired by Eguinaire Baron, *Institutionum Civilium Libri Quatuor* (Pictavii: ex officina Marnefiorum fratrum, 1546), which presents, by way of a comparative *bipartito commentario*, a study of the legal institutions and rules of France and Rome.

and legal systems. Legal science must be, in other words, genuinely comparative in order to uncover the most important parts of this *ius universum* which, Bodin declared, "lies hidden in history" [*in historia iuris universi pars optima latet*].[13] Indeed, it is for this reason that one commentator has called Bodin "the forerunner of comparative law" [*le précurseur du droit comparé*].[14]

Studying *ius universum*, then, had two related, but distinct, tasks. One was pedagogical and inspired by the fashionable legal Ramism of the sixteenth century—to reorganize the whole of jurisprudence into a more systematic and orderly fashion, a system that could, in theory, accommodate not only Roman law but many legal systems. The other was empirical—to gather and sift through the historical legal data efficiently, so that a picture of this grand *ius universum* gradually unfolds and reveals itself to the historically minded lawyer.[15]

The latter was the declared purpose of the *Methodus*, a sort of practical guide for lawyers navigating and efficiently managing the wealth of raw historical data contained in the primary source literature describing past legal practices and institutions. But this comparative empirical research was ultimately intended to supplement the legal cartography being drawn in the *Distributio*.

It was for this reason, then, that Bodin originally (in the 1578 print) chose to present his analysis of the *ius universum* as a Ramist *tableau* of law, some examples of which have been reproduced below. Organized according to the four Aristotelian causes—*forma, materia, efficiens, finis*—that law students would likely have already learned as students in the Arts faculties, Bodin sought to present a visual mapping of this unexplored terrain of jurisprudence according to these familiar "four causes or four questions":[16]

1. ***Forma***: Whether it exists [*An sit*]
2. ***Materia***: In what does it consist [*Quid sit*]
3. ***Efficiens***: In what way does it manifest itself [*Qualis sit*]
4. ***Finis***: Why does it exist [*Cur sit*]

These four questions set the agenda for the *Distributio*. I will discuss the first three in this chapter. The fourth will be treated separately in its own chapter.

[13] *Methodus*, ante Summa Capita.

[14] Michèle Ducos, "'Le Tableau de droit universel' de Jean Bodin et la tradition romaine," *Bulletin de l'Association Guillaume Budé* 1 (1987): 51.

[15] Brown, *Methodus*, 36.

[16] Lloyd, *Jean Bodin*, 58 suggests a possible source in Aristotle, *Posterior Analytics*, trans. Hugh Tredennick and E. S. Forster, Loeb Classical Library 391 (Cambridge: Harvard University Press, 1960), 174–75 [II, 89^b23–24]. It is important to stress how unconventional this Aristotelian approach was, but it was not entirely unprecedented. For example, Bartolus ad D.12.4.16, §13 concerns *emptio-venditio* (contract of sale) and treats of price as the *causa finalis* of sale, whereas classical law usually treats of price as enabling the *venditio perfecta* (the completion of the sale); Accursius ad C.5.12.25, s.v. *mulier*, speaks of the *causa impulsiva vel efficiens* concerning a gift. Wesenbeck, commenting on the opening title of *De iustitia et iure*, would also identify various causes of justice.

The Form of Jurisprudence

The first major section of the *Distributio* opens with a discussion of the *forma* of jurisprudence. The vocabulary selected by Bodin for this discussion is particularly significant. His goal is to provide a conceptual mapping of "law," but he stresses that his focus is specifically on *ius*—not *lex* or *loi*.[17]

Like the French *droit*, the word *ius* carried a broad meaning. It encompassed the sense of legality, legal order, and even that of a whole legal system, the sum-total of legal rules and institutions making up the law as a whole. Hence, *ius civile*, or "civil law," conventionally was understood to mean the whole of Roman law (and not simply promulgated statutes, which are specifically designated *leges*, or singularly, *lex*).[18] But *ius* also meant something more, the general sense of justice or moral rectitude, often thought to be of divine origin, giving moral force to the law and giving rise to the obligation to comply with its rules.[19] With this in mind, Bodin chooses to describe *ius* in this way:

> Law [*ius*] is a ray of divine benevolence and prudence granted to men, and applied by them, for the advantage of human society [*ad utilitatem humanae societatis*].[20]

Ius, however, wasn't the only word in classical Latin meaning "law." The word *lex* also signified law.[21] But the two terms—*ius* and *lex* (cf. *droit* and *loi*)—were not equivalent, a point observed by Cicero in *De Legibus*.[22]

Lex functioned as a general term referring to any legislation formally promulgated by human legislators. Indeed, in classical Roman law, *lex* was a technical

[17] Perhaps a more colloquially accessible translation of *ius universum* into idiomatic modern English might be "law as a systematically organized whole." Cf. James Gordley, "Ius Civile: The Roman Jurists," in *The Jurists: A Critical History* (Oxford: Oxford University Press, 2013), 116.

[18] Modern Continental jurists sometimes specified this particularly broad understanding of *ius* as "objective"—hence, *ius objectivum, droit objectif, objektives Recht.*

[19] It is for this reason that the term *ius* can also mean "right," in the restricted sense of a demand that one can legally make upon another to perform obligations that are legally due, or to restore property. The divine origin of law's rectitude is not exclusively Christian. Cf. Cicero, *De Legibus*, 316–19; 378–81 [I, v §19; II, iv, §§7–8].

[20] *Distributio* fol. A. Cf. D.1.1.10.2. The final clause, *ad utilitatem humanae societatis*, indicates Cicero's influence on this opening section.

[21] There is a celebrated dispute on the etymology of the word *lex*. In the *Tractatus de Legibus*, Aquinas, citing Isidore of Seville (*Etymologiae* V, 3; II, 10), derives the origin of *lex* in *legere*, "to read," because *lex scripta*, "the promulgated law is written." Aquinas, however, also acknowledges another false etymology, *lex à ligando*, that "the law comes from binding." Bodin will revive this false etymology in his own treatment of legislation as a binding-device.

[22] Cicero, *De Legibus*, 314–15; 342–43 [I, v, §§16–17; I, xiv, §42] refers to the *leges tyrannorum*, the "laws of the tyrants"—the Thirty of Athens—to ask whether such laws could be regarded as "lawful" or "just" [*leges iustae*]. Cf. *De Re Publica* III, commenting on the *lex Voconia*, restricting the legal rights of women concerning inheritance and legacies, which is described as an unjust law—or perhaps, more literally, an "unlawful law" [*lex iniuria*]. Note also Bodin's comment on Augustus's exemption of Livia from the Voconian law, at *République* 719; *De Republica* 535 [V, 2].

category of legislation specifying statutes enacted by one of the *comitia*, the popular citizen voting assemblies, of Rome.[23] Justinian put it this way in the *Institutes*:

> A *lex* is what the Roman people [the *populus* as a voting assembly] have decreed, in response to the interrogatory of a senatorial magistrate, such as a consul.[24]

Bodin, however, would repurpose the term *lex* to signify legislation promulgated directly by the commanding will of a sovereign authority (as opposed to an edict promulgated by a magistrate):

> Sanction [*sanctio*] or the command of the prince [*iussum principis*] or of the sovereign authority in a state [*summae in republica potestatis*] is called legislation [*lex*].[25]

Long before Thomas Hobbes or John Austin, then, Bodin was the first to articulate what Anglo-American legal theorists would later call the command theory of law, whereby valid law is always reducible to some imperative act of command.[26]

As Bodin would later explain in the *République*, *lex* was a binding-device which only sovereigns could activate upon their subjects.[27] Borrowing from a Scholastic etymology, *lex à ligando dicitur* ("law is said to derive from binding"), he observed that its purpose was to bind and oblige subjects under some specified legal duty. But just as a sovereign may bind [*ligare*] subjects by commanding legislation, so too could sovereigns release [*solvere*] subjects from legal duty, whether by countermand, derogation from legislation, or full abrogation or repeal.[28]

[23] However, *lex* was not the only form of positive legislation in Rome. Edicts, plebiscites, senatusconsulta, imperial decrees [*constitutiones*], rescripts, and responsa prudentum all were recognized to carry the force of law. The emperor, or *princeps*, was understood to hold the legislative power to make law through decrees, as a result of the *lex regia* (D.1.4.1) by which the Roman people was said to have transferred its collective lawmaking powers to the emperor.

[24] Inst.1.2.4: *Lex est quod populus Romanus senatorio magistratu interrogante, veluti consule, constituebat.* Cf. Gloss ad D.1.3.1, Papinian, s.v. *Lex est*, indicates that *lex* essentially consists of four principal parts. This is the legislative origin of some of the most important sources of Roman law such as the *lex Aquilia*, the *lex Hortensia*, *lex Canuleia* (discussed at length by Bodin), *lex Fufia Caninia*. *Lex* is to be distinguished from *plebiscitum*, which is a legislative instrument exclusive to the plebs assembled under the authority of the plebeian tribunes who alone enjoyed the immunity of *sacrosancta* and the veto power of *ius intercessionis*. The distinction between *leges* and *plebescita* vanish, however, in the Late Republic after the *lex Hortensia*.

[25] *Distributio* fol. A, s.v. *sanctio seu iussum*. Cf. *République* 216; *De Republica* 150 [I, 10].

[26] One distinctive feature in Bodin's command–countermand theory of law is the specifically legal character of command. A legal command is not simply a bare expression of a sovereign's arbitrary will. Nor is it equivalent to a show of coercive force. That is why, to stress its legal character, Bodin often describes the sovereign's legislative command as *droit commandment* or *imperium legitimum*. See Lee, *Right of Sovereignty*, 102–10; 151–59.

[27] Lee, *Right of Sovereignty*, 154.

[28] This point, as I have argued elsewhere, is the quintessential quality of sovereignty, what Bodin called "absolute power"—the sovereign's legal power to "absolve" or release subjects of legal obligation, not unlike the priestly power of absolution from sin, by amending or repealing legislation entirely. Lee, *Right of Sovereignty*, 159–163; cf. *République* 131; 222–23; *De Republica* 85; 155 [I, 8; I, 10]. But this

The point to observe here is that law [*ius*] is more than legislation [*lex*]. The full scope of jurisprudence extends beyond mere legislation and encompasses far more than what human lawmakers have created or will create. This is why, as we'll see, the opening division of law distinguishes between natural law [*ius naturale*] and human law [*ius humanum*], to include natural law, as Ulpian did in the *Digest*, as a valid source of law. While perhaps alien to the habits of modern legal positivism, Bodin's *summa divisio* reflects a well-established principle of classical and early modern jurisprudence, that law (and the obligations emanating from it) derives not only from human promulgated legislation but also from nature itself.

Natural Law and Human Law

Having established the concept of law in general, Bodin proceeds next to the question about sources of law. And he answers that the two principal sources of law—and specifically, of *ius universum*—are "natural law" [*ius naturale*] and "human law" [*ius humanum*].

This division is revealing for several reasons. It uncovers, first of all, Bodin's methodological preference in constructing legal taxonomies by way of dichotomies, rather than trichotomies, as Gaius and Justinian evidently preferred. As he puts it, echoing the classical principle of διαίρεσις, "a dichotomy is far more convenient" than the classical models taught in the law schools.[29]

He is thinking, of course, of the classical tripartite typology in the opening title of Justinian's *Digest*, attributed to Ulpian, which locates the three principal sources of classical Roman private law in natural law [*ius naturale*], the law of nations [*ius*

absolute power is a limited power: No sovereign can alter or amend natural law duties through an assertion of absolute power.

Bodin acknowledges that a sovereign may selectively choose to release a specified class of subjects—or even one individual—by grant of privilege [*privilegium*; *ius singulare*]. On the distinction between "legislation" [*loi*; *lex*] and "privilege" [*privilegium*], Bodin at *République* 216; *De Republica* 150 [I, 10] cites Festus, *De verborum significatione*, on the word *Rogatio*. As he explains, privileges function as a species of legislation, though of limited scope, applicable only to one person or a specific class of persons.

[29] *Distributio* fol. A. Kelley, "Gaius Noster," 622–25. However, as we will soon see, Bodin did not categorically eschew the use of trichotomies. For example, he retains, with a major amendment, the overall architecture of Gaius's trichotomous division of law into persons, things, and "deeds" [*facta*]. The reason for this is that division, as a rhetorical technique, is employed to achieve different ends. Sometimes, the goal is to decompose a complex entity into its basic parts [*partitio*], while in other cases, the goal is to identify the species of a genus [*divisio*]. Cicero, *Topica*, trans. H. M. Hubbell, Loeb Classical Library 386 (Cambridge: Harvard University Press, 1949), 400 [V, §28]: *Definitiones aliae sunt partitionum aliae divisionum.* Inst.1.2 serves as an example of "partition" for Cicero: *si quis ius civile dicat id esse quod in legibus senatus consultis, rebus iudicatis, iuris peritorum auctoritate, edictis magistratuum, more aequitate consistat.*

gentium], and civil law [*ius civile*]. *Privatum ius tripertitum est: collectum etenim est ex naturalibus praeceptis aut gentium aut civilibus.*[30]

What is notable, and most controversial, in Ulpian's definition of natural law is its broadened scope in order to include animals as well as humans. Animals, Ulpian argued, follow natural law, just as humans do, because *natura omnia animalia docuit* ("nature teaches all animals").[31] But lawyers, both ancient and modern, were uncomfortable with Ulpian's broad inclusion of animals as participants in the natural law. Gaius (D.1.1.9) and Paul (D.1.1.11) both rejected Ulpian's theory of law which extended even to animals. So too did Connan.[32]

Bodin felt that Ulpian made an error, leading to unnecessary confusion in determining the distinctive content of natural law:

> Some [i.e., Ulpian and his followers] attribute the procreation of children to the natural law. But this does not pertain to law any more than the appetite for food or sex, which is equally common to beasts and men. There can be no society based on the rule of law [*iuris societas*] among men and beasts.[33] Because they are not capable of participating in crimes, so neither can they participate in any law ... Ulpian's division, which does not even agree with itself... hardly needs refutation.[34]

Rejecting Ulpian's definition of natural law as largely irrelevant to legal science, Bodin effectively transformed the *summa divisio* of law from a tripartition into a bipartition.[35] He had several models to follow in this respect, two of which can already be found in the *Digest*.[36] In addition to Gaius and Paul, Bodin also followed the example of Plato, Cicero, and especially Aristotle, who, in the

[30] D.1.1.1.2: "Private law is divided into three parts. It is gathered from the precepts of natural law, the law of nations, and civil law."

[31] D.1.1.1.3: "From natural law proceeds the union of male and female which we designate as marriage; hence also arises the procreation of children and the bringing up of the same; for we see that all animals, and even wild beasts, appear to be acquainted with this law."

[32] François Connan, *Commentariorum Iuris Civilis Libri X* (Basel: Apud N. Episcopium, 1562), 18 [I, 4, §7].

[33] *Societas iuris* is a Ciceronian phrase, a "legal partnership," appearing at *De Re Publica*, trans. Clinton Walker Keyes, Loeb Classical Library 213 (Cambridge: Harvard University Press, 1928), 76 [I, xxxii, §49]; *De Legibus* 336 [I, xiii, §35]. *Societas* is a type of contract in Roman law, whereby partners [*socii*] agree to pool assets for a common enterprise. This is the model for Cicero's vision of *respublica*, at *De Re Publica* I, §39, which he famously defines as *coetus multitudinis iuris consensu et utilitatis communion sociatus*. See Elizabeth Asmis, "The State as Partnership: Cicero's Definition of *Res Publica* in His Work, 'On the State,'" *History of Political Thought* 25 (2004): 569–98.

[34] D.9.1.1.3: *nec enim potest animal iniuria fecisse, quod sensu caret.*

[35] One advantage of this revision is that Bodin can bypass altogether the medieval distinction between "primary" and "secondary" *ius naturale* and *ius gentium*, attributed to Bartolus of Sassoferrato ad D.12.6.64. There is an echo of this Bartolist distinction in the *Distributio* fol. D, s.v. *obligatio iuris vinculum quo dare facere tenemur*, which introduces a fourfold [*quadruplex*] distinction of obligations: *obligatio naturalis; obligatio naturalis et gentium; obligatio gentium non tamen naturalis; obligatio civilis.*

[36] D.1.1.9 (Gaius); D.1.1.11 (Paul). D.1.1.9 quotes the opening sentence of Gaius's *Institutes*: *Omnes populi, qui legibus et moribus reguntur, partim suo proprio, partim communi omnium hominum iure utuntur: nam quod quisque populus ipse sibi ius constituit, id ipsius proprium est vocaturque ius civile,*

Nicomachean Ethics, formalized the Greek distinction between "natural justice" and "legal justice."[37] Having eliminated Ulpian's tripartite *summa divisio* between *ius naturale*, *ius gentium*, and *ius civile*, Bodin was now in a position to redefine the content of natural law as that body of law concerning "the worship for God, piety for one's relatives, gratitude for the deserving, vengeance for criminals, justice for all."

Equally notable is how Bodin chose to label this dichotomous legal distinction. Whereas one branch of *ius universum* is natural law, the other is labeled "human law" [*ius humanum*], a term that is generally not used in classical Roman law, but rather, in canon law.[38] (For a legal humanist, such usage would clearly be a post-classical interpolation.) Human law, in turn, is further subdivided into Ulpian's (and Gaius's) more familiar categories of *ius gentium* and *ius civile*, thereby yielding the following arrangement (see Figure 2.1).[39]

But civil law, as we have already seen, is almost immediately brushed aside as irrelevant. As Bodin puts it, "civil law, which is specific [*proprium*] to one state or another, does not belong to this science," and the reason is clear.[40] Jurisprudence, which he defines as "the art of rendering to each his due" [*ars tribuendi suum cuique*] for the preservation of human society [*hominum societatem*], is a science that applies universally to all states and all peoples, not just Rome and its civil law.

The real center of attention in Bodin's *Distributio*, then, is the *ius gentium*. While modern legal scholarship typically tends to interpret the *ius gentium* as a synonym for international law, or *ius inter gentes*, Bodin understood the term more in the classical manner of Gaius.[41] It is, as Gaius put it, "the law that natural

quasi ius proprium civitatis; quod vero naturalis ratio inter omnes homines constituit, id apud omnes peraeque custoditur vocaturque ius gentium, quasi quo iure omnes gentes utuntur.

[37] Aristotle, *Nicomachean Ethics*, trans. Horace Rackham, ed. Jeffrey Henderson, Loeb Classical Library 73 (Cambridge: Harvard University Press, 1934), 294–95 [V, vii, §1, 1134^{b}20]. Grotius, at *De Jure Belli ac Pacis* (Amsterdam: Apud Iohannem Blaeu, 1646), 3 [I, 1, §9] makes the same distinction, attributing his distinction between *jus naturale* and *jus voluntarium* (his term meaning essentially the same as positive legislation) to Aristotle.

[38] *Ius humanum* does occasionally appear in the classical Latin literature—e.g., Seneca, *Moral Essays* III: *De Beneficiis*, trans. John Basore, Loeb Classical Library 310 (Cambridge, MA: Harvard University Press, 1935), 160 [III, xviii, §2]. While this has been interpreted to mean "human right"—e.g., in Alex Long, "Seneca on Human Rights in *De Beneficiis* 3," *Apeiron* 54, no. 2 (2021): 189–201—what Seneca actually seems to be stressing is a lawful or juridical relation among humans, including even slaves, a relation which is characterized not only by rights but also by duties and virtues.

[39] This arrangement is noticeably similar to Grotius's legal typology in *De Jure Belli ac Pacis* 3–7 [I, 1, §§9–14], where the concept of law is bifurcated into the two branches of *jus naturale* and *jus voluntarium*, again citing the authority of Aristotle. The latter is then further subdivided into *jus divinum* (divine positive law), *jus gentium*, and *jus civile*. A similar structure is preserved in Grotius's textbook of Roman–Dutch law, *Jurisprudence of Holland*, trans. R. W. Lee (Oxford: Clarendon Press, 1926), 4–5 [*Hollandsche Rechtsgeleerdheid* I, 2, §4], which distinguishes between law [*wet*] that is *aengeboren* ("natural law") and law that is *gegeven* ("positive law"). The original 1631 print included Ramist tables inserted into the volume.

[40] *Distributio* fol. A, s.v. *civile quod.*

[41] Indeed, the term "international law" was coined by Jeremy Bentham.

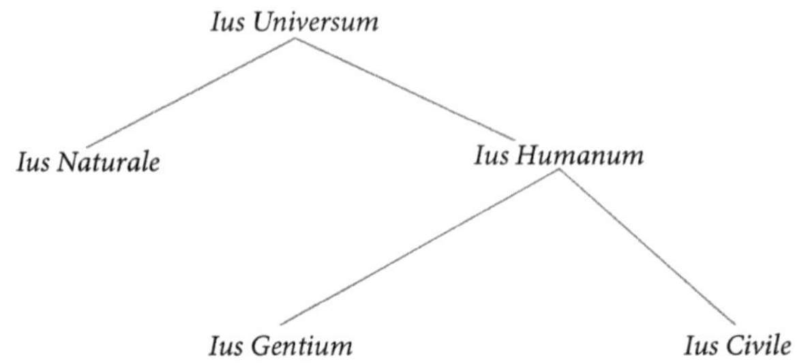

Figure 2.1 Diagram of the various species of the category of *ius universum*, or "the whole law."

reason establishes among all mankind, is followed by all peoples alike, and is called *ius gentium* as being the law observed by all mankind."[42] It is that branch of human law encompassing "what all peoples [*omnes populi*], or a good part of them, have unanimously approved [*consensione probarunt*]."[43] For this reason, he sometimes describes this body of law, synthesized from a methodical comparison between various legal systems, as the *ius omnium populorum* ("the law of all peoples").

Public Law and Private Law

Having identified *ius gentium* as the principal source of the *ius universum* (rather than the *ius civile*, Roman legislation), Bodin turns to the next major division of law—that is, public law [*ius publicum*] and private law [*ius privatum*]. While Bodin is following Ulpian's precedent in the *Digest* who similarly distinguishes between public and private law, Bodin's treatment is especially notable in how much attention he devotes to public law. This is not surprising, considering that Bodin was to become perhaps the most influential early modern theorist of public law and state.[44]

Classical Roman law was almost entirely a system of private law concerning, as Gaius would famously put it, a legal system concerning persons, things, and actions.[45] While Roman jurisconsults acknowledged, in principle, that a body of public law did exist (Ulpian specified that public law concerns matters *in sacris, in*

[42] Gaius 1.1; D.1.1.9: *Quod vero naturalis ratio inter omnes homines constituit, id apud omnes peraeque custoditur vocaturque ius gentium, quasi quo iure omnes gentes utuntur.*

[43] *Distributio* fol. A, s.v. *gentium quod.* The phrase *omnes populi* is a reference to Gaius at D.1.1.9.

[44] Martin Loughlin, *Foundations of Public Law* (Oxford: Oxford University Press, 2010), 55, suggests "Bodin brought about nothing less than a reconstruction of the foundations of public law."

[45] Gaius 1.8; D.1.5.1.

sacerdotibus, in magistratibus), it was unwritten custom originating in the Roman *mos maiorum* and, thus, fell outside the boundaries of legal science.[46]

Bodin's innovation here directly challenged this convention. Public law not only belonged to the *ius universum* but was also an essential component. Neglect of public law was a major deficiency of the Roman *ius civile* that Bodin's *ius universum* could potentially rectify.

What functions did public law perform in Bodin's view? In summary, public law concerns the basic governing functions of state such as "enacting legislation [*leges iubere*], creating and appointing magistrates [*magistratus creare*], taking advice concerning matters of state [*consilium de republica capere*], declaring and ending war [*bellum indicere ac finire*], establishing punishments and rewards [*poenas ac praemia irrogare*], executing actions of law" [*legis actiones exequi*].[47] Readers familiar with Bodin's theoretical writings on sovereignty will recognize this list of public law because it is almost exactly the same list of the various prerogatives and "rights of sovereignty" [*iura imperii, iura maiestatis*] appearing in the *Methodus*.[48] These matters of public law are exclusive—*proprium*—to holders of public *imperium* and cannot be shared with, or delegated permanently to, subordinates.[49]

It is noteworthy that public law—and especially *imperium* ("authority")—holds a vital place in Bodin's vision of jurisprudence, unlike classical Roman law which mostly concerns private law and largely omits treatment of public law.[50] Every legal system must have something like a law governing and classifying the various types of authority. In the *Distributio*, Bodin supplies this, the bare outline of what

[46] Early modern legal historians such as Nicolas de Grouchy and Carlo Sigonio attempted to reconstruct various aspects of Roman public law. The most comprehensive attempt, however, was achieved in the nineteenth century by Theodor Mommsen's multi-volume *Römisches Staatsrecht*, published between 1871 and 1888, which remains the standard modern academic study of Roman public law.

[47] *Distributio* fol. A, s.v. *ius publicum*. The one function of public law that does not appear in Bodin's later analysis of sovereignty was *sacra tueri*. Here is another example of Bodin's application of a Ciceronian rhetorical technique, defining sovereignty by means of a *partitio*.

[48] *Methodus* 260–61 [VI]: *Putabam summum imperium vel magistratuum creatione, vel praemiorum ac poenarum potestate definiri ... Video summam reipublicae in quinque partibus versari. Una est ac praecipua, in summis magistratibus creandis, & officio cuiusque definiendo, altera in legibus iubendis aut abrogandis, tertia in bello indicendo ac finiendo, quarta in extrema procuratione ab omnibus magistratibus, postrema in potestate vitae & necis, cum lex ipsa nec facilitates ullum, nec clementiae locum relinquit.* This is also the same passage where Bodin references (at 262) a now-lost work (or possibly an early working title for *République*), *De iure imperii*, which evidently contained a chapter entitled *De iure maiestatis*.

[49] Bodin often uses the term *proprium* when identifying those powers that are "exclusive" to a particular authority—e.g., *Methodus* 262 [VI]. The reference is to D.1.16.13 [*Legati proconsulis nihil proprium habent*] and D.1.21.1.1 [*Qui mandatam iurisdictionem suscepit, proprium nihil habet*], both of which dealt with the legality of delegated jurisdiction [*mandata*]: Holders of delegated jurisdiction, such as a proconsular legate or a *iudex*, have no authority [*imperium*] of their own [*proprium*] beyond the mere exercise delegated to them. Delegates never have *merum imperium* which is granted by law [*lege datur*] only to the magistrate formally appointed by a *lex de imperio*. Cf. *Distributio* fol. F, s.v. *ex adiunctis iurisdictio*: *iurisdictio alia est propria, eaque vel legitima, iure scilicet magistratus, vel lege soluta, iure maiestatis competens ... alia mandata, à principe, vel à magistratu.*

[50] D.1.1.1.2: *Publicum ius est quod ad statum rei Romanae spectat ... in sacris, in sacerdotibus, in magistratibus constitit.*

modern German lawyers call *allgemeine Staatslehre*, a general theory of state and public law.

Private law, the other chief division of all complete legal systems, concerns everything else. It is "that law which considers interests other than the public."[51] In Bodin's scheme, he organizes private law according to the different levels of application, not unlike the organization of classical Roman law. Some private laws concern towns [*municipia*] and private associations [*collegia*]; others concern the family, in which one can locate those laws governing relations of marriage [*viri & uxoris*], of parents and children [*parentum ac liberorum*], and of masters and slaves [*dominorum ac servorum*]; and still other areas of private law exclusively concern the legal rights and duties of individuals [*singulos*], apart from their connection to any of the above-mentioned associations.

What is only implied at this early stage (and later clarified in the third part of the *Distributio* on the "efficient cause" of law) is that each of these units of private law is, like the state, its own structure of private authority [*imperium privatum*]. Like the state, under the sovereign *imperium* of a prince or people, corporations [*universitas*] and private associations [*collegia*] are united under the sovereign-like authority of their head. Similarly, families are governed under the authority of their head of family, serving in different roles as husband [*manus viri in uxorem*], as father over children [*potestas patris erga liberos*], and as master over slaves [*domini in servos*]. Just as Bodin's vision of the state is pluralistic—an association made up of lesser associations of families and corporate associations—so too is Bodin's vision of public and private law correspondingly pluralistic, a feature that will shape the substance of law.[52]

The Matter of Jurisprudence: Persons, Things, Deeds

The second major part of the *Distributio* concerns the substantive matter, or the *materia*, of jurisprudence and addresses the question—that is, in what does law consist [*Quid sit*]?

Bodin summarizes his reply as follows: "The matter around which every question of law revolves consists in persons [*in personis*], or in things [*in rebus*], or in the deeds and words of persons" [*in factis ac dictis personarum*] (see Figure 2.2).[53]

[51] *Distributio* fol. A, s.v. *ius privatum*.

[52] Lee, *Right of Sovereignty*, chap. 1 details the pluralistic and associational features of Bodin's theory of state.

[53] Cf. the opening *Dedicatio* of the *Distributio*: All matters of jurisprudence concern "persons, things, and deeds [*personis, rebus, et factis*]. In these three [*in his tribus*] is implicated the material cause of this discipline."

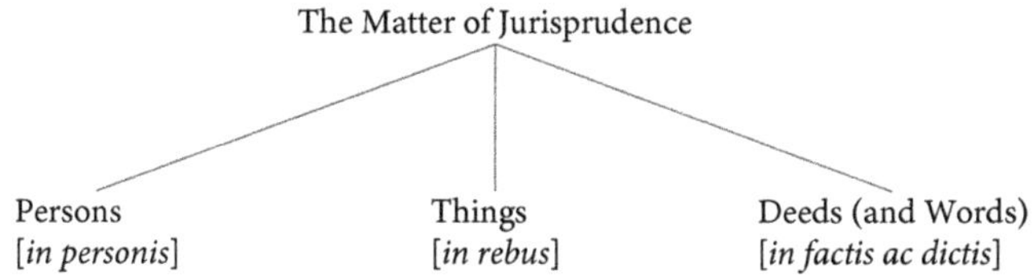

Figure 2.2 Diagram of the three principal areas, or *materia*, of jurisprudence according to Bodin—persons, things, deeds.

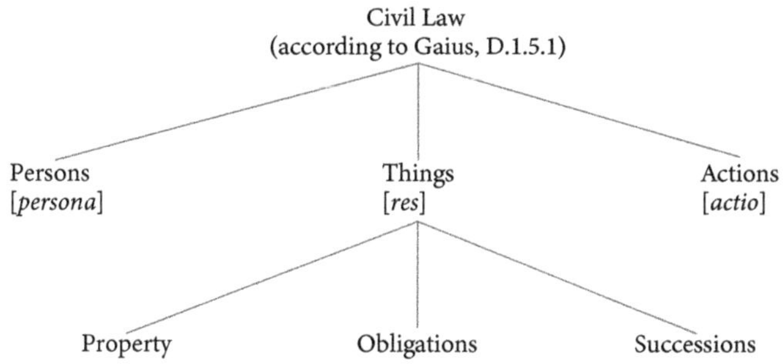

Figure 2.3 Diagram of Gaius's classical taxonomy of civil law, classified according to persons, things, actions. The second category of things, or *res*, is further subdivided into the law concerning property, obligations, and successions.

The form of Bodin's response will be familiar, though suspiciously inaccurate, to any classically trained lawyer, including any classically trained lawyer in sixteenth-century France. Bodin was borrowing from, and purposefully amending, Gaius's own famous tripartite division of civil law, captured in Justinian's *Digest* at D.1.5.1:

> The whole of the law observed by us relates either to persons or to things or to actions.[54]

Bodin even acknowledges his intellectual debt openly where he writes that "Gaius and Justinian had divided all matter of law into things, persons, and actions [*in res, personas, et actiones*]" (see Figure 2.3).[55]

Yet, his deliberate choice to reorganize Gaius's famous tripartition is a testament to Bodin's creativity in designing his own legal system in the *Distributio*.

[54] Cf. Inst.1.2.12; D.1.5.1; Gaius 1.8: *Omne autem ius quo utimur vel ad personas pertinet vel ad res vel ad actiones.*

[55] *Distributio* fol. B, s.v. *Facta.* The reference to Justinian is most likely Inst.1.2.12, which is really just a reference to Gaius.

We can begin, first, with similarities between Bodin's system in the *Distributio* and Gaius's classical system in civil law. Bodin retained the general structure with respect to the first two major areas of law, the law of persons and the law of things.

Persons: Bodin's treatment of the law of persons is organized into three subdivisions: *Personae trifariam dividuntur, ex Sexu, ex Statu, & ex Dignitate.* But in this apparently innocuous presentation, Bodin has actually accomplished something quite heterodox. Every university-trained lawyer (as Bodin was) in medieval and early modern Europe, whether of civil, canon, or common law, knows that the foundational division in the law of persons specifically concerns legal *status* or condition: All persons are either "free" [*liberi homines*] or slaves [*servi*].[56] All other legal classifications of personality—the three traditional aspects of personality in Roman law are *libertas, civitas, familia*—are parasitic on, and flow from, this primary question, what Gaius at D.1.5.3 has called the *summa de iure personarum divisio* ("the chief division of the law of persons").

In classical Roman law, this question of *libertas* concerning status must be addressed first before addressing any other legal question about personality. Gaius's priority rule remained unchanged in the medieval jurisprudence of the Italian Glossators and was well-established dicta among Bodin's legal humanist contemporaries in France. Even the most technically gifted academic lawyers in Bodin's day—François Baudouin, Hugues Doneau, and François Connan—continued to insist on the primacy of Gaius's *summa divisio*, and textbooks of civil law continued to recognize this pedagogical convention.[57]

While Bodin retained the classical treatment of slavery, his presentation of the law of persons in the *Distributio* eliminated this primacy of status entirely, by recognizing, instead, three different and equal dimensions along which legal personality can be established.[58] One was gender [*sexus*]:

Ex Sexu, dicitur vir, foemina, hermaphroditus.

[56] Even the medieval English judge Bracton, once a student of the Bolognese doctor Azo, observes the classical priority of the division between free and slave. Bracton, *De Legibus et Consuetudinibus Angliae*, ed. George Woodbine (New Haven, CT: Yale University Press, 1922), 2:29 [*De Personis*].

[57] Keechang Kim, "L'étranger chez Jean Bodin," *Revue historique de droit français et étranger* 76, no. 1 (1998): 78 gives several examples in the humanist legal scholarship documenting the priority given to the free/slave distinction even during Bodin's lifetime. François Hotman is one example cited, in *Partitiones iuris civilis elementariae* (Basel: Apud N. Episcopium Iuniorem, 1560), 8–9, which states that despite the *multiplex* ways of dividing persons legally, one remains ... *summa & prima, quae bipartita est: ut alii liberi, alii servi dicantur.*

[58] Lee, *Right of Sovereignty*, 131–34. As I noted there, one important reason for this alternative presentation of the law of persons was the recognition that not all states were slaveholding societies, as the Roman Empire was. Bodin's France preserved the ideology that the French were a "frank and free" people and never knew the taint of slavery. Political subjecthood, thus, was to be distinguished from slavery. Bodin allows "the free subject" [*le franc subiect*] to be a free person who nevertheless "holds the sovereignty of another" [*tenant de la souverainete d'autruy*].

Most noteworthy in this division was Bodin's expansive non-binary view of legal gender, beyond a simplistic male/female dichotomy. For Bodin, a complete legal system must acknowledge the reality—and, indeed, the humanity—of hermaphroditism, as a category distinct from male or female. This was a significant departure from Roman law which required the assignment of—and, implicitly, the legal elimination of—hermaphrodites to the "predominant" [*praevalet*] gender.[59] Bodin's position also challenged the Civilian dicta (D.1.5.14) that births *contra formam humani generis* were "monstrous" [*monstrosum*] and, due to their lack of legal humanity, ineligible to be counted as lawful heirs [*liberi*].[60]

The other new dimension, in addition to status (free/slave) and gender (male/female/hermaphrodite), was rank [*dignitas*]:

Ex dignitate, personae dicuntur, publicae, aut privatae.

Dignitas—which might best be translated in terms of personal merit or worthiness—captured the legal distinctions in rank found in both public and private law. Among those designated as "public persons" were included all those in service of the state, at all ranks—from the most powerful magistrates down to minor scribes and notaries entrusted with minor clerical duties.

Bodin's treatment of public persons foreshadows a critical set of distinctions he will introduce in the *République* III—that is, the distinction between officers, magistrates, and commissioners.[61] While all public persons are in service of the state, only some are entrusted with a share of public authority [*cum imperio*].[62] Indeed, many public persons lack authority [*sine imperio*]—what Bodin will sometimes call a "simple officer."[63] The latter include those officers of state charged with some public duty or function—clerks, notaries, recordkeepers, lictors, heralds—but without any authority over another. In the era before modern bureaucratic techniques of routinized record-keeping and computing technology, such roles were

[59] D.1.5.10: *Quaeritur: hermaphroditum cui comparamus? Et magis puto eius sexus aestimandum, qui in eo praevalet.* Cf. D.22.5.15.1 on hermaphrodite witnesses; D.28.2.6.2 specifies that hermaphrodites can appoint a posthumous heir, *si in eo virilia praevalebunt.* In general, see Christoph Rolker, "The Two Laws and the Three Sexes: Ambiguous Bodies in Canon Law and Roman Law (12th to 16th Centuries)," *Zeitschrift der Savigny-Stiftung für Rechtsgeschichte: Kanonistische Abteilung* 100 (2014): 178–222. This is to say nothing of transgender persons and whether transgender was a legal possibility in Bodin's legal universe.

[60] Cf. Baldus de Ubaldis, *Commentaria* III (Venice, 1599), fol. 58vo [ad D.28.2.12]: *monstruosus homo est tamen homo* ("a monstrous human is still a human").

[61] Lee, "Office Is a Thing Borrowed," 409–40; Lee, *Popular Sovereignty*, 208–17.

[62] *De Republica* 259 [III, 2].

[63] Cf. *République* 127 [I, 8]. In *République* III, Bodin sometimes refers to these employees of state as *simples usagers* (441) and *simples execeteurs & ministers des loix & des Princes* (439). It is a vital category for Bodin's theory of the state, to stress that even the lowliest of clerks serve the state, as public professionals, and not as personal servants owing fealty to their *seigneurial* lords. Bodin envisions the depersonalizing of state authority.

Note that Bodin has not yet discussed the juridical quality of *imperium*, a point he will address in the third part of the *Distributio*, when he discusses the *efficiens* of law.

vital for statecraft, and they remain an early modern fossil built into the structure of modern rational bureaucratic states.

Among those entrusted with public authority—that is, *persona cum imperio*—arises another, second distinction. This concerns the terms under which a person is appointed to public office and entrusted with a share of the state's public authority—*ordinario* or *extraordinario*. In some cases, a person is appointed by an "extraordinary charge" [*charge extraordinaire*; *extra ordinem*], when authority is granted *par souffrance*, solely at the continuing pleasure and personal will [*arbitrio*] of the sovereign.[64] These *commissaires* (or "commissioners"), as Bodin will call them later in the *République*, share one basic quality in common—a servile dependence on their sovereign's goodwill and favor.[65] A *commissaire* with such an extraordinary charge can exercise even a vast authority, but only so long as the sovereign permits it. This is why Bodin describes an extraordinary appointment to be *ad incertum tempus*: No one, except the sovereign, really knows for certain when the sovereign's favor will expire and demand the return of the commissioner's borrowed power.[66]

By contrast, a public person appointed by an "ordinary charge" [*charge ordinaire*] exercises a share of public authority that is defined and "limited by the law" [*limitée par edict*; *lege definitum*].[67] Only these public figures, of all ranks (whether *maior* or *minor*) deserve to be called "magistrates." They serve, not as personal dependents of the sovereign—*par souffrance*, as Bodin will put it in the *République*—but as independent officers of the state.[68] Most notable is Bodin's acknowledgment

[64] *République* 378; *De Republica* 263 [III, 2] compares the extraordinary charge *par forme de precaire*—that is, to the Roman contract of *precarium*. He uses the exact same phrasing in perhaps Bodin's most famous work, on the definition of sovereignty, at *République* 122 [I, 8]: *par forme de prest ou de precaire*. The *Distributio* fol. C, s.v. *creditum*, explains that a *precarium* is a type of contract, a *creditum utendi causa domini arbitrio*.

[65] It is the defining quality of those states whose sovereigns are described as *seigneurial*, or "despotic," and whose subjects hold a position comparable to that of slaves. Their sovereignty is exercised, not according to law but through arbitrary will. For this reason, Bodin thinks *seigneurial* states were most common in the earliest stages of human history. By the time Bodin was writing the *Distributio* and *République*, two states exemplified this *seigneurial* style of rulership—the oriental despotic states of the Ottoman Turks and the Muscovites. Bodin's worry is that France's *droit* style of rulership was transforming into a despotic *seigneurial* style of arbitrary rule among the Valois monarchs, influenced by their Medici mother. Perhaps a similar pattern may be observed in the twenty-first-century return to the personal rulership motivated by deep-seated antipathy toward the state. Stephen Hanson and Jeffrey Kopstein, *The Assault on the State: How the Global Attack on Modern Government Endangers Our Future* (Cambridge: Polity, 2024); Lee, *Right of Sovereignty*, 119–28.

[66] Cf. *République* 122 [I, 8]; 378 [III, 2], which indirectly hint at this point in distinguishing between two types of lease involved in appointment of a public person to office—a lease for a prefixed defined period of time, such as a Roman real contract of *depositum* or *commodatum*; and a precarious grant, or *precarium*, "for as much and as long a time as it shall please" the owner. This is why Bodin will often say that public power is a "borrowed" or "leased" [*chose empruntée*] power held by magistrates "on deposit" [*depositaire*].

[67] *République* 372 [III, 2].

[68] In the French case, this independence from the king's will [*arbitrium*] is reinforced by the practice of the *venalité des offices*, by which the monarchy sold public offices to magistrates as a source of public revenue into the fisc. By this practice, magistrates became accustomed to treating their official powers as if they were private property, detached from sovereign control.

in the *Distributio* that even the *princeps* (Bodin's generic term in Latin indicating "sovereign") is also an "ordinary" public person.[69]

So much for public persons: The other main branch of *dignitas* concerns the various legal categories of private persons. Two, in particular, were of special importance. The analysis could take the form of a classification of rank or class [*ex ordine*]. Not only would this distinguish between foreigners [*peregrini*] and citizens [*cives*], it also distinguished among citizens according to the *civium ordo*, of the hierarchical rank of citizens, separating those who are *nobiles* from those who are *plebeii*.[70] In addition, Bodin classified private persons according to occupation [*ex instituto vitae*].[71] As we shall see in Chapter 3, these various hierarchies of citizen rank were directly associated with Bodin's theory of justice as harmony among the different orders.

Things: The second matter of law in Bodin's Ramist schema concerns "things" [*res*]. While this seems prima facie to align nicely with Gaius's classical division, which also concerns "things" [*de rebus*], there is a major difference between the classical Gaian and the early modern Bodinian treatment. But in order to observe how they differ, we need to begin with the generic legal category of *res*.

What did Gaius (and, later, Justinian) mean by "thing" [*res*]? For both these classical authorities of civil law, the Law of Things [*de rebus*] represented a broad substantive area of law that covered all types of assets, in general—anything of value that could be the subject of litigation. These not only included one's property—whether an individual good [*res singulae*] or even an entire estate [*res per universitatem*] capable of testamentary succession—that is, what one owned.[72] They also included incorporeal assets which only exist abstractly in the law, *in iure*, such as obligations—that is, what others owed [*res debita*] you by way of debt, or receivables.[73] While such debts may originate from a contract or from some legally recognized wrongdoing [*delictum*], Justinian's point was that even debt obligations could, from the creditor's perspective, be treated as receivable assets, or "things,"

[69] He will explain later how sovereigns and magistrates, despite both being "ordinary" in their public power, differ.

[70] Citizenship, defined as a quasi-contractual vertical relationship between sovereign and subject, is the main topic of *République* I, 6. Cf. *Right of Sovereignty* 128–34. The Latin *De Republica* III contained a chapter, "*De ordinibus civium*," that was not in the French *République*. Diego Quaglioni, "Una fonte del Bodin: André Tiraqueau (1488–1558), giureconsulto: Appunti su *De Republica* III, 8," *Il Pensiero Politico* 14 (1981): 113–27, has suggested that Bodin essentially plagiarized Tiraqueau's work. Cf. Daniel Lee, "Citizenship, Subjection, and the Civil Law: Jean Bodin on Roman Citizenship and the Theory of Consensual Subjection," *Citizenship and Empire in Europe 200–1900: The Antonine Constitution after 1800 Years*, ed. Clifford Ando (Stuttgart: Franz Steiner Verlag, 2016).

[71] Cf. *De Republica* 330 [III, 7].

[72] Inst.2.9.6.

[73] Inst.2.2.2. Justinian's *rerum divisio* specifies that *res* encompasses incorporeal assets [*quae tangi non possunt*] which consist *in iure*, such as inheritance and obligations, contracted by whatever means [*obligationes quoquo modo contractae*]. Barry Nicholas, *An Introduction to Roman Law* (Oxford: Clarendon Press, 1962), 98–99, develops the Civilian distinction between "owning" and "being owed" in the Roman Law of Things.

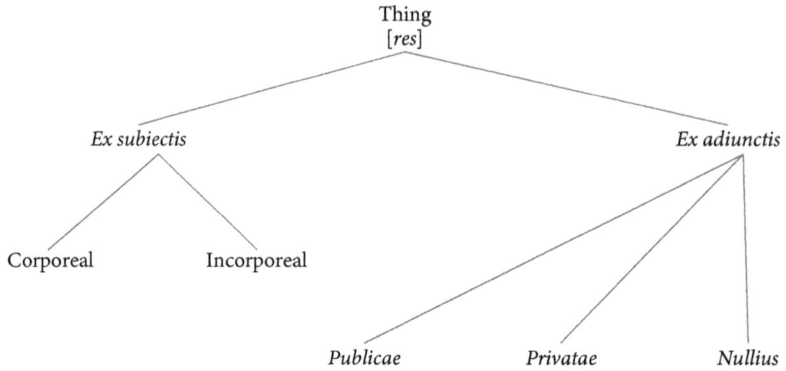

Figure 2.4 Diagram of Bodin's division of *res*, meaning "things" or "assets." Assets can be classified as corporeal or incorporeal. They can also be classified as public, private, or *nullius*, "belonging to no one."

in pursuit of which a creditor could initiate a lawsuit (specifically, an *actio in personam*) in order to obtain the outstanding value of the debt. Bunching these three major areas of civil law—property, successions, obligations—together under the label of the Law of Things was, according to Barry Nicholas, "one of the most characteristic features of the Civil Law... [and] a conscious Romanism."[74]

It was precisely this "Romanism" that Bodin sought to dismantle and reconstruct in the *Distributio*. In this respect, the most important innovation introduced by Bodin was the removal of the Law of Obligations. No longer were obligations to be treated as "things" [*res*], simply as another type of asset. Obligations deserved a separate treatment in Bodin's system, as we shall soon see.

What remained, therefore, was property: Bodin's Law of Things primarily concerned the systematic classification of the different types of property in a complete legal system. Bodin chose to apply an explicitly Ramist classification, bisecting his discussion evenly [*bifariam dividuntur*] into matters *ex subiectis* and matters *ex adiunctis*, as he frequently did in this work (see Figure 2.4).

But even here, the substance of Bodin's analysis, if not the form, bore some resemblance to Justinian's titles, *De rerum divisione* (D.1.8) and *De servitutibus* (D.8.1), as well as the feudal law.[75]

[74] Nicholas, *Introduction to Roman Law*, 98.

[75] Justinian introduces several different divisions of property, none of which are, in any obvious sense, connected to each other. D.1.8.1.pr presents Gaius's first division (Gaius 2.2ff.) which treats the *summa rerum divisio* to be either *res divini iuris* (which includes *res sacrae et religiosae*) and *res humani iuris* (which may be classified variously as *res publicae, res privatae, res nullius, res universitatis, res singulorum*). It is one of the few places in classical law that makes an unusual direct reference to "divine law." D.1.8.1.1 then introduces Gaius's second division between corporeal and incorporeal property. Marcian, however, presents a somewhat different division at D.1.8.2, bypassing "divine law" entirely, and instead distinguishing between *res communia* (things which are *naturali iure* [by natural law]

He acknowledged, for example, Justinian's categories of property distinguishing between "public property" [*res publicae*]; "private property" [*res privatae*], belonging either to individuals [*singulorum*] or to a collective or corporate owner [*municipii, collegii*];[76] and "nobody's property" [*res nullius*], which included sacred or religious properties [*sanctae, sacrae, religiosae*], specifically consecrated to the gods. Notably absent in Bodin's system, however, was Justinian's category of *res communia*—those things which are always "common to all" [*communia sunt omnium*], such as the air, running water, the sea, and the shore, and incapable of private ownership. The absence is less likely due to any antipathy to communism, and more likely due to the fact that *res communia* are features of natural law.[77] Nor was there any mention of the distinctly Roman category of *res mancipi*.[78]

So too did Bodin, under *res ex subiectis*, largely retain the classical distinction between corporeal and incorporeal property, a basic distinction in Roman property law.[79] "Corporeal things" [*corporeae*], he writes, "are either immovables [*immobiles*], such as land [*praedia*] and things attached to land, or movables" [*mobiles*].[80] "Incorporeal things" [*incorporeae*], by contrast, include assets such as the *peculium* (assets entrusted to the care of a son-in-power or a slave), an inheritance, or servitude. The essentials of property law, as Bodin rearranged it, would have been largely recognizable to the classically trained jurist.[81]

Deeds: It was with respect to Gaius's third main category of civil law—*actio*—that Bodin took the greatest risk in departing from classical jurisprudence. In

communia sunt omnium), *res universitatis*, *res nullius*, *res singulorum*. Another vital distinction in classical law that is totally absent in the *Divisio* is the specifically Roman archaic distinction between *res mancipi* (things subject to conveyance by the form of *mancipatio*—such as land, slaves, and beasts of draft and burden) and *res nec mancipi* (everything else). Gaius, who would not have been directly accessible to Bodin, is a major source in Gaius 2.14–22.

By contrast, what Bodin attempts here is a single system that brings together the various Justinianic categories of property into one unified system in the *Distributio*.

[76] Bodin, at *Distributio* fol. B, s.v. *Res ex adiunctis*, studiously avoids the more classically Justinianic term, *res universitatis*, at Inst.2.1.6 (cf. Gaius 2.11), possibly to stress the continuity at other parts of the *Distributio* with Bodin's terminology for corporate and associational bodies, *collegia* and *municipia*, neither of which require the legal qualities of personality exclusive to corporations, the form of *universitas*. See also Lee, *Right of Sovereignty*, 55–60.

[77] Inst.2.1.1.

[78] Nor would there be any reason for Bodin to include a discussion of *res mancipi* in a table on *ius universum* that sought to move away from the gravitational pull of the *ius civile*. Properties subject to the onerous Roman method of conveyance known as *mancipatio* were, even by the time of Gaius, an artifact of early Roman civil "Quiritian" law, exclusive only to Roman citizens.

[79] Inst.2.2.pr–3; cf. Gaius 2.12–13.

[80] *Distributio* fol. B, s.v. *corporeae*. Particularly notable is how Bodin distinguishes between movables in terms of their composition. Some are *simplices ex homogeneis*; others are "mixed" [*mistae*], some of which are "conjoined by art" [*arte coagmentatae*] or "made of separate components with parts collectively forming one body, such as a herd [*grex*] or a people [*populus*]" (referencing D.41.3.30, from which the reference to *grex* and *populus* originates). It is one of the first places where Bodin addresses clearly the composition of a people, a problem that he will later address in conceptualizing "peoplehood" in his own theory of popular sovereignty.

[81] Bodin adds a further distinction concerning property at fol. D of the *Distributio*, concerning the legal powers to acquire and alienate ownership and possession.

short, Bodin eliminated *actio* from his system and, in its place, provided an opportunity for major juridical innovation and reconstruction.[82]

Bodin had a reason for targeting "action." In the *Digest*, the Roman jurisconsult Celsus defined *actio* narrowly as *ius quod sibi debeatur iudicio persequendi* (an *actio* is "the right of pursuing what is legally due to us by means of a judicial proceeding")—in short, a lawsuit or legal remedy litigated in court.[83] So much of formal legal study was the practical study of such "forensic" [*forensis*] actions, the tools necessary for successful litigation in the courtroom exercised to right a legal wrong.

This usage, Bodin felt, was a far too narrow way of interpreting a legal action, limited strictly to contentious legal disputes between parties pleading actions and exceptions, rejoinders and surrejoinders, volleying back and forth against each other in the presence of a judge [*apud iudicem*] or magistrate. Legal acts, he thought, needn't be exclusively litigious or adversarial, a point he emphasized by stressing the function of *voluntaria*, or non-contentious, jurisdictions.[84] Yet, it became conventional among academic lawyers of the Western *ius commune* to restrict *actio* only to those legal remedies pursued by way of litigation in legal disputes—such as the Aquilian actions (for property damage), the Falcidian action (for protection of an heir's successive minimal claim to an estate), the Publician action (for protection of lawful possession), the *actio empti* (for enforcing a sale), the *condictio indebiti* (for unjust enrichment), the *actio iniuriarum* (for outrages), and so forth.

Bodin placed the blame for this well-established convention on Gaius and Justinian:

> Both of them exploited [*usurpavit*] the word, "action" [*actionis verbum*], to mean "forensic action" [*pro forensi actione*], against which Connan argued.[85]

Bodin's passing reference here to François Connan is particularly apposite and revealing. In his *Commentaria* on the civil law, Connan directly criticized Gaius's tripartite division of civil law into persons-things-actions. Connan specifically explained that Gaius's third category of "action" was entirely superfluous. Instead, it was sufficient to organize the whole of civil law according to a dichotomous or "bipartite division" [*bipartitam divisionem*] organized simply on the two

[82] Bodin moved much of the substance of the Law of Actions into the third part of the *Distributio*, which considered *legis actio*.

[83] D.44.7.51: *Nihil aliud est actio quam ius quod sibi debeatur iudicio persequendi.*

[84] He is thinking, for example, of legal acts which are thought to be formal, even liturgical, ritualistic, and "collusive" in nature. These legal acts include the *sollemnia iuris*, indicating certain archaic *ius civile* modes of property conveyances, such as the *mancipatio* involving acts *per aes et libram* (for a *venditio imaginaria*), the *cessio in iure*, manumission *vindicta*. They also include *sollemnia testamenti* for certain categories of wills.

[85] *Distributio* fol. B, s.v. *facta*.

principal categories of "persons" [*personas*] and "things" [*res*]. Under these two basic categories could jurists, then, locate all relevant "forensic actions" [*actiones forenses*]—that is, actions *in personam* (concerning obligations) and actions *in rem* (concerning property).[86] But there is no good reason, according to Connan, why actions should be treated specially, even deserving their own separate area of jurisprudence as Gaius imagined.

Bodin appears to have shared the disapproval of his fellow legal Ramist, Connan, in rejecting the classical Gaian tripartition. But Bodin's approach took a somewhat different turn. For Bodin, the problem was not that action was recognized as a third *sui generis* area of civil law. Instead, the problem was that *actio* was treated far too narrowly to mean the forensic actions of litigation resulting in a legal remedy. Not all legal actions involved contentious litigation or required a remedy for disputes.

> By this [i.e., Gaius's] division, they overlook agreements [*conventiones*], wills [*testamenta*], delicts [*delicta*], obligations [*obligationes*], discharges [*liberationes*], acquisitions [*acquisitiones*], alienations [*alienationes*], from which forensic actions, or the consequential effects of acts, arise.[87]

None of these are technically legal "actions" in the classical Roman sense of a lawsuit or the specific legal remedy sought. Yet, they are nevertheless formal legal acts, sometimes requiring the utterance of set formal words [*sollemnia verba*], and other times requiring the legal authorization or formal recognition of a public official or magistrate to ensure their legal validity.[88] While such legal acts in court may not necessarily involve litigation, they nevertheless deserve just as much recognition for their juridical significance as *actiones*.[89]

Having, then, rejected Gaius and Justinian, Bodin relabeled this enlarged legal category *facta et dicta* ("deeds and words") or, simply, *facta*. What he apparently

86 Connan, *Commentaria Iuris Civilis*, 76 [II, 1, §1].

87 *Distributio* fol. B, s.v. *facta*.

88 These *sollemnia verba* function as performative utterances. They are, as John Searle once labeled them, transformative speech-acts that have the power to change one's legal status or legal relation with respect to another. Such *sollemnia verba* can be found in stipulations creating verbal obligations (Inst.3.15.1), the nuptial rites or *nuptiarum sollemnia iusta* in a *manus* marriage such as *coemptio* or *conferreatio* (Gaius 1.112–13), or adrogations (so called "because both the adopter is asked [*rogatur; interrogatur*], or interrogated, whether he wishes to have the person whom is about to adopt as his lawful son, and he who is being adopted is asked whether he suffers this to take place, and the people are asked whether they sanction its taking place" Gaius 1.99).

89 Bodin was evidently familiar with Labeo's somewhat controversial division (later to be revived by Connan) in D.50.16.19, which introduced the point that all true contracts must be "synallagmatic" in structure involving some kind of bilateral *ultro citro obligatio*, or mutual obligation. Labeo's unconventional classification excludes from the category of συνάλλαγμα varieties of contracts recognized as actionable under Roman law, such as the verbal stipulation, due to its strictly unilateral structure. For Labeo, these one-way obligations, despite their actionability, do not deserve the label of "contract." They deserve, instead, another label—*actum*. *Actum* becomes a *generale verbum* for all kinds of legal transactions handled whether by words [*vi*] or by delivery of property [*re*].

intended to capture under this new unorthodox label coincided closely with what the Austrian jurist Hans Kelsen in the twentieth century would call a *Rechtsakt*, or "legal act."[90] And this is indeed how Bodin described *facta* in the *Distributio*:

> Deeds [*facta*] encompass the words, writings, achievements, and actions of persons—for all these are contained by the word, "doing" [*faciendi*].[91] But it is understood that it includes only those deeds which are associated with law or unlawfulness [*iuris aut iniuriae communionem habet*].[92]

Inspecting the substance of *facta*, however, reveals that Bodin performed a significant amount of reconstructive surgery on the original schema of Gaius and Justinian, and that is because the Law of Obligations (which, as we saw previously, in classical civil law belonged under the Law of Things) now belonged to this novel category in Bodin's legal science, *facta*. Obligations of all kinds, whether delictal or contractual (or even quasi-delictal or quasi-contractual obligations, as Justinian identified), are not technically "things" but legal "deeds"—*facta*.[93]

Bodin's system was heterodox jurisprudence when compared to Gaius or Justinian. But it was not unprecedented, nor was he starting from scratch. Indeed, Bodin's category of *facta* bore some resemblance to the systematization of civil law developed in the first century BC by Quintus Mucius Scaevola, a jurist of the Late Republic (antedating Gaius by some two centuries) who held the honor of being "the first systematizer of Roman legal science."[94]

Facta was a capacious legal category—by far the largest in Bodin's treatment of the *materia* of jurisprudence. Bodin began his analysis by dividing all legal *facta* into two basic categories (see Figure 2.5).

The first was what he called "bare deeds" [*facta nuda*], those deeds "from which questions of law arise" [*unde iuris quaestiones oriuntur*].[95] We learn, in particular, that these comprise acts of agreement [*conventiones*] and delictal acts [*delicta*], both of which happen to coincide with the two major sources of obligations in Gaius's system.[96] It is also the clearest evidence that Bodin appropriated some of

[90] Hans Kelsen, "What Is a Legal Act?" *American Journal of Jurisprudence* 29, no. 1 (1984): 199–212.

[91] Bodin traces this etymology to D.50.16.175; D.50.16.218.

[92] *Distributio* fol. B, s.v. *facta*.

[93] Bodin adds a further specification. Obligations legally "consist in what has been done or not done [*factum vel non factum*]," meaning they are retrospective in orientation. Contracts, by contrast, "consist in what ought to be given or done [*quod dari fieri debeat*]," meaning they are prospective. Classical Roman law does not make use of this distinction, except perhaps when the jurisconsults handle the question of dissolving an existing obligation (i.e., Inst.3.19, *Quibus modis obligatio tollitur*).

[94] Kelley, "Gaius Noster," 622.

[95] *Distributio* fol. B, s.v. *nuda*.

[96] Gaius 3.88: *Obligationes quarum summa divisio in duas species diducitur: omnis enim obligatio vel ex contractu nascitur vel ex delicto*. The important contrast between Gaius and Justinian is the latter's interpolation of two additional sources of obligations, quasi-contracts (Inst.3.27, *obligationes quasi ex contractu*, the two most important of which are *indebitum* and *negotiorum gestio*) and quasi-delicts (Inst.4.5, *obligationes quae quasi ex delicto*, such as *deiectum effusumve*). Bodin relocates these in his system of the *Distributio* in Part III on *legis actio*, under *actio*. Actions *indebiti* are classified as

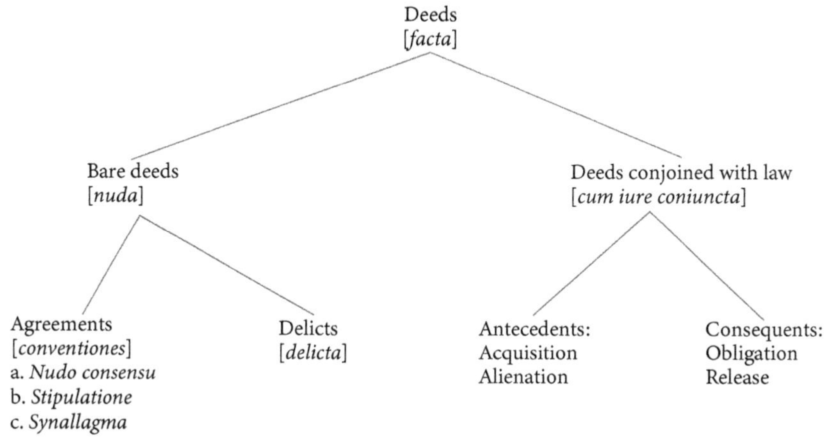

Figure 2.5 Diagram illustrating the various species of *facta*, or legal deeds, in Bodin's system. Bodin initially divides the category into two main branches. One branch concerns "bare deeds," which covers the law of contracts and delicts. The other branch concerns "deeds conjoined with law," concerning legal transactions, such as alienation of property or release from debt obligation.

the Ramist innovations in designing his own system of law. The other main branch in this division concerns "deeds conjoined with law" [*cum iure coniuncta*], which address the various ways in which property and obligations may be legally acquired and alienated.

Since the most innovation takes place in Bodin's treatment of contracts, our focus shall be on the place of contracts in this division.[97]

Contracts

It was under this novel heading of *facta nuda* that Bodin presented his own treatment of contracts, an area of private law that was already undergoing a creative process of radical transformation during his lifetime.[98] Contracts were especially important for Bodin's political thought, and that is because all sovereigns were

certi actions *ex conventione* (i.e., lawsuits seeking a specific defined sum arising from an agreement—though not a quasi-contract), while actions *deiecti & effusi* are recognized simply as actions *ex delicto* (not quasi-delicts). *Indebitum*, in particular, is classified as a type of real contract, *creditum* (cf. *res credita*: the sum of money given in a loan), wherein *creditum sub conditione vel errore contractum*.

[97] Bodin's treatment of delict is brief, compared to the detailed attention he pays to contracts. Delict is defined as an "offense inflicted against law." Bodin then proceeds to introduce three divisions of delicts, none of which correspond in any obvious way with Justinian or Gaius or the *lex Aquilia*.

[98] Decock, *Theologians and Contract Law*, chap. 3.

theoretically bound by their contractual obligations. Contracts constitute, in fact, a substantial portion of Bodin's famous discussion of sovereignty in *République*.[99] Sovereigns may be *legibus soluti*, but they nevertheless remain obliged, like any private person, to perform their contractual obligations.[100] Even an exercise of "absolute power" cannot exempt a sovereign prince from contractual duties owed to another party.

Bodin's term of choice for contract, in the most generic and most inclusive possible sense, was *conventio* ("agreement").[101] He explains:

> An agreement [*conventio*] is the consensus of several people into one engagement to give or to do something [*plurium in idem consensus dandi aut faciendi causa*].[102]

It is perhaps worth reflecting, first of all, on the significance of Bodin's contribution to the emerging early modern theory of contracts. *Conventio* was meant to function as a generic, abstract concept of contractual agreement, inclusive of all kinds of contractual agreements. This term included all those specific contractual forms recognized and enforced in Roman law by their name [*nominati*], such as *stipulatio* (verbal obligation, enforced by *condictio*), *depositum* (deposit, enforced by *actio depositi*), *mutuum* (loan for consumption, enforced by *condictio*), *emptio-venditio* (sale, enforced by *actio empti* or *actio venditi*), *locatio-conductio* (hire, enforced by *actio locati* or *actio conducti*), *societas* (partnership, enforced by *actio pro socio*), *mandatum* (mandate, enforced by *actio mandati*), and so forth.[103] For classical lawyers, the only contracts that mattered legally were those recognized by

[99] *Right of Sovereignty* 82–94. *République* 135; 52–54 [I, 8].

[100] This is because even sovereigns are bound by the law of nature, a fundamental rule of which is the obligation to perform contracts.

[101] This term corresponds to the French *convention* in the *République*. It is notably the same term that Rousseau will later use in developing his own political theory of the social contract.

[102] *Distributio* fol. B, s.v. *conventio*. This is a direct reference to D.2.14.1 in *De Pactis*, a title in the *Digest* which opens with Ulpian's etymology, *pactum autem a pactione dicitur* ("Pact is said to derive from peace") and his definition, *pactio duorum pluriumve in idem placitum et consensus* ("An agreement is the consensus of two or more persons in the same thing agreed upon").

It is also here that the word *conventio* is famously introduced in the legal literature as a *verbum generale* ("a general word"; cf. Gloss ad D.2.14.1, s.v.: *generale*: *magis quam pactionis*) inclusive of all types of contracts. It is so called because, in all agreements, the parties are said "to-come-together" [*convenire dicuntur*] upon one opinion [*in unam sententiam*; cf. Gloss ad D.2.14.1, s.v.: *sententiam*: *id est, voluntatem*] from different feelings of mind [*ex diversis animi motibus*], just as in a meeting [*conventio*] people come from different places to converge in one place [*ex diversis locis in unum locum*].

One other noteworthy point on D.2.14.1 is the Gloss, s.v.: *contractum*, where it is explained, *contractum praecedit obligationem, & obligatio actionem, ut diximus*. This is the same point that Bodin will make in the Latin *De Republica* 100 (but not in the French *République*) in the similar connection he makes concerning the force of *conventio*, *obligatio*, and *actio* deriving from natural law upon a sovereign. See *Right of Sovereignty* 91–92.

[103] What gave these contractual forms their legal validity and force was their recognition by law courts through the grant of an effective legal remedy, whether by legislation or by the praetorian, or other magisterial, edict.

courts by their specific name (e.g., *societas, emptio-venditio, depositum*) and, more important, those enforced by means of specific actionable remedies (e.g., *pro socio, actio empti, actio depositi*).[104] Other "unnamed" (or "innominate") agreements may have resembled some features of contract but generally lacked legal force and validity.[105]

As Alan Watson once put it, "in fact, the Romans had no abstract concept of 'contract'... [and] the Romans never developed a system of contract but only of individual [nominate] contracts," grouped into four main categories of contract—*re, verbis, litteris, consensu*.[106] To construct something like a general theory of contract would have been a decidedly un-Roman move.

Yet, that is precisely what Bodin (and many of his sixteenth-century contemporaries) attempted. The most advanced work in this effort at creating something like a "general theory" of contracts emerged from the jurisprudence and moral theology of the Second Scholastic, based primarily (though not exclusively) in sixteenth-century Spain.[107] This effort involved a creative synthesis of Aristotelian ethics, Thomist moral theology, and contract doctrine in Roman and canon law.[108] What these Neo-Scholastic theologians crafted was a new legal taxonomy of contracts, the influence of which would extend across several centuries to the nineteenth-century Pandectists.[109]

Bodin, for his part, offered his own general theory, the closer inspection of which reveals the influence of Scholastic reasoning with respect to contracts. As a genus, *conventio* was divisible into three main species in Bodin's taxonomy of contractual forms. These were:

(a) agreements contracted by bare consent [*nudo consensu*];
(b) those contracted by a verbal stipulation [*stipulatione*] involving the utterance of specific legal words [*verbis legitimis*]; and

[104] This point, I believe, can partly explain Bodin's division between *facta nuda* and *facta cum iure coniuncta*. Not all agreements give rise to legal obligation, nor can they all be the basis of a legal claim. Barter (*permutatio*, or *do ut des*), for example, is recognized as a *factum nudum*, under "remunerative" or "onerous" [*mercenarium*] transactions and may even resemble some elements of the contract of sale. Yet, for much of Roman legal history, they lacked a remedy for enforcement.

[105] In later Roman law, courts recognized a generic remedy, called *praescriptis verbis*, to protect the party that performed first in an innominate contractual agreement that could not be protected under any other formal action.

[106] Alan Watson, "The Evolution of Law: The Roman System of Contracts," *Law and History Review* 2, no. 1 (1984): 2–3, referencing J. A. C. Thomas, *A Textbook of Roman Law* (Amsterdam: North Holland, 1976), 226.

[107] Some of the most creative Scholastic jurisprudence on contracts was produced by Leonardus Lessius, who was a Flemish Scholastic theologian. Wim Decock, "Lessius and the Breakdown of the Scholastic Paradigm," *Journal of the History of Economic Thought* 31, no. 1 (2009): 57–75.

[108] James Gordley, *The Philosophical Origins of Modern Contract Doctrine* (Oxford: Clarendon Press, 1991), 69ff.

[109] See, e.g., T. B. Smith, "*Pollicitatio*—Promise and Offer: Stair v. Grotius," *Acta Juridica* 41 (1958): 141–52.

(c) those involving a bilateral or "synallagmatic" obligation [*contractu facta cui synallagma inest*].[110]

The distinction between the first two categories of *conventio* concerned whether a legally valid agreement can be engaged simply by the consenting will alone, through a bare promise, or whether it requires something more than an act of will, such as the utterance of stipulated formal words or another outward sign, in order to activate the agreement.[111] While it is not unusual that Bodin should include stipulations in this typology of contractual agreements, what is perhaps more notable is that Bodin acknowledged that even promissory agreements contracted by bare consent—specifically, "pollicitations" and "pacts"—ought to be treated as legally valid and binding agreements.[112]

Not everyone accepted this view. For centuries, Civilian jurists were generally skeptical that bare promises, staked on the will alone, can have any legal force in a court of law. Unlike actionable contracts recognized in civil law, such as sale [*emptio-venditio*], mandate [*mandatum*], loan [*commodatum*], or deposit [*depositum*], promissory agreements based only on the consent of the promisor could be obligatory only under natural law—which is equivalent to saying that they are not, properly speaking, contracts.[113]

[110] Cf. Robert Joseph Pothier, *A Treatise on the Law of Obligations, or Contracts*, trans. William David Evans (London: A. Strahan, 1806), 1:3–5 [I, 1, 1, 1 §§1–2] follows roughly the same arrangement. Citing D.2.14.1.1, Pothier defines agreement as "the consent of two or more persons to form some engagement." Contract is "an agreement by which two parties reciprocally promise and engage ... to give some particular thing, or to do or abstain from doing some particular act." A pollicitation, by contrast, "is a promise not yet accepted by the person to whom it is made" (D.50.12.3).

[111] Bodin evidently was aware of the potential controversy in treating verbal stipulations as *sui generis*. Stipulations generally functioned as the all-purpose contractual form to reinforce any contractual obligation, since stipulations are enforceable by way of *condictio*. They are also unilateral, with the debt incurred only by the promisor due to the stipulator. This is perhaps why Bodin inserts a note referencing an interpretive debate between Bartolus of Sassoferrato, Alexander de Tartagnis Imolensis, and Louis the Roman on *l.1.de verborum obligatione* [D.45.1.1] concerning "whether a *stipulatio* belongs to law or deed [*iuris vel facti*; or perhaps the meaning is better captured as '*de iure* or *de facto*'], since it is evident that it is implicated in fact, and law arises from it."

[112] The two main types of promissory agreements, or *conventio nudo consensu*, were pollicitations and pacts. Both were, in Bodin's scheme, theoretically consensual, but with one key difference. Simple promises, even bare or informal promises that were not accepted (the juridical term of art was *pollicitatio*), were binding only on the promisor (but not the promisee) and, thus, one-sided or "unilateral." As Bodin put it, a pollicitation was *unius promissum* ("a promise made by a single person"). Pacts, by contrast, were mutually binding on both (or all) engaging parties and, thus, bilateral (or, to borrow a Kantian term, omnilateral) in their obligatory force. Cf. D.50.12.3.pr: *Pactum est duorum consensus atque conventio, pollicitatio vero offerentis solius promissum.* Gordley, *Philosophical Origins of Modern Contract Doctrine*, 71–73, observes that, while *pacta* were governed by expectations of commutative justice, *pollicitatio* were marks of liberality.

Stipulations, by contrast, activated obligations "by legal words" [*verbis legitimis*], in addition to voluntary consent—two distinct features in the juridical analysis. While even these were also unilateral (binding only on the promisor, but not the stipulator), stipulations functioned as a kind of template form of contract that could be used to create and strengthen almost any kind of contractual obligation.

[113] That is because there are no available actions to plead to enforce a promise.

Canonists, however, saw pollicitations and pacts somewhat differently, and their influence spilled over into Scholastic moral theology and eventually the modern Natural Law school. This is summarized in the Decretal, *Antigonus* (X.1.35.1): *Pacta quantumcumque nuda servanda sunt* ("Pacts, howsoevermuch naked, are binding").[114] Canonistic recognition of the binding force of naked pacts clashed directly with Civilian doctrine which clumsily adopted a doctrine of *vestimenta pactorum* ("clothed pacts") to provide actionable remedies, despite the rule of D.2.14.7.4, *nuda pactio obligationem non parit.*[115]

Ultimately, it was the work of Neo-Scholastic theologians, especially De Soto, Cajetan, Molina, and Lessius, who crafted the basic outlines of a general "consensualist" theory of contract by synthesizing elements of Roman and canon law with Thomist moral theology to isolate the main features that all contracts must share in common—*causa* and acceptance.[116] According to this analysis, then, even pollicitations and promises, freely accepted and made for reasons either of liberality or strict commutative justice, can be regarded as obligatory contracts. By following the Neo-Scholastic treatment of promises and pacts, Bodin took a quantum leap away from classical Roman law in visualizing his own theory of contract, as inclusive of nominate as well as innominate and informal varieties.

* * *

It was, however, the third species of *conventio*—bilateral or "synallagmatic" agreement—that demanded the most attention. Most contracts in Justinian's system of civil law were, in Bodin's view, essentially synallagmatic—that is, agreements involving a commercial exchange, or *synallagma* [συνάλλαγμα], of some kind. What is exchanged—whether money, grain, wine, oil, livestock, land, personal services—is less important than the requirement that the exchange itself be fair. One party in a synallagmatic exchange must not gain unfairly at the expense of the other.

The term is most famously associated with Aristotle's theory of commutative justice [συναλλάγμασι δίκαιον] and establishes the principle that justice requires equality in commercial exchange.[117] This same term, *synallagma*, appears

[114] Decock, *Theologians and Contract Law*, 121–30; Reinhard Zimmermann, *The Law of Obligations: Roman Foundations of the Civilian Tradition* (Oxford: Clarendon Press, 1996), 542–44.

[115] Zimmermann, *Law of Obligations*, 538–40.

[116] Gordley, *Philosophical Origins of Modern Contract Doctrine*, 73.

[117] *Commutativa* was the medieval Scholastic Latin term assigned by Robert Grosseteste to translate the Greek, συναλλάγμασι. Aristotle, *Nicomachean Ethics*, 272–73 [V, iv, §§1–2, 1131^{b}25–26]. In such a commercial exchange, the value of what I do for, or give to, you must equal the value of what you do for, or give to, me. Bodin observes in the final part of the *Distributio* that commutative justice, which is based on arithmetic proportions, is called συναλλακτική: *semper aequalis facta factis, res rebus ... eaque potissimum elucet in rebus creditis, mutuis, pignore, commodato, deposito, & similibus.* Chapter 3 will discuss this point in more detail.

The principle of equality in exchange is restated in Grotius's *De Iure Belli ac Pacis* II, 2, §8 as foundational to his natural law theory of contract. The party who benefits less in such an exchange is entitled to legal action—or war—against the other party. Cf. James Gordley, "Equality in Exchange," *California Law Review* 69 (1981): 1587–656.

prominently in a text by Labeo, possibly influenced by the Peripatetic vocabulary, reproduced in the penultimate title of Justinian's *Digest* (D.50.16.19) on the "meaning of words" [*De verborum significatione*] in civil law:

> **D.50.16.19**: Contractum autem ultro citroque obligationem, quod Graeci συνάλλαγμα vocant, veluti emptionem venditionem, locationem conductionem, societatem.
>
> A "contract," however, involves a mutual obligation, what the Greeks call "synallagma," such as the contract of sale [*emptio-venditio*], hire [*locatio-conductio*], and partnership [*societas*].

Labeo's purpose here was to define contract specifically so that a genuine contract must, at its core, involve a bilateral or "synallagmatic" transaction of some kind, thereby creating a mutual obligation [*ultro citroque obligatio*].[118] *Synallagma*, thus, could be construed broadly so that the exchange agreed upon may involve, in principle, any commercial exchange of goods or services [*ex facto vel datione*]. Whatever the nature of the exchange, Labeo's point was that all contracts must, in principle, be reciprocal or bilateral—both contracting parties must do, or give, something of value in exchange for the other's benefit.[119]

Labeo's synallagmatic interpretation of contract effectively eliminated a range of unilateral contracts that Roman courts classically recognized as legally valid and enforceable, despite their unilateral, one-sided structure, such as verbal stipulations. Labeo, instead, classified such one-sided verbal stipulations simply as legal "acts" rather than as "contracts":

> The word, "act" [*actum*], is a general term encompassing anything accomplished legally by words [*verbis*] or by delivery of property [*re*], such as in a stipulation.[120]

[118] Zimmermann, *The Law of Obligations*, 562, n.111 suggests that Labeo's synallagmatic interpretation of contract as involving *ultro citroque obligatio* is "possibly spurious." Hans-Peter Benöhr, *Das sogenannte Synallagma in den Konsensualkontrakten des klassischen römischen Rechts* (Hamburg: Cram, De Gruyter, 1965), 10ff.; Constantin Despotopoulos, "La notion de Synallagma chez Aristote," *Archives de philosophie du droit* 13 (1968): 115–27; Raimondo Santoro, "Il contratto nel pensiero di Labeone," *Annali del Seminario Giuridico dell'Università di Palermo* 37 (1983): 5–304. Roberto Fiori, "The Roman Conception of Contract," in *Obligations in Roman Law: Past, Present, and Future*, ed. Thomas McGinn (Ann Arbor, MI: University of Michigan Press, 2012), 45–48.

[119] This was a controversial position because Labeo's synallagmatic theory would eliminate a range of unilateral contracts and promises of liberality, including stipulations that, in principle, burden only the promisor with a debt. This is the principal reason why, in Bodin's *divisio conventionum*, stipulation appears as its own *sui generis* category of contractual agreement. Bodin cites three other authorities on this point, Accursius's Gloss and Cinus da Pistoia on D.18.6.1 and Baldus de Ubaldis on D.2.14.58.

[120] D.50.16.19. In this text, Ulpian is referring to two main categories of contracts—contracts *verbis* (verbal contracts, such as stipulation) and contracts *re* (real contracts by delivery, such as deposit, pledge, and loan-for-use)—in the Roman law of obligations. Observe here the linguistic proximity of *actum* and *actio*.

Perhaps for this reason, Labeo's position was ignored for much of Roman legal history and even after its medieval revival.[121]

It was only in the sixteenth century that Labeo's synallagmatic doctrine was revived, and not without controversy, by the legal Ramist François Connan.[122] Following Labeo, Connan stated in his *Commentaria* that all legally valid contracts were fundamentally "synallagmatic," involving a mutual obligation of some kind, whether that involved an exchange of goods, services, or money.[123] It was one of the reasons that would later lead Grotius to conclude that Connan was "an ordinary man of very little learning" [*vir eruditionis minime vulgaris*].[124]

Bodin, for his part, thought highly of Connan's system.[125] Bodin even credited Connan, by name, with rejecting the excessively narrow understanding of the word *actio*, adopted by Gaius and Justinian as an all-encompassing label for suit or legal remedy.[126] Instead, he saw the value of Connan's synallagmatic theory. Most contracts, even those familiar nominate contracts of Roman law, could be classified neatly in synallagmatic terms. But it still left room for him to classify other types of imperfect or unilateral agreements—pollicitations, pacts, stipulations—as related species belonging to one common legal genus.

In his treatment of contracts, Bodin thoroughly reveals himself to be a "Connanite."[127] Most contractual forms, including those recognized in classical Roman law, were synallagmatic. Because of this expansive variety of synallagmatic contracts in Roman law, Bodin felt the need to introduce a sharper and more intuitively accessible system of distinctions to classify them for the lawyer in training. But it was a new arrangement that departed far from the familiar Justinianic presentation of contracts in terms of real [*re*], verbal [*verbis*], scripted [*scripta*], and consensual [*consensu*] forms (see Figure 2.6).

[121] Bartolus on D.50.16.19, for example, has very little to say about Labeo, other than a criticism of the gloss on the same.

[122] Connan was Grotius's principal target in *De Jure Belli ac Pacis* 219–20 [II, 11, §1] on promissory obligations. Decock, *Theologians and Contract Law* 121. See also Italo Birocchi, *Causa e categoria generale del contratto: Un problema dogmatico nella cultura privatistica dell'età moderna* (Turin: Giappichelli Editore, 1997), 95–136.

[123] François Connan, *Commentariorum Iuris Civilis Libri X* (Basel: Apud N. Episcopium, 1562), 474 [V, I, §4]

[124] Grotius, *De Jure Belli ac Pacis*, 219 [II, 11, §1].

[125] *Distributio* fol. B, s.v. *facta*. Bodin names Connan in the opening dedication of the *Methodus* fol.*4vo, alongside Du Faur, Bohier, Baron, Tiraqueau, and others, for "useful" [*utilitates*] lessons in civil life. Bodin also cites Connan as an authority in *République* 103; 218; 369, particularly on the legislative powers of the Roman senate via senatusconsulta.

[126] This, too, was likely inspired by Labeo at D.50.16.19, where he defines an "actum" as a *generale verbum* indicating anything legally accomplished whether by words or by delivery of property [*sive verbis sive re quid agatur*].

[127] Franklin, *Jean Bodin and the Sixteenth-Century Revolution in the Methodology of Law and History*, 36, ultimately crediting the "Connanite" label to Mesnard, *Oeuvres Philosophiques de Jean Bodin*, 69–70. In addition to Connan, Mesnard points to the Ramist systematic method in François Baudouin, François Hotman, and Antoine Le Conte.

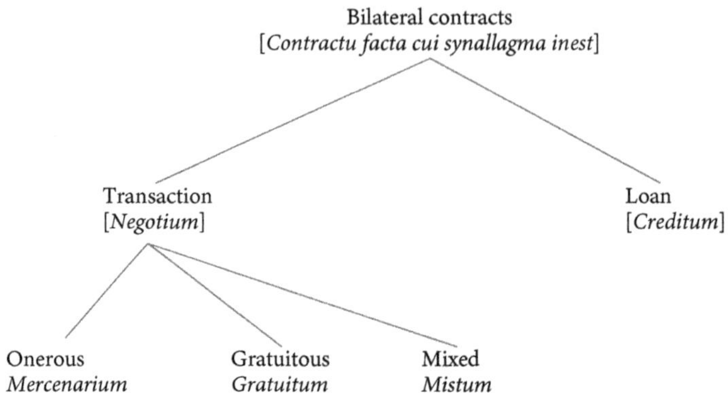

Figure 2.6 Diagram classifying the varieties of bilateral or "synallagmatic" contracts in Bodin's system. Such contracts originate either by loan [*creditum*] or by a transaction [*negotium*], the latter of which can be further subdivided into onerous, gratuitous, or mixed contracts.

Instead, Bodin distinguished between two principal forms of bilateral contracts—what he called *negotia* and *credita.*

Negotium: The first broad category, *negotia,* concerned bilateral contractual agreements enabling the lawful completion [*perfectio*; cf. *venditio perfecta*] of some commercial transaction. These could be, as one might expect in commerce, "those things which are done in return for payment [*mercede*]," or, if not pecuniary, some other form of recompense.[128] These "onerous" [*mercenarium*] contracts, as Scholastic moral theologians and modern natural lawyers labeled them, covered a whole range of familiar Roman nominate contracts, including sale [*emptio-venditio*], hire [*locatio-conductio*], partnership [*societas*], and dowry [*dos et donatio propter nuptias*]. They also included innominate contracts that, despite their "synallagmatic" onerous structure, typically were unrecognized and unactionable (and thus, unremedied) in Roman law.[129]

The difficulty of the classical Roman law of contracts was its apparently haphazard arrangement. Why should a contract of hire (a consensual contract) be treated differently from, say, deposit (a real contract)? Why should mandate (a consensual contract) be treated differently from, say, deposit (a real contract)?

[128] Bodin cites D.3.5.1–48(49); C.2.18(19).1–24; D.19.3.1.

[129] The classification of contracts as *oneroso* and *gratuito* ultimately originates in Thomist moral theology. Its revival in Neo-Scholastic literature provides a new convenient classification for lawyers reforming the law of contracts. It becomes especially useful for natural lawyers: Samuel Pufendorf, for example, utilizes the Scholastic distinction in his treatment of contractual obligations at *De Jure Naturae et Gentium Libri Octo* (Amsterdam: Apud Joannem Wolters, 1698), 477 [V, ii, §8] between contracts *beneficios* and *onerosos.*

Bodin evidently echoed the frustrating groans from prior generations of law students studying contracts.

Bodin's strategy was to treat nominate contracts (i.e., contracts with a specific name and associated remedy—for example, *societas* with *actio pro socio*; *mandatum* with *actio mandati*) as a species of the innominate contractual genus they most closely resemble. In this way, the boundary separating nominate from innominate contract vanishes—a strategy especially characteristic of the treatment of contracts in the modern Natural Law School.[130] Instead, onerous contracts are arranged in the following way:

> *Do ut des* (or a thing for a thing) contracts include barter [*permutatio*], as well as the contract of sale [*emptio-venditio*] and money-exchange [*pecuniam pro pecunia*].[131]
>
> *Do ut facias* contracts include the actionable contract of hire [*locatio-conductio*].
>
> *Facio ut facias* contracts give rise to "infinite agreements" [*infinitae conventiones*], including contracts of partnership [*societas*], betrothals [*sponsalia*], and contracts of marriage [*nuptiarum contractus*].[132]

By arranging contracts in terms of what is (or is not) given [*dandi*] or done [*faciendi*] in exchange, Bodin can, in principle, classify every form of bilateral onerous contract, even beyond those documented in Justinian's Roman law.[133]

Not all contracts, however, are onerous. Bodin recognized another category of transactional *negotia*—what he labeled *gratuitum*, or "gratuitous" contracts. These consisted of contractual transactions done "gratuitously"—that is, by way of a contractual agreement that there should be no recompense, so that only one party, by mutual agreement, performs for the other. This agreement is what keeps gratuitous contracts synallagmatic, even though only one party benefits. These included contracts:

> *In faciendo tantum*: These were agreements engaged on the understanding that one party performs some service without recompense, such as serving as a surety

[130] Cf. Grotius, *De Jure Belli ac Pacis*, 229 [II, 12, §3]: *Jus naturae ignorat haec discrimina: neque vero qui innominati ab illis dicuntur contractus... Imo permutatio, quae innominatis accensetur, emtione* [sic] *& simplicior est, & antiquior.*

[131] Grotius, at *De Jure Belli ac Pacis*, 229 [II, 12, §3], similarly recognizes money-exchange (he calls it "collybum") as a species of *do ut des* contract under natural law.

[132] Bodin, at *Distributio* fol. B, s.v. *mercanarium quod*, also allows for various combinations of these three basic innominate forms—e.g., *do ac facio ut des, contrave* and *facio ut des ac facias, contrave.*

[133] Bodin, thus, anticipates some of the major structural features of the system of onerous contracts developed in the Natural Law School of Grotius and Pufendorf. Bodin's insight is revealed in his careful treatment of "giving" and "doing," by observing that "the word, giving [*dandi verbum*], equally well signifies a deed [*factum*], as for example a transfer [*traditionem*]," while also citing D.19.1.1, 19.1.11, and 19.5.5.2.

> [*fideiussio*], the contract of mandate [*mandatum*], and the quasi-contract (as Justinian labels it) of unauthorized agency [*negotiorum gestio*].
>
> *In dando et faciendo mistum*: These gratuitous contracts consisted chiefly in supervisory roles connected to guardianship and agency, such as tutors of pupils [*tutela*], curators of minors [*minoris*], spendthrifts [*prodigi*] and madmen [*furiosi*].[134]
>
> *In dando tantum*: Gifts [*donatio*], whether pure or conditional, can also legally be considered contractual.[135]

Bodin finally acknowledged a third hybrid category of "mixed" transactions [*negotia mista*], as he put it, "when a thing is partly given gratuitously [*partim donator gratuito*], and partly in order to create an obligation [*partim obligando*], such as in wills or codicils."[136]

This is an unusual interpolation. Classical Roman law treated the law of succession, governing wills, legacies, trusts, and intestate succession, as its own area of law, separate from contracts. Bodin, however, apparently thought that wills, in general, were continuous and overlapping with contracts, on the theory that testators entered a kind of contract with their heirs. Some classical Roman jurisconsults explicitly resisted this interpretation, most notably Labeo, who, at D.50.16.20, states: *Verba contraxerunt gesserunt non pertinent ad testandi ius* ("The words, 'they contracted,' or 'they transacted,' do not pertain to the legal right of making a will.")

[134] Bodin cites D.39.5.6 and most likely D.39.5.9 (the incipit reads *In aedibus*, while Bodin cites *Qui in aedib* under the rubric on donations). Classical Roman lawyers did not ordinarily treat guardianship in tandem with contracts, preferring instead to view guardianship as a feature of the family. But, as Bodin argues, wills can be seen as functioning as a sort of contract between testator and heirs and trustees burdened by a will or other instrument. Since guardians can be appointed *testamentaria* ("by will"), guardians may be seen as "agreeing" gratuitously to serve in this role. Unlike gratuitous contracts that require some form of acceptance, testamentary guardians were sometimes appointed unwillingly, prompting them to seek legal "excuses" [catalogued in *De excusationibus*] to avoid serving as someone else's guardian.

[135] This distinction appears in one of the most famous excerpts in the *République* at 128 [I, 8], *De Republica* 82–83, where Bodin addresses the question whether sovereignty can be delegated or transferred to another party, as when Charles IX empowered his brother, Henri de France as Duke of Anjou (before his accession to become Henri III), to become the lieutenant-general of France. It depends ultimately on the terms under which that sovereignty is conceded and transferred. A sovereign may "give their absolute power purely and simply" [*donner purement & simplement la puissance souveraine*; *pure donare potest*] to another party, just as "an owner can give away his property purely and simply, without any other reason than his liberality. Only this is a proper gift" [*le propriétaire peut donner son bien purement & simplement, sans autre cause que de sa liberalité, qui est la vraye donation*, D.39.5.1. The Latin *De Republica* 82 adds a citation to C.8.54(55).4] because it has no conditions attached to it. It is "complete and accomplished at once" [*estant une fois parfaicte & accomplie*]. By contrast, "other gifts which carry terms and conditions are not real gifts" [*les autres donations, qui portent charge & condition, ne sont pas vrayes donations*]. Cf. *Popular Sovereignty* 208–10.

[136] D.3.5.15; C.2.4.7. His principal authority for this hybrid category was the jurist, Aristo (as recounted by Ulpian), D.39.5.18.pr: *Aristo ait, cum mixtum sit negotium cum donatione, obligationem non contrahi eo casu, quo donatio est.*

Bodin, for his part, explained his reasoning in one of the explanatory marginal texts appended to the *Distributio*, and it displayed Bodin's aspiration for a much broader and comparative law of contracts beyond Justinian:

> What the testator bequeathed [to the heir] cannot be considered a loan. And yet, he is said to make a contract with the heir [*dicitur tamen contrahere cum haerede*].[137] From here arguments are also drawn from contracts to wills, and vice versa[138] ... All of France, Germany, Italy, and Spain are accustomed to mix wills in with contracts. The Hebrews also use the same word, Berith [[139]ברית], for agreements and wills, and the Greeks often confound will [διαθήκην] with agreement [συνθήκῃ].[140]

The result, in Bodin's theory, is a much more elastic and encompassing concept of contracts that potentially can extend across generations.

Creditum: So far, Bodin has only classified *negotia*—that is, those synallagmatic contracts intended to facilitate the completion of some transaction, whether onerous or gratuitous, or a hybrid mixture of those two.

The other main branch of synallagmatic contracts in Bodin's *Distributio* consisted of *credita*—that is, loans which were activated by simple delivery and generated an obligation of restitution.[141] Bodin is thinking here chiefly of the "real contracts" (contracts *re*; *contrats réels*) of Roman law—*mutuum*, *commodatum*, *precarium*, *depositum*, *pignus*, as well as the quasi-contract of *indebitum* by error.

The real contract of *mutuum* (from *meum-et-tuum*, "mine-and-yours"), for example, offers an illustration of how Bodin seems to have understood *res credita*. One of the oldest contractual forms in Roman law, the *mutuum* was a loan for consumption, usually of a fungible good such as grain, money, wine, or oil. Once delivered by the creditor, the debtor would be entitled to consume the *res credita* but would also be burdened by the strict obligation to return, at a later due date, the equivalent amount (without interest) to the creditor.[142]

[137] Here, in addition to C.6.23.17, Bodin here mistakenly cites "§*sed neque, de haeredibus instituend. Lib I.Institut*," when he was most likely citing the rubric for *De testamentis ordinandis*, yielding Inst.2.10.10. This excerpt states that *hoc totum negotium, quod agitur testamenti ordinandi gratia, creditur hodie inter testorem & heredem agi*.

[138] Bodin cites three authorities at this point: D.30.[1].46, which compares a promise to give something as comparable to a legacy; 28.1.20.3, which compares a will to a *negotium*; D.35.1.24, which treats cases where one interested party deliberately prevents the other party from fulfilling conditions for legacies as comparable to similar cases in stipulations.

[139] Berith, ברית, is the Hebrew term for "covenant."

[140] *Distributio* fol. C.

[141] Simon Goyard-Fabre, *Exposé du droit universel*, 35, n.29, suggests that *res credita* might best be translated as *obligation de restitution*, the sort of obligation arising from a real contract such as a *depositum* or *mutuum*.

[142] Failure to do so exposes the debtor to a *condictio*, a *stricti iuris* remedy by which the creditor may sue for the value of the *res credita*. In litigation, the *stricti iuris* nature of the suit prevents the judge from applying any equitable flexibility in resolving the dispute. This is why, later in his discussion of commutative justice, Bodin points to these real contracts requiring strictly the return of the same, or an equal

Such loans, in Bodin's view, were reciprocally synallagmatic, even though they may appear one-sided in favor of the creditor. Debtors in such real contracts, such as the *mutuum*, were, of course, burdened by the duty of restitution to their creditors, a duty enforced by the strict remedy of *condictio*. Likewise, depositaries (*depositarii*: those to whom some good is delivered for the purpose of safekeeping) and lessees (*commodatarii*: those to whom some good is delivered for the purpose of limited use) are similarly burdened by a duty of restitution. Even those mistakenly enriched by someone else's error in making an unowed payment [*indebitum*] to them are similarly obliged.[143]

What is less clear, however, is that even creditors are reciprocally burdened by obligation to their debtors. Bodin interprets this as something like a duty of non-interference. Once something has been delivered for the purposes of, say, a *mutuum* or *depositum*, it is understood that the original creditor cannot arbitrarily interfere, contrary to the specified terms of the agreement, to retrieve the *res credita*. In Bodin's view, the creditor must wait until the contractual term of the loan expires or seek due process by way of an appropriate legal remedy.

Bodin's thesis that real contracts are synallagmatic in structure had, however, a much larger purpose. In classical law, real contracts were usually intended to manage legal debts arising from tangible goods such as grain, wine, olive oil, horses, and the like. Bodin proposed viewing *res credita* much more broadly, even inclusive of abstract things—like public authority, or *imperium*. To wit: Even the authority of the state can, like oil or grain, be handed over to another party, as if by a real contract, activating an obligation of restitution.

When a share of the state's public authority is formally entrusted to a government official—"magistrate," as Bodin will call them *in genere*—something like a debt relation, not unlike the *creditum* arising from a real contract, is created between the sovereign and the subordinate magistrate. In the *République*, Bodin will famously describe government magistrates, of all ranks, as "lessees," "borrowers," and even "depositaries" entrusted with the safekeeping of public *imperium*.[144] For this reason, public offices, and the powers attached to them, are described as *res commodata* ("borrowed things").[145]

amount, to the creditor: *eáque potissimum elucet in rebus creditis, mutuis, pignore, commodato, deposito, & similibus.* Any added interest or fee of some kind would change the nature of the contract into a contract of hire, or *locatio-conductio*.

[143] This last example of *indebitum* is treated in Justinian, Inst.3.27.6–7, as a "quasi-contract" and has become the model for cases of unjust enrichment in civil law. Like the other real contracts, such cases of unjust enrichment are also actionable by way of a strict action, the *condictio indebiti*.

[144] For a prominent example, see *République* 122, 124–25 [I, 8].

[145] Lee, "Office Is a Thing Borrowed," 420–24. Lee, *République*, 378: *Office est comme une chose empruntee, que le propriétaire ne peut demander, que le temps prefix ne soit expiré. De Republica* 263: *quasi commodato* [III, 2], also referencing D.2.1.6. Cf. *Popular Sovereignty* 212.

Magistrates, however, enjoy a degree of discretion and independence in their office, while in the capacity of a public officer of state. This is due entirely to the synallagmatic structure of their appointment. While we learn that the right of appointing magistrates [*ius magistratuum creandi*] is among the core rights of sovereignty, the formal constitutional act of creating and distributing powers to an office (by defining the official powers and terms of office) functions much like *res credita*. While magistrates are burdened by a duty of restitution, of "returning" the lawful powers in their public charge to the state at the expiration of their term, the state is understood to be likewise burdened by a duty of non-interference. What Bodin calls *droit government*, then, is an autonomous layer of political professionals—bureaucratic officialdom—empowered to manage affairs of state, while distanced from the *arbitrium* of the sovereign.

Not all states choose to govern through magistrates. Bodin recognized that, historically, some sovereigns, preferring instead to have a much tighter, direct, and personal control over the affairs of state, established a regime subsumed entirely under their personal will—or, as he put it, their *arbitrium*. These "seigneurial" rulers, as he labeled them, characteristically treated their state as their personal property and their subjects as their personal slaves.[146]

These *seigneurs* also need subordinates to exercise their rule effectively (Bodin bids us to think of sultans ruling through viziers). In seigneurial regimes, however, these subordinates are not properly magistrates but instead are regarded as their personal "commissioners," whose charge is entirely at the pleasure [*par souffrance*; *arbitrio*] of the sovereign. One critical difference separates the two: Whereas magistrates are legally [*droit*; *legé*] bound and protected by the synallagmatic contract creating their public office, commissioners are no better than personal servants of the sovereign whose precarious hold on power depends entirely on the continuing favor of their *seigneur*. Unlike the real contracts of *mutuum*, *depositum*, *commodatum*, and the like, which sustain a government of magistrates, a government of commissioners depends solely on the sovereign's *precarium*, which is defined here in the *Distributio* as *creditum utendi causa domini arbitrio* ("a precarious grant for use by the permissive will of the owner").[147]

Deeds conjoined with law: In addition to the preceding discussion of "bare deeds," the category of legal deeds [*facta*] also included another branch, what Bodin called deeds "conjoined with law" [*facta quae cum iure coniuncta*]. These, in turn, were subdivided, in Ramist fashion, into two broad areas of antecedents and consequents—one concerning the acquisition or alienation whether of property or

[146] *Seigneur* was Bodin's French equivalent of the Latin *dominus* (meaning "owner" and "master") and the Greek δεσπότης ("despotis"). Cf. *Popular Sovereignty* 208–16; *Right of Sovereignty* 119–28, especially on the historical significance of Nimrod as the first seigneurial sovereign.

[147] *Distributio* fol. C, s.v. *creditum*.

of a right [*rei iurisve*], and the other concerning engagement and release from an obligation [*obligationis solutio*].

Gaius and Justinian traditionally treated these topics as integral aspects of the law of property and the law of obligations. Bodin, by contrast, treated these separately. That is because the legal mechanics by which property can be acquired or alienated, or by which obligations can be engaged or dissolved, was understood to be a higher-order aspect of law, beyond the substantive law governing property and obligations.[148] These were *facta*-concerning-*facta* and specifically functioned in order to explain how legal changes take place.

Under the first "antecedent" heading, Bodin catalogues the various modes of acquiring and losing property. Acknowledging the classical Roman legal distinction between ownership and possession, he proceeds to document no fewer than nine ways of acquiring ownership—nine ways whereby a non-owner can become an owner of some property. These may be counted as examples of deeds "conjoined with law," which include the legal use of just force [*vi iusta*] in a lawful war or licit hunting [*venationis licitae*],[149] occupation of abandoned property [*occupatione rei derelictae*],[150] and "transfer with a just cause" [*traditione ex iusta causa*].[151] All of these exemplify the higher-order quality of *facta cum iure coniuncta*, whereby non-owners can legally become owners.

The same point can be made under the second "consequent" heading concerning the engagement and release from legal obligations. Beginning with Justinian's definition of obligation as a "legal bond" [*vinculum iuris*] by which we are required to give or do something, Bodin declares that legal obligations can be classified in four ways [*quadruplex*].[152] These included natural obligations (those arising from the *ius naturale*), civil obligations (those arising from the *ius civile*), obligations arising from the *ius gentium*,[153] and obligations of both the *ius naturale* and the *ius gentium*. These different bodies of law not only define what an obligation is but also how one can become bound by one.

[148] The closest analogy in modern jurisprudence to illustrate this might be the Hohfeldian "power," the higher-order legal ability to alter one's first-order rights, whether by restricting or conferring one's liberties, or by validating or negating one's claims. See Wesley Newcomb Hohfeld, "Some Fundamental Legal Conceptions as Applied in Judicial Reasoning," *Yale Law Journal* 23, no. 1 (1913): 16–59.

[149] Cf. Inst.2.1.12 [*ferae bestiae*]. Bodin's translation of Oppian, *Oppiani de Venatione* (Paris: Apud Michaëlum Vascosanum, 1555), displays his early interest in the practice of hunting. The legal significance of hunting is illustrated in Bodin's own theory that the Biblical Nimrod, "the mighty hunter before the Lord," was the world's first sovereign in Scriptural history, whose title was established by conquest. *Right of Sovereignty* 123–28.

[150] Cf. Inst.2.1.47.

[151] D.47.2.65(64), C.1.2.23.

[152] Lee, *Right of Sovereignty*, 79, n.48 shows that Bodin's *obligatio quadruplex* attracted some notice. Doneau, perhaps the most influential of the Ramist legal systematists and a teacher of Grotius, cited Bodin's *divisio obligationum* in his *Commentariorum de Iure Civili: Opera Omnia* (Lucca: Typis Joannis Riccomini, 1763), 3:col. 425 [12.2.2].

[153] Bodin's evidence for this category is D.1.5.4 and D.12.6.60.

Most remarkable is the obverse, how one may be released from a prior obligation. His answer is "the performance of that obligation" [*obligationis solutio*], but this is somewhat misleading. Sometimes release [*liberatio*] from a prior obligation need not involve the debtor's performance but rather the creditor's grace, whereby a debt can be forgiven or transferred to another party.[154] Debt-forgiveness (or any kind of debt restructuring) that alters the terms of the original obligation may be regarded as an example of a legal deed. The result is a hodgepodge of legal means by which one can be released from obligations, including set-off [*compensatio*], "confusion" [*confusio*], judicial decision [*re iudicata*], and even by prescription of time.[155] Even the *cessio in iure*, understood in classical law to be a *ius civile* mode of conveying property before a judge, is said to have "the force of performance, if the debtor cedes the thing sought from him."[156]

* * *

Taken together, Bodin's division of the *iuris materia* provides a far different system of law, grouped into persons, things, and deeds, than the traditional system of Gaius. The biggest difference in Bodin's *Distributio* is the notable absence of actions—legal remedies and procedures pursued in court for enforcing the rules of law as they have just been outlined. This topic constitutes the third major part of Bodin's system.

The Efficient Cause of Jurisprudence: *Legis Actio* and *Officium Iudicis*

Part III of the *Distributio* is dedicated to a study of the "efficient causes" of law—that is, what animates the law (and its institutions: courts). It answers the question, *Qualis sit*: In what way does the law manifest itself? Bodin's response constitutes the largest part of the work and is structured upon a fundamental legal distinction between what Bodin calls *legis actio* and *officium iudicis*, a distinction that appears throughout Bodin's corpus of theoretical writing.[157] These are, however, among

[154] In Justinian's system, the title, *Quibus modis obligatio tollitur* (Inst.3.29), documents the principal ways in which release from obligation can be achieved without performance such as *acceptilatio* (Inst.3.29.1; D.46.4.6) and *novatio* (Inst.3.29.3; D.17.1.34). Bodin acknowledges this double-meaning of *solutionis verbum* and distinguishes here between release *naturalis et legitima* that is achieved strictly through performance, and *solutio* in a broader sense which "embraces every release from debt" [*debiti liberationem*], as D.46.3.49.

[155] C.4.31.4; C.2.3.7; D.12.6.60; C.7.39.3; C.7.39.4.

[156] *Distributio* fol. D, s.v. *ipso iure quoties*.

[157] The distinction appears most notably in the *Methodus* 263 [VI], and *République* 440 [III, 5], where Bodin addresses the question concerning those features of *imperium* which are "exclusive" [*proprium*] to sovereigns and magistrates. His point is that, just as those discretionary aspects of magistracy called *officium iudicis* are exclusive to magistrates, so too are the fundamental rights of sovereignty similarly exclusive.

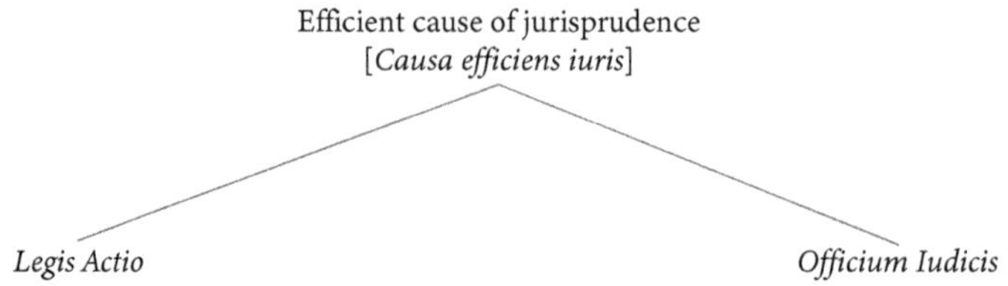

Figure 2.7 Diagram of the two efficient causes of law in Bodin's system—the *legis actio* and the *officium iudicis*.

the most technically difficult concepts in all of Bodin's legal theory and, for this reason, deserve a closer look.

The two branches of study under this heading of efficient cause, *legis actio* and *officium iudicis*, originate in Roman law (see Figure 2.7).[158]

In Bodin's *Distributio*, they are repurposed specifically as markers to explain the distinctive role of courts and judges in a legal system.

His main observation concerns the defining quality that judges, of all ranks, share in common: Judges stand both inside and outside the law. They are inside, in that their judicial powers are defined and granted by law and, thus, they are bound to follow the law in their impersonal exercise of jurisdiction. But they also stand outside the law, in that the exercise of their jurisdiction in resolving legal disputes implicitly entails an equitable discretion that may call for exceptions from the law, for the sake of justice.[159]

These two terms, *legis actio* and *officium iudicis*, signaled this dual identity of judges, respectively, as standing inside and outside the law—or, as he preferred to frame it, as agents both of law [*lex*] and of equity [*aequitas*].[160] Together, they empowered judges to bring "disputes and lawsuits [*controversias ac lites*] to a close."[161]

[158] *Legis actio* was the earliest form of civil procedure and litigation, described by Gaius in Book IV of his *Institutes*. The most notable feature of the *legis actio*, when compared to the later formulary procedure, was its quasi-ritualistic rigidity requiring strict adherence to the form of legal actions, described by jurists as *stricti iuris*.

Officium iudicis, by contrast, was the penultimate title of Justinian's *Institutes*. It addressed the varieties of judicial duties—that is, the duties of a person nominated and appointed by formula to exercise *iurisdictio* in a case. The term *officium iudicis* was later used by medieval canon lawyers to designate an equitable remedy.

[159] Bodin often uses the language of D.1.1.7.1 in describing praetorian legislation as a body of law introduced by praetors *adiuvandi vel supplendi vel corrigendi iuris civilis gratia propter utilitatem publicam*. For example, *De Republica* 155 [I, 10] cites the example of the *lex Laetoria* which permitted the urban praetor "to supplement, correct, and emend the laws" [*leges supplere, corrigere, emendare*], to show that magistrates can bend [*flectere*] the laws as equity demands [*tum ad lenitatem tum ad acerbitatem*].

[160] The action of law and the duty of the judge pertain to its execution [*legis actio & iudicis officium ad exequendum*]. Just as legislation is to the action of the law, so also is equity to the duty of the judge.

[161] *Distributio* fol. E, s.v. *efficiens*.

Beyond the *Distributio*, these two terms appear prominently elsewhere in Bodin's corpus, specifically in his treatment of the role and powers of high magistrates and judges in the state. In a difficult, well-known passage in the *Methodus*, Bodin attempts to explain how the authority of an ordinary magistrate—such as a judge—can be both constrained by law and yet also characterized by discretionary license. This dual aspect of judges is captured, respectively, by the terms *legis actio* and *officium iudicis*:

> None of the interpreters of civil law up to now has explained what the difference is between *legis actio* and *officium iudicis* [*quid inter legis actionem & iudicis officium intersit*] ... There are two aspects of the law taken as a whole [*duo capita iuris universi*]—law and equity—on which *legis actio* and *magistratus officium* depend. The relationship of the law to its action [*ratio legis ad eius actionem*] is the same as that of equity to the duty of the magistrate [*eadem est aequitatis ad officium magistratus*].[162]

He explains this distinction between *legis actio* and *officium iudicis* by referring to that famous passage in the *Digest* (D.1.21.1.pr), cited earlier, on "delegated jurisdiction":

> Papinian, Ulpian, and the ancient jurisconsults opined thus: Whatever authority is conferred by law [*quaecunque lege tribuuntur*] to a magistrate may not be entrusted [*committere*] to another.[163] He has no more than the bare exercise of lawful authority [*nudam duntaxat habere legis actionem*]. And this is because such authority does not belong to the magistrate [*non tam eius esse propria*] so much as it does to the law itself [*quam legis ipsius*]. But whatever is permitted to his equity [*eius aequitati*] may be entrusted to another by his own right [*pro suo iure*].[164]

His examples explaining this point are particularly revealing. Criminal matters illustrate how even magistrates of the highest rank, such as the praetors and

[162] *Methodus* 263; *Method* 174. The distinction is addressed in *République* 440; *De Republica* 305 [III, 5].

[163] Cf. D.1.21.1.pr: *Quaecumque specialiter lege vel senatus consulto vel constitutione principum tribuuntur, mandata iurisdictione non transferuntur.* Bodin saw this text as a model to explain the delegation of certain functions of sovereignty to inferiors. In its original context, however, this text is referring to the Roman magisterial practice of delegating jurisdiction to a lay judge appointed (in the *nominatio*, for the first sentence, of a magistrate's formula: "Gaius iudex est") specifically for the purpose of adjudicating a civil case. While magistrates, such as the praetor or a provincial governor, derive their authority [*imperium*] by a specific legislative act—usually a *lex de imperio*—such authority does not also transfer over to the lay judge, along with the delegation of *iurisdictio*.

[164] This passage is additionally notable for Bodin's use of the Ciceronian phrase *ius ipsum*. The powers of magistracy belong, not to the magistrate but to the very law itself [*ius ipsum*] which creates the magistrate. The phrase *suo iure* is a technical legal term appearing in D.1.21.3 and D.2.1.5.

provincial governors, are constrained in carrying out official acts of *legis actio*—"as if held by chains" [*quasi vinculis constringerentur*]—and legally prohibited from delegating their authority to others [*aliis imperium illud mandare non poterant*] or from modifying legal sanctions [*nec in iudicando legis acerbitati aut lenitate detrahere, aut addere quicquam*].[165]

Civil matters, however, permitted magistrates, like the urban and peregrine praetors of Roman law, a wide degree of latitude in resolving legal disputes according to their own sense of equity, sometimes beyond the strict requirements of law and sometimes even contrary to the law [*pro sua aequitate ac religione, multa praeter legem, aut etiam interdum contra legem*].[166] It was also by this same *officium iudicis* that Bodin explained the equitable powers of judges to "promulgate, at their sole discretion [*arbitratu suo*], edicts in which they could emend [*emendarent*], alter [*flecterent*], moderate [*lenirent*] the laws, or make the laws more severe [*exacerbarent*]," so that the law better approximates equity.[167]

How did Bodin handle these two joint concepts in the *Distributio*? One feature that becomes immediately apparent from inspecting the original tabular presentation of the *Distributio* is the disproportionally lopsided treatment of the two concepts (see Figure 2.8).

Bodin had very little to say about *officium iudicis* in the *Distributio*, despite its outsized importance in the overall structure of the work. He is even able to summarize it in two sentences:

> The *officium iudicis* is involved with those things that are not comprehended by legislation, or are said too obscurely, or which seem unjust [*iniqua*] as applied to the case at hand. It operates, above all, in supplementing the laws [*in legibus supplendis*, D.1.1.7] and in moderating the severity or lenience of the laws [*in legum acerbitate vel lenitate temperanda*, D.48.19.11; D.48.19.13].[168]

This brevity of treatment is deliberate. This is because all matters falling to the *officium iudicis* of a public official appeal, not to the law, but to their equitable discretion to carve out exceptions from the law.[169] However, exceptions, by their

[165] *Methodus* 264 [VI]. Bodin comments that "Papinian proposed this example" [*hoc enim exemplum proposuit Papinianus*]. This is a reference to D.1.21.1.pr, Papinian's text concerning the *Lex Iulia de Vi*. The *Lex Iulia* is one of the *quaestiones perpetuae* or *iudicia publica* established in the Late Republic to address specially defined criminal acts such as treason, adultery, and assassinations.

[166] *Methodus* 264 [VI]; Bodin is referring here to the body of praetorian legislation giving rise to *bonae fidei* actions, empowering judges with flexibility to decide cases equitably, beyond the strict requirements of civil law, in particular the civil law of the XII Tables which, by the time of the praetorian legislation making up the *ius honorarium*, was already felt to be outdated and inequitable.

[167] *Methodus* 264 [VI].

[168] *Distributio* fol. F, s.v. *iudicis officium*.

[169] At *Popular Sovereignty* 183, n.118, I stressed Bodin's reliance on the Bartolist distinction between *officium nobile* and *officium mercenarium*. While the former is a proper office, the latter is to be regarded simply as a "slavish" [*servile*] process of the law. *Officium iudicis* was not only the penultimate title of Justinian's *Institutes* 4.17, it was a canon law remedy actionable *in foro interno* (i.e., in the

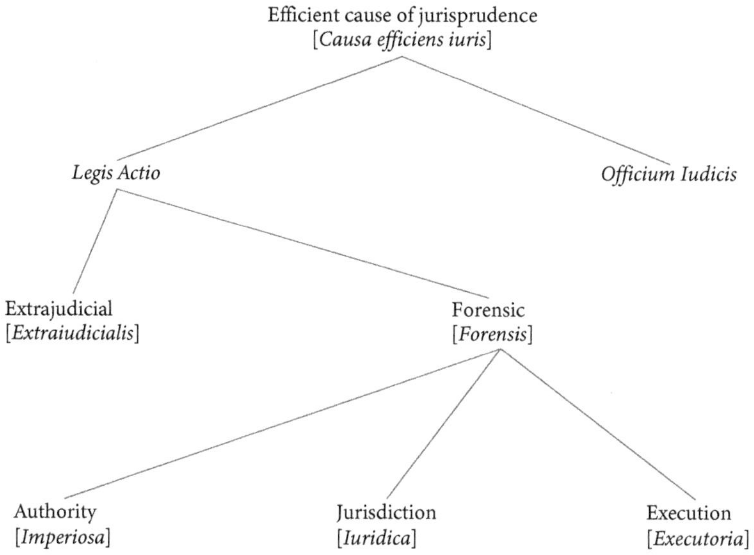

Figure 2.8 A more detailed diagram of the efficient causes of law. The category of *legis actio* is subdivided according to extrajudicial and forensic causes. Forensic causes, in turn, are further subdivided according to authority [*imperiosa*], jurisdiction [*iuridica*], and execution [*executoria*].

very nature, cannot be defined. Rather, as Carl Schmitt will famously later note, declaring a legal exception always represents a momentary arbitrary and decisive act of will that must be applied individually, case by case.[170]

The far greater share of Bodin's attention, then, is devoted to *legis actio*, which he defines as "the law's very execution, force, and power."[171] It is, as Cicero once put it, the *lex loquens* ("the speaking law"), the law personified in the words and deeds of a judge.[172]

One way to interpret *legis actio*, then, is to treat it as Bodin's catalogue of the essential judicial powers and legal functions and processes of courts. While intended to be a general statement on all legal systems, Bodin is very clearly thinking about

confessor's court) to enforce performance of *pacta nuda*. Cf. *Right of Sovereignty* 70, n.19; Decock, *Theologians and Contract Law*, 92–93; 124–29.

[170] Carl Schmitt, *Political Theology: Four Chapters on the Concept of Sovereignty*, trans. George Schwab (Chicago, IL: University of Chicago Press, 1985), 8–10. Schmitt cites Bodin on this point. In *Distributio* fol. A, s.v. *ius sine sanctione*, Bodin observes, "Equity [*aequitas*] is law entrusted to the judgment of the one deciding [*arbitrio statuentis permissum*], whether of the sovereign ... or of the magistrate."

[171] *Distributio* fol. E, s.v. *legis actio*.

[172] Cicero, *De Legibus*, 460 [III, i, §2]: *vereque dici potest, magistratuum esse legem loquentem*.

the Parlements in the *pays du droit écrit*, which, over centuries, assimilated and preserved Vulgar Roman law in the courts of Southern France.

The *summa divisio* of *legis actio* separates the "extrajudicial" from the "forensic" aspects of *legis actio*—or, to put it more simply, what happens outside the courtroom and what happens inside the courtroom necessarily involving the authority of a judge.[173] Aside from a perfunctory acknowledgement of the "extrajudicial" functions of *legis actio*, the far greater part of the discussion is devoted to an exploration of the "forensic"—the procedural rules governing litigation.[174]

The forensics of court proceedings were further subdivided into three main branches, which Bodin described as the *imperiosa* (that aspect of *legis actio* concerning authority, or *imperium*), the *iuridica* (that aspect of *legis actio* concerning jurisdiction, or *iurisdictio*—i.e., involving a judge), and the *executoria* (that aspect of *legis actio* concerning the execution or enforcement of judicial decisions). The relationship between these three areas was a matter of intense academic controversy in sixteenth-century French legal scholarship. It is a controversy that requires some explanation of the contextual background.

The Tree of Jurisdiction: The Context of Bodin's *Legis Actio*

The controversy originates in the very concept of *iurisdictio* in classical Roman law.[175] Ulpian illustrates some of the qualities of *iurisdictio* in two well-known passages in the title *De Iurisdictione* in the *Digest*:

> **D.2.1.1**: *Ius dicentis officium latissimum est: nam et bonorum possessionem dare potest et in possessionem mittere, pupillis non habentibus tutores constituere, iudices litigantibus dare.*
>
> "The powers of one who administers justice (*ius dicentis*) are most extensive. For he can grant *bonorom possessionem* (i.e., the right of succession to the estate of a deceased person), order *missio in possessionem* (i.e., a praetorian remedy allowing a creditor to take over a debtor's property in order to protect a creditor's interest after a judgment pronounced in his favor), appoint tutors for a pupil lacking one, and nominate judges for litigants."
>
> **2.1.3**: *Iurisdictio est etiam iudicis dandi licentia.*

[173] Bodin describes the latter as *quae in iure, id est apud iudicem*, which correspond to the two stages of trial in the formulary system—before and after joinder of issue [*litis contestatio*] and praetorian issuance of a formula to a judge. Jerphangnon, in *Exposé du droit universel* 59, renders "forensis" as *l'action judiciare*.

[174] On this point, Bodin cites D.11.1.4.1 (which specifies that answers to interrogatories must be *apud magistratus populi romani vel praesides provinciarum*); D.1.1.11–12 (which clarifies that the word *ius* can mean *locus in quo ius redditur*: "the place in which justice is administered"); Inst.1.1.4 (which concerns the formal judicial *datio libertatis*—that is, manumission).

[175] I originally presented this analysis in *Popular Sovereignty* 83–90.

"Jurisdiction includes also the right of appointing a judge."

Ulpian's description in these famous passages indicate that *iurisdictio* was fundamentally a legal power of magistrates, especially the praetors and provincial governors. Of course, many features of the magistrate's *iurisdictio* touched upon litigation. This was captured in Ulpian's observation that a principal function of *iurisdictio* was the "nomination" and formal appointment of a judge in specific legal disputes, without whom a trial cannot take place.

But *iurisdictio* needn't always be a tool to manage *contentiosa* litigation. *Iurisdictio* even encompassed those matters designated *voluntaria*, or non-contentious, legal transactions represented as collusive "feigned controversies" before a judge, such as the *cessio in iure* (property conveyance in the presence of a judge, which Bodin regards a kind of *liberatio*, or release from obligation), manumission, emancipation, or (in Ulpian's example above) the judicial appointment of tutors.[176]

But magistrates, whether praetors, provincial governors, or otherwise, could not be expected personally to handle all the matters brought before them. The Romans, therefore, devised an efficient legal division of labor, whereby some aspects of the magistrate's *iurisdictio* could be "delegated" [*iurisdictio mandata*] to others with strict instructions (documented in the praetor's *formula*). This system is described in the *Digest* under the title *De officio eius, cui mandata est iurisdictio* (D.1.21: "On the duty of those persons to whom *iurisdictio* is delegated").

D.1.21.1.1: *Qui mandatam iurisdictoionem suscepit, proprium nihil habet, sed eius mandavit, iurisdictione utitur.*

"He who receives a magistrate's *iurisdictio* by delegation does not hold that *iurisdictio* as his own, but merely exercises the *iurisdictio* of the magistrate who originally delegated it."

This was fundamental to the formulary system of Roman litigation. Upon hearing the basic facts of the case from the parties, the praetor documents in a "formula" the legal issues that must be tried and decided. Having arrived at this "joinder of issue," the praetor can then delegate his *iurisdictio* to the private person "nominated" to serve as the judge overseeing the trial.

What can this private judge do with his delegated *iurisdictio*? The most important duty is captured in the word itself—*ius dicere* ("to declare a verdict"). And, as Bodin will observe, pronouncing the judge's verdict, whether absolution

[176] Ulpian is referring there to the category of *tutela dativa*, legal guardians appointed for the care of wards by the praetor or other official, originally introduced by the *lex Atilia*. Marcian introduces the distinction between *contentiosa* and *voluntaria* jurisdictions at D.1.16.2.pr. The latter becomes the "jurisdiction gracieuse" in the French Civil Code and a vital feature of most Civil Law systems.

or condemnation (or an inconclusive finding of *non licqet*), is the essence of the magistrate's judicial power. This is not in dispute.

The core of this interpretive dispute, however, concerns what the private judge or other delegate *cannot* do with this delegated power. What holders of delegated *iurisdictio* lack, above all, is the coercive power of enforcement—variously called here *animadversionem*, *coercitionem*, and, most important, *imperium.*[177] On this principle, the *Digest* supplies some examples. Deputies of proconsuls, for example, who are delegated the proconsular *iurisdictio*, lack the coercive right of punishment [*animadversionem*]. Papinian explains why:

> **D.1.21.1.1**: *Verius est enim more maiorum iurisdictionem quidem transferri, sed merum imperium quod lege datur non posse transire.*
>
> "Although it is true that a magistrate's *iurisdictio* may be transferred to another, as the *mos maiorum* (Roman customary norms governing economy and society) allows, the *merum imperium*, which is conferred by law, can never be so transferred."

Some confusion and interpretive disagreement, however, attached to the term *imperium*. Paul acknowledges that, when a magistrate's *iurisdictio* is delegated to another agent, it is understood that at least some minimal degree of coercive enforcement powers are also transferred as well:

> **D.1.21.5.1**: *Mandata iurisdictione privato etiam imperium quod non est merum videtur mandari, quia iurisdictio sine modica coercitione nulla est.*
>
> "When a magistrate's *iurisdictio* is delegated to a private person, it is observed that all *imperium* which is not *merum imperium* is also delegated. This is because there is no *iurisdictio* without even a minimal right to inflict moderate punishment."

Papinian, who disagreed with this position, acknowledged Paul's view that delegation of *iurisdictio* entails a delegation of at least some *imperium* as well:

> **D.1.21.1.1**: *Paulus notat: et imperium, quod iurisdictioni cohaeret, mandata iurisdictione transire verius est.*
>
> "Paul observes: It is true the magistrate's *imperium*, which is connected to *iurisdictio*, is transferred whenever magistrate's *iurisdictio* is delegated."

[177] There are additional points of difference. Holders of delegated *iurisdictio* cannot convoke their own *consilium* (D.1.21.2.pr) or hold their own inquiry [*quaestio*] in matters involving the sale of property *in tutela* (D.1.21.2.1).

The original disagreement, then, concerns *imperium*. When a magistrate delegates *iurisdictio* to an agent or deputy, does he also transfer *imperium* as well?

The controversy called for a clarification on Paul's usage of the term *imperium*. In this classical context, *imperium* was simply the execution and coercive enforcement of a legal decision—including potentially the capital penalty of death, the *merum imperium*.[178] What Paul's dictum indicates is that *imperium* needn't be *merum*. Not all penalties and enforcement measures require a capital penalty of execution. In principle, then, Paul recognizes that *imperium* is a genus admitting of various degrees and species. In these sources, he famously distinguishes between *merum imperium* and *modica coercitio*. Ulpian, too, offered another typology in D.2.1.3, distinguishing between *merum imperium* and *mixtum imperium*, the latter of which indicated those judicial powers that can be delegated to private judges and deputies, along with *iurisdictio*.[179] What is clear in this cluster of legal explanations is that a magistrate's *merum imperium* (assuming he has it) can never be delegated, because a special legal authorization (a *lex de imperio*) is required even for the magistrate to hold it. It is never a magistrate's discretionary right to delegate away the *merum imperium* specifically granted to him.

But that was classical law. When the *Digest* was recovered in the Middle Ages, Bartolist medieval lawyers of the *ius commune* interpreted the relation between *iurisdictio* and *imperium* somewhat differently. *Iurisdictio*, in particular, presented some interpretive complexity because it was thought the term carried an unavoidable double meaning. It could mean, on the one hand, the ordinary judicial power of magistrates and delegated private judges in the context of litigation in court. This aligned with the classical understanding of Papinian and Paul we saw above.

But, as we saw in Chapter 1, medieval lawyers also recognized that *iurisdictio* indicated something beyond this narrow meaning. Jurisdiction was *iuris-ditio* ("the authority of law"), functioning as a generic term for legal authority of all kinds, and not just the authority of judges presiding over a trial proceeding.[180] Because of this double meaning, medieval lawyers of the *ius commune* distinguished (in unclassical fashion) between two types of *iurisdictio*:

> *iurisdictio in genere sumpta* (corresponding to the latter broad generic sense of *iuris ditio*);

[178] Ulpian at D.2.1.3 famously defines *merum imperium* as *gladii potestatem ad animadvertendum facinorosos homines, quod etiam potestas appellatur* ("Merum imperium is the magistrate's *potestas gladii* (i.e., the right to inflict capital penalties) over criminals. It is also simply called *potestas*." Cf. D.50.16.215.

[179] Ulpian at D.2.1.3 defines *mixtum imperium* as *imperium cui etiam iurisdictio inest quod in danda bonorum possessione consistit. Iurisdictio est etiam iudicis dandi licentia* ("*Mixtum imperium*, to which *iurisdictio* is attached, consists in the right of granting *bonorum possessio*. *Iurisdictio* includes also the right of appointing a judge."

[180] Accursius ad D.2.1.3 s.v.: *Mixtum est*; Bartolus ad D.2.1.3, s.v.: *Imperium*, §§3–4, who observes *potestas et iurisdictio idem sunt, ut dixi: et est potestas iuris.*

iurisdictio simplex (corresponding to the former narrowly specific sense of judicial power).

The relationship between the two is species to genus: *Iurisdictio simplex* is understood to be but one species, or "branch," of the broader class of legal authority signified generically by *iurisdictio*. But it is not the only species, a point visualized, as we saw earlier in Chapter 1 (see Figure 1.1), in the famous "tree of jurisdictions" accompanying the Bartolist commentary on D.2.1.1, the *l.Ius dicentis officium*.

The other "branch" on this tree of *iurisdictio* was *imperium*. But here, the Bartolists transformed the concept of *imperium*. Unlike classical jurists who defined it narrowly as the magistrate's right of enforcement of a decision following a trial, the Bartolists interpreted *imperium* as a versatile, all-encompassing term for lawful public authority in all its forms. Whereas *merum imperium* treated public matters of state, *mixtum imperium* treated private matters.

Another question remained to be answered. Who can lawfully wield these powers of *imperium*, and especially the highest *maximum* powers of *merum imperium*? This question was originally the basis of a famous, possibly apochryphal, thirteenth-century public debate argued between the Glossators Azo and Lothair, in the presence of the Holy Roman Emperor Henry VI.[181] The Emperor, no doubt, had a political interest in how jurists answered this question. To avoid encroachment on his authority as "lord of the whole world," he needed to ensure that his *imperium* remained supreme and exclusive, so that no subordinate, such as an inferior magistrate or another prince, could claim any part of the *merum imperium*.

The Emperor asked his lawyers whether the *merum imperium* was exclusive to the Emperor alone [*An sit merum imperium proprium principis*], or whether it could be shared with others. Lothair replied that *merum imperium* was indeed reserved to the *princeps* alone, while magistrates exercised authority simply as a concessive delegation of imperial authority.[182] Azo, by contrast, disagreed, arguing instead that emperors and magistrates each had, by right, their own form of *merum imperium*, albeit corresponding to different ranks.

The Emperor ultimately favored Lothair's reply and awarded him with a horse [*equus*], leading to Azo's pun that he lost a horse [*equum*] even though he defended what was just [*aequum*]. But it was Azo's dictum and its more flexible understanding of *merum imperium* that would become the standard doctrine of the Western medieval *ius commune*. The Bartolist tree of jurisdictions with its multiple layers and ranks of *imperia* was simply an expansion of Azo.

[181] Lee, *Popular Sovereignty*, 86–8. This story is recounted in Gilmore, *Argument from Roman Law*, 17–20; Kenneth Pennington, *The Prince and the Law, 1200–1600: Sovereignty and Rights in the Western Legal Tradition* (Berkeley: University of California Press, 1993), 19–20. It can be located in Azo's *Summa* ad C.3.13 and Odofredus, *Lectura Super Digesto Veteri* (Lyon, 1550), fol. 38, ad D.2.1.3, s.v. *Imperium*.

[182] Cf. the distinction at D.2.1.5 between jurisdiction held *suo iure* and *alieno beneficio*.

It was only in the sixteenth century, when humanist scholarship began to expose the interpretive license on Roman law, that the predominant Bartolist teaching on *imperium* and *iurisdictio* began to crumble. Alciato, the founder of the legal humanist school of Bourges, can once again claim credit for this achievement. In addressing the concept of *merum imperium*, he returned to the old debate between Azo and Lothair and undermined centuries of medieval jurisprudence constructed around the Azonian and Bartolist doctrine by revitalizing Lothair's strict position that *merum imperium* belongs exclusively to the *princeps*: Magistrates simply exercised that coercive power as agents on behalf of the imperial authority.[183]

But Alciato's explanation entailed something even more consequential. This was his observation, recorded in his *Paradoxorum*, that *imperium* was not really a species or "branch" of *iurisdictio* at all, as medieval jurists believed.[184] It was something entirely separate. For Alciato, the *Digest* was sufficiently clear that *iurisdictio* was, above all, a narrowly judicial function, requiring a judge to pronounce a legal decision in a specific legal dispute.

Enforcing such a decision, however, was a different matter altogether and called for a different power—this is actually what Ulpian designated *imperium*. It was not so much a kind of *iurisdictio*, as it was the carrying out, or execution, of the court's *iurisdictio*. It is also the reason why Alciato could not see *imperium* as a kind of *iurisdictio*. There was simply nothing in the sources to justify treating *iurisdictio* generically as *iuris-ditio*, legal authority of all kinds.

Merum imperium, in particular, has nothing to do with the emperor's exclusive authority. It is, instead, "nothing other than the power of the sword to punish wicked men" [*merum imperium nil aliud esse quam potestatem gladio animadvertendi in facinorosos homines*].[185] It is a power that belongs properly to magistrates [*haec potestas magistratibus tribuitur*], not to the emperor.

Humanist jurists of the sixteenth century that followed Alciato's line of reasoning came to see that *iurisdictio* and *imperium* actually corresponded to different stages of trial proceedings in civil law. Whereas *iurisdictio* indicated the first stage requiring a judge, *imperium* indicated the latter stages after judgment that were only tangentially judicial.[186] This led humanists to treat these terms as part of a trial timeline. Ioannis Gillotus, as Guido Rossi explains, "sharply divided the legal proceeding in three phases: *cognitio*, *sententia*, and *executio*. While *cognitio* and *sententia* pertain to *iurisdictio* and *mixtum imperium*, *executio* is the province of *merum imperium*. *Executio* is wholly detached from the legal proceeding because

[183] Andrea Alciato, *Paradoxorum ad Pratum, Libri Sex* (Milan: Alexander Minutianus, 1518), fol. 17ro [II, vi].

[184] Alciato, *Paradoxorum*, fol. 17ro–17vo [II, vii].

[185] Alciato, *Paradoxorum*, fol. 17vo [II, vii].

[186] Bodin specifies that the forensic functions of *legis actio* are all, by definition, *apud iudicem*. The stages introduced here, therefore, do not directly correspond to the classical division in the formulary procedure between *in iure* and *apud iudicem* stages of litigation before a judge.

it is only concerned with executing the judgment (*sentential effectus*)."[187] Others, seeing that *merum imperium* was reduced simply to the work of an executioner, attempted to reconnect it to the jurisdictional *cognitio* of judges. Pierre Loriot, for example, narrowly defined the function of *sententia* literally as the declaration of a verdict, so that *merum imperium* could be reconnected to the discretion associated with *iurisdictio*.[188] Later humanists, such as François La Douaren, António de Gouveia, Jean de Coras, Eguinaire Baron, and Hugues Doneau, contributed even more to this interpretive debate on *imperium* and *iurisdictio*, making it one of the central interpretive disputes in humanist legal scholarship of the sixteenth century.

Bodin was immersed into this flood of legal scholarship on *imperium* and *iurisdictio*. He even attempted to produce his own topical treatises on the subject. The original versions did not survive but would be incorporated into his later works in the *Methodus*, *République*, and the *Distributio*. It is within this context of academic lawyers debating how best to interpret and understand *imperium* and *iurisdictio* that Bodin's own efforts must be evaluated.

The Forensic *Legis Actio*: *Imperium, Iurisdictio, Executio*

How does Bodin approach this broad category of forensic *legis actio*? Bodin accepts, to a limited degree, Alciato's basic position. Like Alciato, Bodin acknowledges that there is no generic concept of *iuris-ditio*, a capacious juridical notion of authority encompassing both the judicial power of judges [*iurisdictiones simplices*] as well as the coercive power [*imperia*] of magistrates. Instead, *iurisdictio* and *imperium* designate different stages of legal proceedings. Bodin, however, adds one crucial element—*executio*—that later humanist jurists, like Gillotus and Loriot, introduced into their analysis.

In sum, Bodin identifies three distinct aspects, or stages, of *legis actio* in the operation of courts—the *imperiosa*, the *iuridica*, and the *executoria*. All three, as he defined it, are essentially "forensic," which is to say they are legal powers necessitating an authority of some kind, whether a judge or someone else. Let us work in reverse order, starting with *executio*.

Executio: The "executive" [*executoria*] aspects of *legis actio* concern the carrying out of the legal decisions of a court. Bodin has little to say, except to observe that forensic *executio* can take one of two forms—"against one who voluntarily complies [*qui sponte obsequitur*], and against one who is compelled by force" [*qui vi cogitur*].[189] The distinction reflects Marcian's distinction, at D.1.16.2.pr, between

[187] Rossi, "Deconstructing *Iurisdictio*," 66–67, commenting on Ioannis Gillotus, *De iurisdictione et imperio*.
[188] Rossi, "Deconstructing *Iurisdictio*," 67–68. Petrus Loriotus, *De iurisdictione et imperio*.
[189] *Distributio* fol. F, s.v. *executoria duplex*.

iurisdictio contentiosa and *iurisdictio voluntaria*. When parties voluntarily submit to the jurisdiction of a court in order to effect a legal transaction (such as master and slave in a manumission, paterfamilias and child in an emancipation, or seller and buyer in a cession of property), compliance with execution of the order must likewise be regarded as voluntary.

Who wields the *executoria* functions of *legis actio*? Is it the same official or judge who exercises jurisdiction (which, as we'll see, Bodin treats as a distinct function)? Or someone else? This was the interpretive problem that humanist commentators on *imperium* and *iurisdictio* encountered: Execution appeared to be the carrying out of someone else's decision, thereby reducing it the role of the "mere executioner" but without any decision-making discretion or autonomy.[190] It is perhaps one of the ancestral ideas that would eventually be interwoven into the modern doctrine of the separation of powers.[191]

Imperium: Under the heading of authoritative [*imperiosa*] actions are those basic functions which take the form of commands, prohibitions, and permissions [*in iussis, vetitis, & permissione*] (p. 159).[192] These can happen in courts on the order of judges.

Bodin places here a familiar typology of *imperium* ("authority" or "command," from *imperare*) that extends outside the forensic setting of the courtroom. Indeed, the old Roman distinction between *merum* and *mixtum imperium* is missing here in the *Distributio*.[193] What appears, in place of Ulpian's division (at D.2.1.3), is a new comprehensive typology of authority, perhaps the first time Bodin offers a preview of the novel theory of the *République* (see Figure 2.9).

Imperium, Bodin explains, encompassed both public and private forms of authority. Following the earlier distinction between public and private law (the latter of which, as he put it, "pertains to towns, private associations, and families"), Bodin now specifies the kinds of authority that animate public and private law. In the private sphere, *imperium* includes the paterfamilial *potestas* over the Roman family, the *dominium* of a master over a slave, and the procuratorial authority over a corporate or collegial body.[194]

Imperium also encompassed the various forms and ranks of public authority over the state. While it included the "lawful authority" [*imperium legitimum*] of officials, of all ranks, appointed to the lawful exercise of some share of the public *imperium*, Bodin's main purpose here was to isolate that one form of *imperium*

[190] Rossi, "Deconstructing *Iurisdictio*," 68.

[191] M. J. C. Vile, *Constitutionalism and the Separation of Powers*, 2nd ed. (Indianapolis: Liberty Fund, 1998), 59–62 [chap. 3] points to George Lawson's *Politica Sacra et Civilis* as an example of the confusing uses of "executive power"—the one meaning the execution of judge's sentence following "as a distinct act of Jurisdiction," the other meaning "all acts that tend to the execution of the Lawes."

[192] *Distributio* fol. E, s.v. *imperiosa*. Cf. D.1.3.7: *Legis virtus haec est imperare vetare permittere punire.*

[193] Bodin dismisses the old interpretive debate on *iurisdictio* and *merum imperium* at *Methodus* 263 [VI], complaining that the jurists have left the matter *in magna obscuritate*.

[194] Cf. *République* 19; *De Republica* 14; *Right of Sovereignty* 99–102.

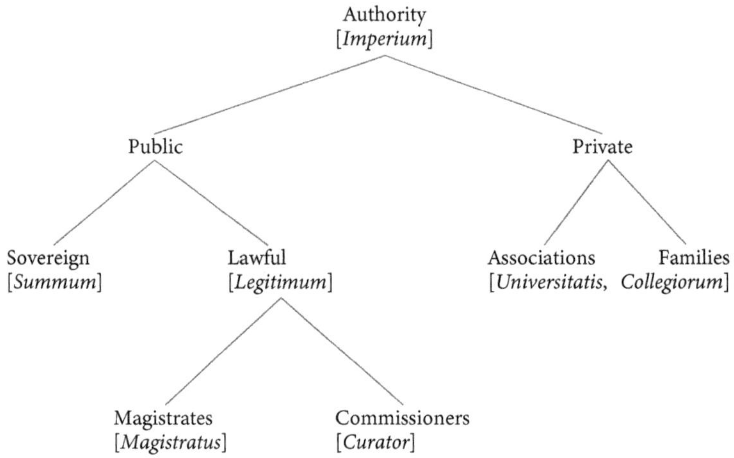

Figure 2.9 Diagram of the varieties of *imperium*, or authority, in Bodin's system. Authority can be either public or private. Public authority can be sovereign or *legitimum*, the latter of which covers the subordinate authority of magistrates and commissioners. Private authority concerns the authority in private associations and families.

irreducible to all these others. This was the supreme, or "sovereign," authority [*summum imperium*] of the state, positioned above the authority of all inferior magistrates. Even at this early stage, Bodin resisted duplicating the mistake he apparently felt other jurists treating the topic of *iurisdictio* and *imperium* had made, in regarding the prince's (or people's) sovereign authority as coextensive with the judicial functions of magistrates. And that is because, unlike magistrates whose authority is defined and legally limited according to the law governing the offices of magistrates [*iure magistratus competit*], only the sovereign's is "exempt from the law" [*lege soluta*].[195]

Though it traverses across the private-public boundary, all forms of *imperium* share one feature in common—namely, that it is a form of command that can create obligations binding others (Bodin will later call this *le droit commandment*).[196] In this sense, Bodin not only anticipates the basic insight of the command theory of law, advanced by theorists such as Thomas Hobbes and John Austin, but also the connection between law and obligation fundamental to Grotius and Pufendorf.

195 *Distributio* fol. F, s.v. *propria*. Cf. D.1.21.1; D.1.3.31: *Princeps legibus solutus est*.

196 For Bodin, command entails its reverse de-imperative function of countermand. Whereas an act of command creates a new binding obligation, countermand (the negation of prior command) has the opposite effect of release (*liberatio*; *solution*) from an obligation. Hans Kelsen had categorized such countermands generically as "negative legislation." Cf. *Right of Sovereignty* 155–59.

Iurisdictio: By far the largest part of Bodin's analysis of the forensic *legis actio* concerns *iurisdictio*—or, more precisely, the *iuridica* aspects of *legis actio*. One point that is immediately clear from the outset is that Bodin is deliberately choosing to interpret the term only in the narrow sense of the judge's *ius dicentis officium* (what medieval Bartolists would have called the *iurisdictio simplex*)—jurisdiction in the courtroom. This is especially apparent from how Bodin divides the concept of *iurisdictio*, in Ramist terms of "causes" and of "adjuncts" (indicating how *iurisdictio* is held).

For both of these, Bodin has relatively little to say. He explains, following the standard doctrine of D.1.21.1 and D.2.1.5, that *iurisdictio* can either be held as one's own [*propria*], as in the case of lawfully appointed magistrates, or it can be delegated [*mandata*] to another, such as a proconsular deputy. He also identifies three "causes" of *iurisdictio*—causes which are *ex materia*, *ex forma*, and *ex efficiente*. Whereas "material" aspects of jurisdiction concern simply whether the matter before a court is civil, criminal, or some hybrid, the "formal" aspects address the origin and scope of the jurisdiction.[197] The latter includes the ordinary jurisdiction of an "ordinary" judge, the permanent office and power as defined by law or by custom [*ex lege vel ex more consueto*]. It also includes the extraordinary jurisdiction, the power and decision of a judge [*iudicis arbitrio*] appointed outside the usual legal procedures of appointment, including especially commissioners [*curatoris*] with precarious tenure and provisional judges appointed directly by the sovereign [*a principe dati*].[198]

It is the third cause, the efficient cause [*ex efficiente*], that occupies the bulk of Bodin's attention in discussing jurisdiction. This concerns the core of litigation and Bodin's attempt at constructing a detailed theory and catalogue of all the major actions that take place in trial. While the individual technical details are extensive, it is possible to identify some general features and patterns of what is perhaps the most technically complicated area of the *Distributio* (see Figure 2.10).

The first division is a familiar one in civil law. It is, as we saw earlier, Marcian's division (at D.1.16.2.pr) of *iurisdictio* into "voluntary" and "contentious" forms. Bodin supplies some standard examples to illustrate the former for "feigned" or collusive controversies requiring the formal presence of a judge to effect a legal transaction, such as an adoption or emancipation of a child from *paterfamilias*, the manumission of a slave from *dominium*, and cession of property from one party to

[197] With respect to jurisdiction *ex forma*, Bodin's inspiration for the distinction between ordinary and extraordinary jurisdiction appears to be canonistic in origin. Cf. *Distributio* fols. B–C on persons *ex dignitate*, Bodin's discussion of "public persons" divided according to whether they hold authority *ordinario* or authority *extraordinario* which is, in turn, defined as a tenure *ad incertum tempus* and dependent on the *arbitrium* of the sovereign.

[198] Bodin's description of the extraordinary judges as exercising their discretionary *arbitrium* recalls the distinction between *droit* government based on law and *seigneurial* government based on will. Bodin's point seems to be that these extraordinary "seigneurial" judges decide solely according to arbitrary will, unrestrained by the ordinary limits imposed by law and custom.

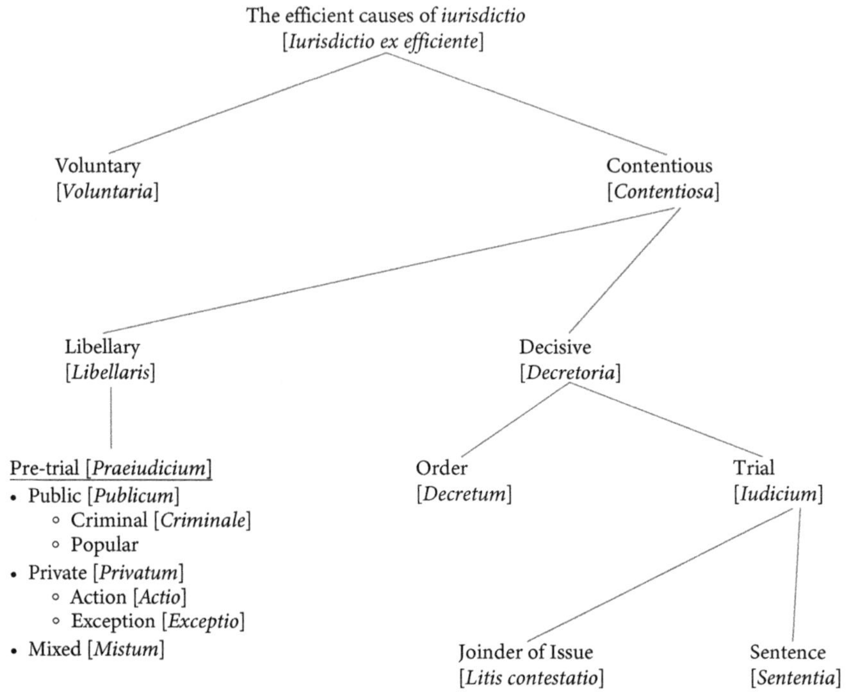

Figure 2.10 Diagram of the efficient causes of *iuisdictio*. Jurisdiction can be either voluntary or contentious. The latter is further subdivided according to "libellary" [*libellaris*] matters, which concern pre-trial motions, as well as "decisive" [*decretoria*] matters, which concern the trial and its outcome.

another in the presence of a judge. Because they must take place *in iure*, they are regarded as aspects of a judge's *iurisdictio*, even though there is no dispute or judicial examination of facts.

Disputes are treated in cases involving a court's exercise of "contentious" *iurisdictio*. One way to read this final branch is to treat it as Bodin's attempt to catalogue all the basic types of actionable legal remedies and motions that may be pleaded before a court, as well as the basic stages of trial involving contentious *iurisdictio*. And the analysis is remarkably similar to the humanist analysis on the exercise of *iurisdictio* and *imperium* we observed above in litigation.

Bodin divides contentious *iurisdictio* into two branches—what he calls the "libellary" [*libellaris*] and "decisive" [*decretoria*]. They correspond broadly to the two major stages of a trial where contentious jurisdiction is exercised—the "pre-trial" [*praeiudicium*] stage and the "trial" itself [*iudicium*]. What separates the two is joinder of issue [*litis contestatio*], the moment when all parties agree on the legal issues that are in dispute and must be tried before a judge. Under the formulary system, joinder of issue marked the final pre-trial stage, *in iure*, when the magistrate documented the basic elements of the case in his *formula*, which "nominated" and "delegated" the *iurisdictio* to a judge with strict instructions and designated the specific legal issues that must be tried in court.[199]

Bodin's division, however, relies not on the formulary procedure but rather the *cognitio extra ordinem* procedure, which historically replaced the *formula* in the third century. The principal difference in the *cognitio* was the role of the magistrate. Whereas the *formula* nominated and delegated jurisdiction to a private judge, the *cognitio* (literally, a judicial "examination") assigned all responsibility in managing and deciding a case to the public magistrate with *iurisdictio*.

These two vital concepts—*cognitio* and *litis contestatio*—allow Bodin to establish the principal stages of a trial. The first, "libellary," stage is characterized by the initial submission and exchange of written pleadings and replies [*libellis*], but specifically without *cognitio*—that is, before the presiding magistrate in court has even had a chance to examine the litigants' claims—and all before joinder of issue [*sine contestatione*]. Indeed, the bulk of Bodin's discussion concerns what might approximate initial "pre-trial" motions [*praeiudicium*].

It is under this broad category of "libellary" jurisdiction where Bodin finally locates the substance of Gaius's law of actions. These are classified in three ways, in terms of public actions (which include criminal and "popular actions"), private actions, and mixed actions ("when public and private things are mingled, and when at the same time we pursue what is of both public and private interest").[200]

Bodin's principal focus, not surprisingly, concerns private actions—legal remedies for civil disputes. In treating actions, Bodin preserves here many of the fundamental classical distinctions found in Gaius and Justinian. For example, having defined an *actio* as the plaintiff's "private pre-trial action [*privatum praeiudicium*] brought about by entering a civil plea,"[201] Bodin acknowledges Gaius's teaching that all actions are either "real" [*realis*], "personal" [*personalis*], or "mixed" [*mista*].[202] He preserves the basic distinction between actions *stricti iuris* and

[199] Gaius 4.39–44 outlines the principal features of a standard praetorian *formula*.

[200] "Popular actions" [*populares actiones*] are likely a reference to the public prosecutions [*publica iudicia*] described in the final title of Justinian's *Institutes* (Inst.4.18). These include prosecutions of treason, embezzlement, and adultery under the *lex Iulia*; assassination under the *lex Cornelia*; and parricide under the *lex Pompeia*. Bodin distinguishes criminal actions from civil "popular actions not involving a crime," but it is not clear how this distinction works, since public prosecutions were reserved specifically for prosecution of the most serious crimes.

[201] *Distributio* fol. E, s.v. *privatum praeiudicium*. Cf. D.44.7.51: *Nihil aliud est actio quam ius quod sibi debeatur iudicio persequendi*. Inst.4.6.13 explains the function of *praeiudiciales actiones*. Bodin at *Distributio* fol. E, s.v. *praeiudicilias* explains that it is a type of personal action, "by which a dispute is carried out concerning the status, rank, sex, or condition of persons." It includes the *actio liberalis*, the *actio peregrinitatis*, the *actio de iure magistratuum*, the *actio de liberis legitimis*, among other remedies.

[202] Cf. Gaius 4.1–3; Inst.4.6.1, distinguishing between actions *in rem* and actions *in personam*. Bodin cites C.3.31.7 to illustrate the category of mixed actions. He also cites the actions *familiae erciscundae*, *communi dividundo*, and *finium regundorum* which are described as "mixed actions" in Inst.4.6.20, along with other examples at Inst.4.6.16, 4.6.18, and 4.6.19.

bonae fidei, while also acknowledging *actiones arbitraria* (Inst.4.6.31), those which depend solely on a judge's individual ruling [*ex arbitrio iudicis*]. Finally, alongside the plaintiff's *actio* is the defendant's *exceptio*, which is "exercised in exclusion of an *actio*" as an affirmative defense against the plaintiff's claim. Taken together, these various actions and exceptions constitute the preliminary raw materials from which a potential dispute can take shape in a justiciable form that can be tried in court. But that can only happen when a formal decision is made that the elements of a trial are present.

Such decision requires the other main branch of contentious jurisdiction, concerning the "decisive" [*decretoria*], or decision-making, stages of a trial, where formal *cognitio*, or judicial examinations, of the case can take place.[203] Here, Bodin is careful, acknowledging that a magistrate with jurisdiction may decide matters, only pertaining to the case in the form of a court order [*decretum*], such as adjournments or praetorian grants of *bonorum possessionis*,[204] without pronouncing final judgment of the case itself. Distinguishing between these two types of judicial pronouncements requires joinder of issue. Whereas a pre-trial court order [*decretum*] is technically the result of a judicial *cognitio* but prior to joinder of issue [*sine litis contestatione*], the trial itself [*iudicium*], as defined by joinder of issue, is an exercise of jurisdiction that results in the court's final *sententia*—either absolution or condemnation. Only after a court has pronounced its sentence can the "executive" [*executoria*] function of the court (p. 166) take effect, which ultimately brings Bodin's outline of the efficient causes of law to a close.

As a whole, Bodin's division of jurisdiction presents a schematic of how trials proceed, from start to finish. What is remarkable about his version is the palpable influence of humanist legal scholarship on *iurisdictio*. Just as humanists divided trials into the *cognitio*, *sententia*, and *executio*, Bodin too envisioned the exercise of *iurisdictio* as a sequence from pre-trial and trial to enforcement. The Roman law of actions provides only a partial glimpse into what *iurisdictio* entails, a deficiency that Bodin's system has remedied.

Conclusion: The Bodinian Division of Law

Bodin's *Distributio* presents a systematic Ramist division of law [*ius*] that moves beyond the classical forms of Gaius and Justinian. This chapter has investigated Bodin's choices in designing what he regarded to be a general system of law, such as the division of law into "natural" and "human" forms; the subject-matter of law

[203] On this point, Bodin cites D.1.16.9.1 which discusses the duty of proconsuls to pursue a proper *cognitio* where litigants request, *per libellum*, a proconsular order, or *decretum*, to dismiss [*expedire*] a case.

[204] Bodin is referring here to the possessory interdict, *quorum bonorum*, which granted possession of the estate of a deceased person, especially where the heir entitled to succession may be in dispute.

as concerning persons, things, and deeds; and the division of the efficient causes of law in terms of *legis actio* and the equitable *officium iudicis* of judges.

What remains to be explored is the ultimate purpose, or *finis*, of jurisprudence. Bodin's answer gestures toward Ulpian's opening statement of the *Digest* (D.1.1.1.pr), observing that *ius* ("law") is so called because it is derived, *a iustitia* ("from justice"). The *Distributio* is not only a theory of law. It also prefigures a theory of justice.

3

Harmonic Justice

Introduction

The *Distributio* closes with a relatively brief discussion in Part IV on the aims, or the *finis*, of jurisprudence. Referencing the opening title of Justinian's *Digest—De iustitia et iure* ("On justice and law")—Bodin declares that the ultimate purpose of law [*ius*] is to achieve justice [*iustitia*]. And justice, in turn, is defined narrowly in the classical language of "requital" [Τὸ ἀντιπεπονθὸς] as a reciprocal moral exchange of deed and return. This is how Bodin chose to interpret that Ciceronian description of justice as *suum cuique tribuens* ("the rendering unto each his due").[1]

But how much, whether of rewards or punishments, must one render to another, in order to achieve justice? There is, as Aristotle once taught, no uniform answer to this question, since the answer depends on the context in which a question of justice arises. Consider, for example, the everyday commercial exchanges, or "synallagma" [συνάλλαγμα], taking place in the marketplace. Here, justice demands the full payment, delivery, or performance of whatever is strictly due, and not a penny less, regardless of the personal character of the recipient. Hence, in a sale, justice requires that a buyer must always pay what is due, even if the seller may be lacking in virtue. Likewise, a debtor must always repay what is due on an outstanding loan, even if the creditor may be undeserving of such repayment. Failure to do so can count as injustice that calls for legal remedy. Lawyers sometimes referred to this mode of justice as *ius strictum*, reinforced by legal remedies later described in Roman law as *stricti iuris* actions.[2] Aristotle simply called it rectificatory or "commutative justice."[3]

[1] Cicero, *On Ends*, trans. Horace Rackham, Loeb Classical Library 40 (Cambridge: Harvard University Press, 1914), 468–71 [*De Finibus* V, 67]; Cicero, *On the Nature of the Gods*, trans. Horace Rackham, Loeb Classical Library 268 (Cambridge: Harvard University Press, 1933), 320–21 [*De Natura Deorum* III, xv, §38]; Ulpian at D.1.1.10, which Bodin cites in the final part of the *Distributio* fol. F, s.v. *finis iustitia*.

[2] Gaius 3.18, for example, describes the law of the XII Tables as *strictum: Quod ius quemadmodum strictum fuerit palam est intellegere*. The term *ius strictum* is of Byzantine origin peculiar to jurists. Jacobus Spiegel, *Lexicon Iuris Civilis* (Lyon: Apud Sebastianum Gryphium, 1548), s.v.: *stricti iuris*, which cites in turn Guillaume Budé, *Annotationes in Quatuor et Viginti Pandectarum Libros* (Paris: Ab Iodoco Badio Ascensio Impressae, 1508), fol. 2ro; Johannes Calvinus, *Lexicon Iuridicum* (Frankfurt: Impensis Johannis Marnii Haeredum, 1610), col. 1889, documents uses of the phrase at C.3.1.8; Inst. 4.6; D.13.6.3.2; D.12.3.5; D.29.2.86.pr; D.4.13.5.30; C.3.42.8; D.5.3.50; and D.40.7.28.pr.

[3] Aristotle, *Nicomachean Ethics*, 266 [V, ii, 1131^{a}2]; 272 [V, iv, 1131^{b}26] uses the term συνάλλαγμα, meaning commercial exchange or private transaction to illustrate commutative justice.

Divisions of Law. Daniel Lee, Oxford University Press. © Daniel Lee 2026. DOI: 10.1093/9780191847806.003.0004

Justice, however, needn't always concern what is strictly due. The principle, *suum cuique tribuere*, could be understood as a rule which says that the deserving ought to get their just deserts, even if such rewards (or punishments) may not be *strictly* due, as in a sale or loan. This is a justice of proportional merit, where the worthier justly deserve and merit greater rewards, while the less worthy (or worthless) merit fewer rewards. Rewards and punishments, on this theory of justice, are to be distributed in proportion to one's merit and worth—*pro dignitate*, as Cicero once put it in *De Officiis*.[4] When each receives what they deserve, a different form of justice is realized, what Aristotle called "distributive justice."[5]

These two types of justice—commutative and distributive—have been the main pillars upon which the theory of justice has been constructed in Western philosophy and jurisprudence. And these two types of justice have, in turn, been interpreted and represented metaphorically and mathematically in terms of arithmetic and geometric sequences, respectively. Commutative justice, and its requirement to render what is strictly due to others, is reflected in the strict numerical equality separating the terms of an arithmetic sequence (2, 4, 6, 8, 10 ...). By contrast, distributive justice is reflected in a geometric sequence (2, 4, 8, 16, 32 ...), where terms are conjoined to each other by a common ratio.

Is there an alternative to these two principal forms of justice? Aristotle had suggested equity, a "better justice" in the form of exceptions from the strictures of commutative or distributive justice.[6] Stoic and Christian commentators stressed the ancient virtue of liberality (or benignity) as a supererogatory show of grace, not required by law or justice.

Bodin proposed another, third alternative to these two classical forms of justice, one overlooked in the modern scholarship on the theory of justice and its intellectual history. Bodin called this third way *la justice harmonique*, or "harmonic justice," a concept that, he claims, "neither Greek nor Latins" have discussed.[7] He described it as a mixture or blend of commutative and distributive justice, inspired by the various forms of Pythagorean harmony emerging from the early modern theory of polyphonic music. The best form of justice, Bodin argued, arises when a moderate mixture combining principles of equality and similitude produce a kind of harmony among the different members of a society, even a society divided by religious intolerance.

[4] Cicero, *De Officiis*, trans. Walter Miller, Loeb Classical Library 30 (Cambridge: Harvard University Press, 1913), 46–47 [I, xiv, §42], where *dignitas*, like the Greek αξία, is best translated to mean "worth."

[5] In medieval moral theology, departures from just distribution were sinful, a sin captured by the label *acceptio personarum*. The term "distributive justice" is often a source of unnecessary confusion among modern readers who, perhaps more familiar with John Rawls's *Theory of Justice* and his account of distributive justice, interpret it as a theory of social justice.

[6] Aristotle, *Nicomachean Ethics*, 314–15 [V, x, 1137^{b}10–11].

[7] *République* 1015 [VI, 6].

This chapter presents Jean Bodin as a theorist of justice and explores his novel theory of "harmonic justice." The first part of the chapter reconstructs the essentials of the three principal forms of justice, what Bodin calls "the three daughters of Themis." His criticisms of commutative (or arithmetic) and distributive (or geometric) justice open the way for his theory of harmonic justice and his use of Pythagorean music theory and early modern ideas of polyphony to conceptualize the value of *concordia*. The chapter will then focus on the application of harmonic principles to the structure of government. Contrary to much of the existing scholarship, I show in this chapter that Bodin promoted a normative political theory, based on his analysis of harmony, that he called "harmonic government."

The Three Daughters of Themis

The French historian of political and legal thought, Michel Villey, once described harmony as the "leitmotiv" of Bodin's social and political thought.[8] Indeed, justice, according to Bodin, was essentially a form of harmony. But Bodin was hardly the first to use harmony as an organizing principle to envision a just, well-ordered society and politics. He was the beneficiary of a long intellectual tradition in social and political thought that valorized this ideal of harmony.

In fact, harmony, understood as the proper proportional blending of dissimilar social elements and orders, is an old ideal rooted in Antiquity, with which Bodin demonstrated intimate familiarity. It was central, for example, to the social and political philosophy of the Academics and the Peripatetics. Cicero, who was among Bodin's major classical influences, best captured how harmony could be achieved in a state, in a famous passage in his main work of political theory, the *De Re Publica*. Speaking through Scipio, Cicero treated harmony as a concept that could apply both to music as well as to politics because both dealt with the challenge of blending dissimilar elements together to produce a new orderly whole:

> Just as in the music of harps and flutes or in the voices of singers a certain harmony of the different tones must be preserved, the interruption or violation of which is intolerable to trained ears, and as this perfect agreement and harmony is produced by the proportionate blending of unlike tones, so also is a state made harmonious by agreement among dissimilar elements [*civitas consensu dissimillimorum concinit*], brought about by a fair and reasonable blending

[8] Michel Villey, "La Justice Harmonique selon Bodin," *Verhandlungen der Internationalen Bodin Tagung in München*, ed. Horst Denzer (Munich: Verlag C.H. Beck, 1973), 69. See also Diego Quaglioni, *À une déesse inconnue: La conception pré-moderne de la justice*, trans. Marie-Dominique Couzinet (Paris: Éditions de la Sorbonne, 2019), chap. XI.

> together of the upper, middle, and lower [*ex summis et infimis et mediis interiectis ordinibus*] classes, just as if they were musical tones. What the musicians call harmony in song [*quae harmonia a musicis dicitur in cantu*] is concord in a state [*in civitate concordia*], the strongest and best bond of permanent union in any commonwealth [*in re publica vinculum*].[9]

It was Cicero's closing message in *De Re Publica* II that likely caught Bodin's attention as he developed his own theory of social and political harmony: "Such concord can never be brought about without the aid of justice."[10] Harmony and justice must go together.

Harmony in a state—this "fair and reasonable blending" of classes and orders—requires justice, which Bodin would define, in general, as "the rightful distribution of rewards and punishments" [*le droit partage des loyers & les peines*].[11] But it can only be achieved with justice of the right sort, what Bodin called *la justice harmonique*. Not all forms of justice, however, were "harmonic."

In fact, Bodin acknowledged that justice could take one of three possible forms, a principle he declared in the concluding section of the *Distributio* on *finis iurisprudentiae*, or the "aim of jurisprudence." In sum, these three forms of justice were commutative, distributive, and harmonic. Bodin called these three forms "the three daughters of Themis, Eunomia [Εὐνομία], Dikaiosunē [Δικαιοσυνη], and Eirēnē [Εἰρήνη] - each corresponding respectively to *aequa lex, iustitia, pax*."[12] The first represented the commutative justice reinforced indifferently by law, or *nomos* [νομός], according to the equality in an arithmetic sequence [*ad arithmeticas rationes*]. The second, by contrast, stood for the distributive justice achieved, not by law, but by equity [*aequitas*], or *epieikeia* [ἐπϊείκεια: "fairness"; "clemency"], which reflected the idea of similitude of proportional value in a geometric sequence [*ad geometricas*]. For the third, Bodin coined a Greek term, *epeikonomia* [επιεικονομία], a hybrid neologism which combined, by way of a kind of harmony [*ad harmonicas*], the commutative and distributive elements of justice achieved through law and equity.[13]

[9] Cicero, *De Re Publica*, 180–83 [II, 42, §69]. The *De Re Publica*, which was recovered as a palimpsest, was mostly inaccessible in the sixteenth century and known only indirectly through quotes in other sources, most notably Augustine. This passage, however, was accessible, because it was quoted by Augustine in *De Civitate Dei* II, 21, and reproduced in the Monarchomach text, *Francogallia*, by the humanist jurist, François Hotman, whose theory of popular sovereignty would become one of Bodin's major targets. François Hotman, *Francogallia*, ed. Ralph Giesey, trans. J. H. M. Salmon (Cambridge: Cambridge University Press, 1972), 295.

[10] Cicero, *De Re Publica*, 182–83 [II, 42, §69]. Keyes's translation of this passage does not, in my view, entirely capture the content of Cicero's original text: ... *eaque sine iustitia nullo pacto esse potest.*

[11] *République* 1014 [VI, 6]; cf. *Colloquium Heptaplomeres* 4: *praemiorum ac ponearum potestatem.*

[12] Cf. *Methodus* 456 [VI]. Themis was the second wife of Zeus. Grotius refers to Themis in *De Iure Praedae Commentarius: Commentary on the Law of Prize and Booty*, trans. Gwladys Williams and Walter Zeydel (Oxford: Clarendon Press, 1950), 1:8 [II].

[13] My thanks to Daniela Cammack for inspecting possible etymological origins for this neologism.

To distinguish between these three species of justice, Bodin sought the precision of a mathematical analysis that could explain justice in terms of the differences and relations between numbers in sequence. The first two would already have been familiar to his readers through the legacy of Peripatetic philosophy and Scholastic moral theology.

Commutative Justice

Commutative justice, which captured the principle of equality, was expressed mathematically in an arithmetic progression such as the following:

Arithmetic progression: 2. 4. 6. 8. 10.

In this sequence of numbers, the difference between each term is, by definition, numerically equal. Each term in the sequence gains by exactly the same amount as both the prior term and the following term—in this example, by two. Aristotle uses this in the *Nicomachean Ethics* as a mathematical metaphor to illustrate the basic principle which characterizes commutative justice (*iustitia in commutatibus*), which is strict equality—especially in commercial transactions involving συναλλαγμα, a mutual exchange in a sale or hire.[14]

As Bodin puts it in the *Distributio*, justice of this kind "always renders equivalent things equal [*aequalis*], deeds to deeds [*facta factis*], things to things [*res rebus*], without discrimination of persons."[15] The result is a stringently egalitarian society: Regardless of each person's social position, merit, or moral worth, everybody gets the same and everybody is treated indifferently. It is the sort of justice characteristic of democratic societies which, Bodin observes, are anchored in this basic idea of strict equality in all the laws.[16]

Bodin, who attributed this principle of commutative justice not to Aristotle but ultimately to Xenophon, illustrated how this arithmetic abstraction of justice could materialize into a strict and inflexible law.[17] Roman real (or *re*) contracts—that is, strict obligations which are legally contracted simply by the delivery of some property [*res*], with the expectation of return, and enforced by *stricti iuris* remedies—exemplified this egalitarian principle of commutative justice. As he put it, commutative justice "shines forth above all in loans [*in rebus creditis*], such as

[14] Gordley, *Philosophical Origins of Modern Contract Doctrine*, 14. The term for a commercial exchange, συναλλαγμα, is central to Aristotle's understanding of commutative justice, as transactions requiring equality or evenness on all sides.

[15] *Distributio* fol. F, s.v. *rationes arithmeticae.*

[16] *République* 937 [VI, 4].

[17] *République* 1014–15 [VI, 6]. Xenophon, *Cyropaedia*, trans. Walter Miller, Loeb Classical Library 51 (Cambridge: Harvard University Press, 1914), 1:40–43 [I, 3, §§16–18]. Grotius cites this same passage in Xenophon in *De Jure Belli ac Pacis* I, 1, §8.

loans for consumption [*mutuis*], pledge [*pignore*], loans for use [*commodato*], deposit [*deposito*], and the like."[18] Both the meritorious and the meritless, the heroic and the cowardly, the highborn and the lowborn, men of virtue and of vice, must all equally perform their contractual obligations, as the law strictly requires.

Punishment, too, can also serve as a device to implement the principle of commutative justice. Pecuniary fines, for example, which levy the same penalty indifferently for some legally defined infraction, without regard to social rank or wealth, are characteristic of democratic societies governed according to the principle of isonomia.

Bodin supplied one notable example from Roman law. In Bodin's narration of Roman legal history, the XII Tables, promulgated by the Decemvirate at *ca.*451 BC early in the Republic, exemplified a strict body of legislation intended to apply indifferently to all Romans, whether of plebeian or patrician rank. Bodin cited the example of Table VIII (§4): *Si iniuriam [alteri] faxsit viginti quinque poenae sunto* ("If anybody commits an outrage against another, the penalty shall be twenty-five *asses*.")[19] This rule, a draconian penalty in the Early Republic, served as a quintessential illustration of arithmetic justice in Roman law.

But such isonomic pecuniary punishment was not exclusive to the ancient world. Even a status-sensitive monarchy, such as Bodin's native France, can sometimes choose to implement a practice of democratic justice. In support of this point, Bodin cites a draconian "law of apparel" promulgated by Charles IX which fined transgressors 1,000 crowns, regardless of the transgressor's status.[20]

The defining quality in all these laws embodying commutative justice is their impersonal rigidity or strictness to ensure legal equality, where the law shows, as Bodin puts it, "no respect of persons."[21] But it is precisely this quality that most worried Bodin. Since commutative justice requires that the law must be equally and indifferently enforced, without exception, it effectively minimized the role and discretionary license of courts and the judges who served in them from making case-by-case equitable exceptions (the equitable judicial power of magistrates which Bodin called *officium iudicis*). In such cases, judges are left with no discretionary

[18] See Chapter 2 concerning the distinction between contracts *res negotia* and *res credita*. In the *Distributio*, *res credita* is Bodin's label corresponding to the general category of "real contracts" in the Roman law of obligations, which include the real contracts of *mutuum*, *pignus*, *commodatum*, and *depositum*.

[19] Lex Duodecim Tabularum ("The Twelve Tables") in *Fontes Iuris Romani Antejustiniani, in usum scholarum*, ed. S. Riccobono et al. (Florence: Apud G. Barbera, 1909), 44 [Tabula VIII, iv]. Cf. Inst. 4.4.7; Gaius 3.220, 3.223; Aulus Gellius, *The Attic Nights of Aulus Gellius*, trans. John Rolfe, Loeb Classical Library 195 (Cambridge: Harvard University Press, 1927), 3:168–69; 410–11 [*Noctes Atticae* XVI, 10, §8; XX, 1, §12].

[20] *République* 1032 [VI, 6]. By contrast, Bodin praises an *ordonnance* of Philip the Fair which fined transgressions by the nobility at one hundred livres, while lesser landholders, knights, clergy, and commoners paid far less.

[21] *République* 937 [VI, 4], *acception de personne*, referring to *acceptio personarum*, the sin against distributive justice. Cf. Acts 10:34–35: "Of a truth I perceive that God is no respecter of persons" [προσωπολήμπτης: *prosopolemptes*].

license in the execution of the law. Citing the practice of Italian republics, Bodin concluded that in states adopting the strict equality of commutative justice, "judges are commanded to follow the law strictly as it is written."[22]

What emerges from Bodin's treatment of commutative justice is his dissatisfaction: Commutative justice is, taken by itself, unjust. Part of his criticism concerned the principle of strict equality. Justice cannot always be achieved through reinforcing a strict equality, and that is because people are not strictly equal. Some are more heroic, some cowardly. Some are wealthier, some poorer. Some are virtuous, some vicious. For any society to treat everyone indifferently, where the heroic are rewarded just the same as the cowardly, or where the poor are fined just as heavily as the rich, can itself count as injustice.

A proper, more complete theory of justice, therefore, must also be tailored to reflect these interpersonal differences in proportion. There ought to be, as Bodin suggested, "unequal punishments for unequal persons."[23] The same principle applies to distribution of rewards as well. If justice is about achieving the proper distribution of rewards and punishments, strict equality will inevitably result in injustice, given the natural differences between persons and the need for equitable exceptions.[24] Justice thus requires loosening the unyieldingly strict adherence to equality.

Distributive Justice

This is the basic insight of distributive justice, which Bodin attributed to Plato and was captured by Aristotle in the geometric progression illustrating the principle of proportionality intrinsic to distributive justice.

Geometric progression: 2. 4. 8. 16. 32.

In a community organized according to the principle of distributive justice, the less deserving will get less (e.g., a payout of 2), while the more deserving will get more (e.g., a payout of 32). A prima facie first glance will perhaps prompt an observer to treat this community as inegalitarian.[25] And they might be right.

But "inegalitarian" needn't be "unjust." And that is because people naturally differ in their merit and relative value (a critical background assumption in

[22] *République* 1023 [VI, 6], citing also Alexander Tartagnus Imolensis, *Consilium*, 86.

[23] *République* 1032 [VI, 6]: *les peines inegales à personnes inegales*.

[24] Bodin, thus, avoids entirely the question of how to neutralize, or minimize, the effects of the morally arbitrary inequality of unmerited natural endowments or natural goods which is at the core of John Rawls's *Theory of Justice*.

[25] And even this critical observation of inequality would be incorrect, since classical mathematicians will point out that geometric sequences embody the equality of ratios between any two consecutive terms. Thus, 1/2 = 2/4 = 4/8 = 8/16 = 16/32, etc.

Bodin's theory of justice). Some will show greater virtue and be deemed worthier than others. Given these differences, it is only just—on a principle of distributive justice—that distribution of rewards and benefits should be proportional to, and reflective of, these interpersonal differences in merit and worth.[26] The inevitable result of such an arrangement, however, would be a stratified hierarchy, where people of similar characteristics and abilities are grouped, like with like, together in the same rank or grade, proportional to their merits.[27]

Again, Bodin illustrated this geometric expression of distributive justice—or, as he borrowed from the Aristotelian lexicon, διανεμητική (*dianemētikē*)—with reference to specific areas of law implementing the principle of proportionality that rewards and punishments ought to be proportional to merit or status.[28] The *Distributio*, for example, cites several authorities in Roman law illustrating this principle in the title *De poenis* ("On punishments") in the *Digest*.[29] Bodin cites, for example, the law, *in servorum* (D.48.19.10.pr), which concerns the punishment of Roman slaves compared to the punishment of free persons of the lowest rank:

> **D.48.19.10.pr**: *In servorum persona ita observatur, ut exemplo humiliorum puniantur. Et ex quibus causis liber fustibus caeditur, ex his servus flagellis caedi et domino reddi iubetur: et ex quibus liber fustibus caesus in opus publicum datur, ex his servus, sub poena vinculorum ad eius temporis spatium, flagellis caesus domino reddi iubetur.*
>
> "It is observed that slaves are to be punished just as persons of the lowest rank. And so, in cases where a free person would ordinarily be cudgeled, a slave should instead be scourged and ordered to be returned to his master. And where a free person, after having been cudgeled, is sentenced to labor in public works, a slave in the same circumstances shall, after being kept in chains for a period of time, be ordered to be scourged and returned to his master."

Proportionality is implemented likewise in the law governing punishments for arson (D.47.9.12.1):

> **D.47.9.12.1**: *Qui data opera in civitate incendium fecerint, si humiliore loco sint, bestiis obici solent: si in aliquo gradu id fecerint, capite puniuntur aut certe in insulam deportantur.*

[26] The same principle of proportionality applies to demerit or vice, so that the severity of punishment should be incrementally proportional to the degree of a person's demerit or vice, with the right to impose capital penalties, *merum imperium*, reserved only for the most wicked.

[27] For this reason, Bodin observes that the result of a society based on distributive justice is "*similitude*" or "*semblables*" where like are grouped together with like. *République* 1014, 1016 [VI, 6].

[28] The term διανεμητική signals proportional distribution as Aristotle describes the justice of distribution according to merit, or ἀξία. *Nicomachean Ethics* 268 [V, iii, 1131^{a}24–27].

[29] *Distributio* fol. F, s.v. *ratione geometrica.*

> "Persons of low rank who designedly cause a fire in a town shall shall be thrown to wild beasts, and those of superior station shall suffer death, or else be banished to some island."

This principle of proportionality is again illustrated in the civil law by rules governing the imposition of capital penalties for particularly heinous crimes. But geometric justice isn't only about crimes. It is also about the bestowal of public honors for especially meritorious service.[30] In all of these examples, the point remains the same: Strict equality entailed by commutative justice would be itself an injustice.

Perhaps the most notable feature in Bodin's treatment of distributive justice in the law, however, concerns its origin. While distributive justice, by definition, necessitates differentiated treatment of people in proportion to relative differences in merit (or demerit, as the case may be), such differentiation does not typically originate by legislative design. It originates, rather, by exception.

Understanding this point requires some understanding of Bodin's legal theory and how he conceptualizes law. As we have seen in the previous chapter, legislation [*loy*; *lex*], in Bodin's legal theory, is generally conceptualized as the general legal command of a legislative sovereign authority directed indifferently to subjects of all ranks and qualities, who, by definition, are obliged to obey the sovereign's commands, without exception.[31] Because it indifferently burdens all subjects under an obligation to obey the law, I have elsewhere characterized Bodinian legislation as "binding-devices."[32] However, Bodin recognizes that legislation can sometimes be a blunt tool of government and potentially even a source of profound injustice, precisely because it treats all subjects—unfairly, he seems to think—on a basis of strict equality.

One solution around this difficulty is the use of "privileges" (or "*iura singularia*"), which Bodin defines, following the precedent of Roman law, as a legal command of a sovereign directed—not to all subjects indifferently—but to one specific class of subjects, or even to a named private individual (not unlike a private member's bill in modern legislatures).[33] Such privileges, which target specific persons, or classes of persons, may release the privilege-holder from a legal

[30] D.48.19.28; D.50.4.11.

[31] Bodin's radical definition of the citizen, at *De Republica* 45–46 [I, 6], as the *liber homo qui summae alterius potestati obligatur* ("a free person who is duty-bound to the sovereign power of another") highlights the egalitarian leveling force of law. In the presence of the sovereign, even the highest magistrate or wealthiest oligarch becomes just another subject. Cf. *République* 68: *le franc subiect tenant de la souverainete d'autruy*.

[32] *Right of Sovereignty* 154. Moreover, "absolute power" is the sovereign's exclusive power to dissolve such obligatory bonds created by legislation. Like the priestly power of "absolution" [*potestas absolvendi*] to dissolve the bond of sin, the sovereign's absolute power dissolves and releases [*absolvit*] the subject from the legal bond of obligation.

[33] Rousseau, perhaps thinking of Bodin's comment here on the difference between legislation and privileges in the *République*, insists that privileges, because they are directed only to a particular class or a private individual, lack the force of the general will. *Social Contract* II, 6.

obligation otherwise burdening everyone else, or immunize them from being so burdened in the future. They may also empower or "enfranchise" privilege-holders with special entitlements beyond what the law allows (or, as Bodin puts it, *praeter legem*)—such as an exclusive right of monopoly.

But the far more important vehicle for fine-tuning legislation, so as to make it fairer and more equitable, was not legislative, but judicial—the use of carefully crafted exceptions to a general legal rule, which fell under the judicial purview of courts. In Roman law, this responsibility fell chiefly to the praetors who, by way of their edicts, had the judicial authority to fine-tune and reshape the law and its application in the courts. As we have seen in Chapter 2, Bodin referred to this equitable responsibility as the *officium iudicis*.[34] It is relevant particularly in those moments when judges, realizing that the ordinary application of a settled rule of law in a particular case might actually introduce an injustice by rewarding or punishing the undeserving, choose instead to deviate exceptionally from legislation for the sake of equity.[35] In this way, Bodin observed that courts, with their equitable function of *officium iudicis*, possessed the ability to "bend the law and its interpretation, either to soften or to toughen it ... [and] to supplement and correct the laws."[36]

One prominent example of such judicial equity refers to Bodin's earlier example of the XII Tables penalty of twenty-five *asses* for acts of outrage. Twenty-five *asses*, as we saw above, was a draconian penalty in the Early Republic, when the rule was first promulgated by the Decemvirate. But it was a relatively light fine by the time of the Late Republic, especially for the very wealthy who could afford to pay the fine with hardly any financial hardship. In commenting on this inflationary effect on the force of the law, Bodin referred to a comment by Labeo on the XII Tables concerning the "exceptionally rude" [*egregie improbus*] jurist, Neratius, who reportedly "struck people's faces by the palm of his hand for his own amusement" [*delectamento os hominis liberi manus suae palma verberare*]. Undeterred by the light monetary penalty set in Table VIII, Neratius made his slave follow him with a money bag, immediately paying his victims the twenty-five *asses* due to them

[34] Cf. Inst. 4.17. Note also that, in canon law, *officium iudicis*, was introduced by Huguccio as a remedy to enforce performance of a *pactum nudum*, thereby circumventing the principle of D.2.14.7.4: *Nuda pactio obligationem non parit, sed parit exceptionem* ("A bare pact does not give rise to an obligation, but it does give rise to an exception."). Decock, *Theologians and Contract Law*, 124.

[35] Bodin uses this language frequently throughout his writings to describe the equitable *officium iudicis* of courts and, ultimately, of sovereigns, acting in a judicial capacity. He is borrowing this language from D.1.1.7.1, where the praetors are said to have the power of "supplementing or correcting the civil law for the sake of the public good" [*supplendi vel corrigenda iuris civilis gratia propter utilitatem publicam*].

[36] Bodin, *On Sovereignty*, ed. Julian Franklin (Cambridge: Cambridge University Press, 1992), 58; *République* 223 [I, 10]. Bodin uses this language of "supplementing and correcting the laws" frequently in describing the equitable function of magistrates exercising *officium iudicis*, beyond the law—e.g., *Distributio* fol. A, s.v. *magistratus*. He is taking this from Papinian's description of praetorian legislation at D.1.1.7.1, *quod praetores introduxerunt adiuvandi vel supplendi vel corrigendi iuris civilis gratia propter utilitatem publicam*.

under the Law of Delicts. The apparent injustice of the situation forced the Roman praetors to repeal [*absolvere*; *abrogandae legis XII praebuit occasionem*] this portion of the XII Tables and leave the penalty instead to the equitable discretion—the *officium iudicis*—of the Roman courts.[37] In this way, the arithmetic justice of the XII Tables transformed into the geometric justice epitomized by the praetorian edict.

While a geometrically patterned distributive justice was a marked improvement over a world governed strictly according to commutative justice, Bodin nevertheless expressed some apprehension. Distributive justice diminished the status of law by handing over authority to judges to emend and alter it as equity demanded. A distrust of judges pervades Bodin's unwillingness to abandon the rule of law entirely. However imperfect legislation may be, there must be a place for law in well-governed states.

Harmonic Justice

We see that justice in some situations called for the strict arithmetic equality of commutative justice. In other circumstances, it called for the meritorious geometric proportionality of distributive justice. Bodin, however, was dissatisfied with both. Treating everyone on terms of strict equality, without exception, can sometimes be an injustice, particularly when questions of differential merit or worth are involved. By contrast, treating everyone on terms of merit or worth and asking a judge to decide what each deserves calls for a discretionary judgment of those qualities that can exceed the strictures of law. These were the two classical forms of justice—Bodin attributed them to Plato and Xenophon—that have shaped Western moral reasoning for centuries.

But it needn't be restricted only to these two. Bodin's third way was intended to be an alternative that avoided the disadvantages of these two classical forms of justice. This was "harmonic justice," or *la justice harmonique*, a form of justice that "obeys musical harmony" and harmonic proportions in the same way that "the middle voice between the bass and the treble blend together to produce a soft and melodious chord."[38] The challenge, however, was to identify those proper blends, in order to avoid the dissonances that destroy harmony. Justice cannot be attained but by a moderate mixture, as he put it, of "equality and similitude."[39]

[37] *République* 1038; *De Republica* 763–64 [VI, 6]. Cf. Jakob Spiegel, *Lexicon Iuris Civilis* (Basel: Apud Ioan. Heruagium, 1554), col. 74 [*De iniuriis, aliis que delictis*]. I discuss Bodin's reference to Neratius in *Right of Sovereignty* 164.

[38] *République* 1018 [VI, 6]: *la voix moyenne entre la basse & le dessus pour faire un accord doux & melodieux*; *De Republica* 749: *quasi media voce inter summam & infirmam interiecta.*

[39] *République* 1014 [VI, 6]: *proportion d'equalité & de similitude ensemble.*

Figure 3.1 Standard musical notation indicating the E-natural on the treble clef.

Ultimately, this task required a study of mathematics, and that was because harmony itself was fundamentally a "musico-mathematical" concept.[40] That is, it was a concept both in music theory as well as in mathematics.[41] As a musical concept, harmony was realized by way of polyphony with the proper interval—or *juste proportion*—between notes. In the age before Johann Sebastian Bach, the sixteenth century—encompassing the work of Byrd, Gibbons, Josquin, Monteverdi, and Palestrina—was a golden age of Western polyphonic music and reinforced the possibilities of polyphonic harmonization and notation in the early modern musical imagination.

Theorists of early polyphonic music, most notably Gioseffo Zarlino's *Istitutioni harmoniche* (1558), the most important early modern treatise on harmony, attempted to document those rules establishing the intervals which can be counted as proper, or *droit*.[42] These rules of harmony, before the standardization of twelve-tone chromaticism performed on "well-tempered" instruments, prioritized certain intervals, such as octaves, perfect fifths, and perfect fourths, while prohibiting other intervals—above all, the *diabolus in musica*, the tritone (an interval of three whole steps). The goal was to avoid all such intervals in polyphonic music thought to be discordant, displeasing, and even "offensive" to the Renaissance ear.[43]

Harmony was not just an aesthetic principle in music. It was mathematical as well, a feature of harmonics observed in Antiquity by the Pythagoreans. Pythagoras himself reportedly studied the mathematics of harmony by studying the properties of strings on a lyre. Two strings of identical length, thickness, and tension on a lyre will produce the same pitch—say, for example, an E♮ (see Figure 3.1).

Comparing the lengths of the two strings, Pythagoras documents the first mathematical principle of harmony: A ratio of 1:1 generates unison.

[40] Kate Van Orden, *Music, Discipline, and Arms in Early Modern France* (Chicago, IL: The University of Chicago Press, 2005), 54. On the mathematically formal presentation of political theory in Bodin, see Philippe Desan, *Naissance de la méthode: Machiavel, La Ramée, Bodin, Montaigne, Descartes* (Paris: Nizet, 1987).

[41] And, for this reason, harmony played a central role in the arts curriculum of the old quadrivium. The influence of Plato on Bodin's thought governing music and mathematics is palpable. See Van Orden, *Music, Discipline and Arms in Early Modern France*, 68–69.

[42] Gioseffo Zarlino, *Le Istitvtioni Harmoniche* (Venice, 1558). See, in particular, Zarlino 47, which summarizes the differences between the three types of proportions, "arithmetica, geometrica, harmonica."

[43] *Colloquium* 112: *sensus teneros ... offendit.*

Figure 3.2 Standard musical notation indicating the high and low E-natural on the treble clef.

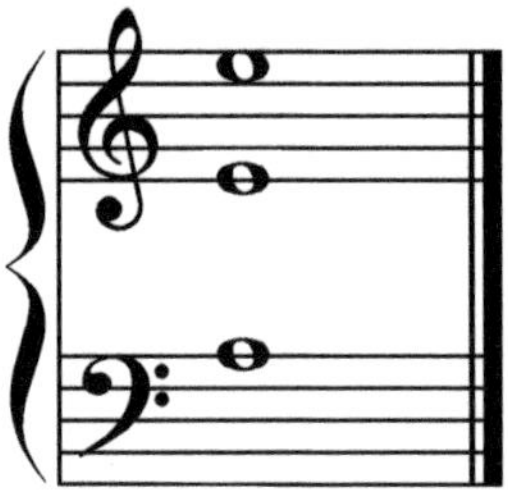

Figure 3.3 Standard musical notation indicating the high and low E-natural and an A-natural on a grand staff.

Suppose we were to double the length of one of those strings, thereby halving the frequency. Pythagoras discovered that doubling the string length will produce the same note, but one octave lower (see Figure 3.2).

Here, then, was a second principle of Pythagorean tuning: A ratio of 2:1 generates an octave.

Suppose now we were to triple the length of the original string. Tripling the original string length results in a different note, an A♮, positioned a perfect fifth lower than the E♮ produced by the second string (see Figure 3.3).

A third Pythagorean principle emerges: A ratio of 3:2 generates a perfect fifth.

Pythagoras continued this line of investigation by quadrupling the length of the original string. This quadruple-length string produces another E♮, positioned a perfect fourth lower than the A♮ of the third string (see Figure 3.4).

This observation yields a fourth Pythagorean principle: A ratio of 4:3 generates a perfect fourth.

In summary, musical intervals constitutive of key harmonic intervals corresponded to mathematical ratios, as follows:

Unison	1:1
Octave (diapason)	2:1
Perfect Fifth (diapente)	3:2
Perfect Fourth (diatessaron)	4:3

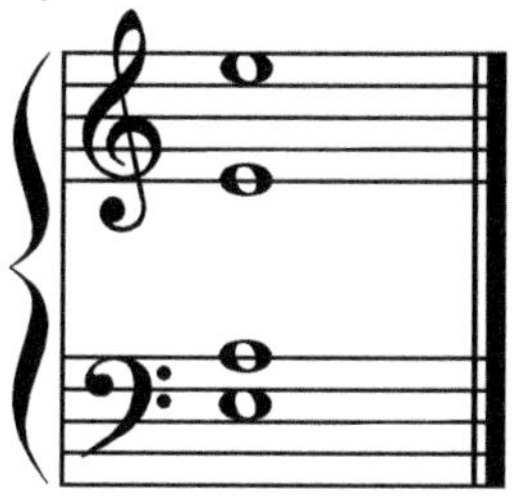

Figure 3.4 Standard musical notation indicating the high and low E-natural, an A-natural, and a bass E-natural on a grand staff.

This Pythagorean analysis of the ratios undergirding musical harmony would have a profound influence on Western thought.[44]

For Bodin, these ratios were essential for the numerical sequence that he would call the harmonic progression.[45] In the *République*, Bodin described this harmonic progression as a "mixture" of arithmetic and geometric progressions. Specifically, this involved inserting the arithmetic mean between the two terms of the corresponding geometric progression, as follows:[46]

Geometric progression:	2. 4. 8. 16. 32.
Harmonic progression:	2. 3. 4. **6.** 8. **12.** 16. **24.** 32.

Harmonic progressions preserved the Pythagorean ratios that generated the main harmonic intervals. Octaves, which corresponded to 2:1 ratios, were preserved in the geometric progression (2/4; 4/8; 8/16; 16/32). Perfect fifths corresponded to 3:2 ratios in the sequence (2/3; 4/6; 8/12; 16/24). And perfect fourths corresponded to 4:3 ratios in the sequence (3/4; 6/8; 12/16; 24/32).

[44] One prominent example is Plato, *Timaeus*, 35^{a}–36^{b}, which considers different mixtures of the categories of "same" and "different" as corresponding to different proportions. Ptolemy and Boethius are two others. See Calvin Bower, "The Modes of Boethius," *Journal of Musicology* 3 (1984): 252–63. Cf. *Methodus* 455 [VI], where Bodin explains that the octave is in the ratio *ab uno ad binarium in dupla ratione*; the perfect fifth *diapente* is in the "*sesquialtera*" (3/2) ratio, *intervallum duorum at trium*; and the perfect fourth *diatessarωn* [sic: in the 1572] is in the ratio where *quartum* is not included. Bodin, at *Colloquium* 112, similarly investigates the "sweetness in tone" [*suavitas in voce*] when the diapason, diapente, and diatessaron are blended together. Marion Daniels Kuntz, "Harmony and the Heptaplomeres of Jean Bodin," *Journal of the History of Philosophy* 12, no. 1 (1974): 35: "This statement of Coronaeus is extremely interesting because, as [Edward] Lowinsky points out, the new chromaticism in the music of the Renaissance met with a hostile attitude from the Church."

[45] Note that this is not actually a harmonic sequence.

[46] The arithmetic mean of the first two terms is 3 = (2 + 4)/2. The arithmetic mean of the second and third terms is 6 = (4 + 8)/2. And so on. On the harmonic progression, compare with Bodin's *Universae Naturae Theatrum* (Lyon: Apud Iacobvm Rovssin, 1596), 143–44 (Lib. II). The *marginalia* of *Methodus* 457 [VI] includes an illustration of the three progressions: "G.1.2.4.8; M.2.3.4.6; A.3.4.5.6."

The lesson to be taken from this study of the harmonic progression is not simply aesthetic. It is also normative, harnessed in the principle that harmonic mixture, by "uniting together the extremes," can produce a better whole. This is to be observed in the polyphonic mixture of voices in a choir.

It is a principle also to be observed in society, as Bodin explores in several memorable illustrations of harmonic justice in the *République*. One illustration is the banquet.

Suppose the host of a banquet has invited guests of various backgrounds and classes and is considering seating arrangements. One option would be to seat his guests on a first-come first-served basis, without distinguishing by sex, condition, or age.[47] Bodin advises against such an arrangement of "arithmetic" equality. The other "geometric" arrangement, where the host seats "the worthiest [*les plus dignes*; *dignissimos*] in the place of supreme honor" while the others are seated elsewhere, so that "the wise [sit] with the wise ... the aged with the aged ... women with women ... the young with the young ... and the foolish together," would also be undesirable, by reinforcing division and envy among ranks.[48] Harmonic justice, however, calls for a different seating arrangement:

> The wise symposiarch will gently seat [*entrelacera*] the fool between two wise men, the peaceful man between two quarrelsome ones, the temperate man between the sophists, the old babbler with young apprentices, the envious (or stingy) man joined with the generously wealthy, the choleric man between two cold and stale men. In grasping this, he will not only avoid the envy of some and the jealousy of others, which is not easy to escape when it is a matter of rank. Instead, from such a beautiful order, a sweet and pleasant harmony of one with another, and of all together, will result.[49]

The social advantages of "harmonically" mixed seating arrangements also inspired Bodin's criticism of Scipio Africanus. Scipio's policy governing the Roman theater, as referenced in Livy XXXIV, reserved the best seats of the theater exclusively for the senatorial class and separated them from the plebs. It was an "unheard-of arrogance" that not only exemplified a geometric arrangement reflecting social difference in rank but also contributed to the eventual destruction of the Roman

[47] *République* 1018 [VI, 6]: *sans discretion des grands aux petits*; *De Republica* 749: *nulla sexus, conditionis, aetatis habita ratione.*

[48] *République* 1018 [VI, 6]: *les sages aupres des sages ... les vieux avec les vieux ... les femmes aupres des femmes ... les jeunes avec les les jeunes ... les fols ensemble*; *De Republica* 749: *sapientes sapientibus, senibus senes, foeminas foeminis, stultos simul.*

[49] *République* 1018 [VI, 6]. The corresponding passage at *De Republica* 750–51 is somewhat different, including a new observation treating table talk as *quasi medicina* that can cure the foolishness of the insane. This example of the feast foreshadows the structure of the *Colloquium*, as a discussion between interlocutors over a meal.

Republic.[50] Bodin stressed that Scipio's policy departed from the long-established custom (Livy states 557 years by the time of Scipio), dating from the founding of Rome when "patricians observed the games in common [*promiscue*] with the plebs."[51] A harmonic arrangement, by contrast, would intersperse patricians and plebeians together by a just proportion, so the Roman theater would neither be segregated by order nor indifferent entirely with respect to rank.

The law governing marriage also provided an opportunity for a comparative illustration of the three forms of justice. Marriage was a central concern of the Roman Law of Persons, in part because the restrictive legal right of *ius connubii* (the legal right to enter a legal *manus* marriage, thereby establishing *patria potestas* over heirs) was an essential element of Roman *civitas*, or citizenship. Early Roman law, codified in the XII Tables (at Table XI), effectively prohibited intermarriage and, for this reason, Bodin interpreted traditional *manus* marriage as a geometric system preserving matrimonial segregation between the worthier from the *humiliores*. Patricians may only marry patricians, while plebs may only marry plebs. Above all, Romans may not legally marry peregrines, nor may peregrines acquire agnatic *patria potestas* under this rule.

But, as Bodin observed at various places, this restrictive system would not last. The plebeian demand for the right of intermarriage was realized through the *lex Canuleia* (named for the tribune, Gaius Canuleius), which repealed the restrictive XII Tables rule on marriage. For this reason, Bodin saw the *lex Canuleia* as a decisive moment when the Roman Republic transitioned from aristocratic government of the patricians and ultimately to the popular government of the plebs.[52]

But it is in criminal law and the meting out of punishments where the distinctive quality of harmonic justice can be most clearly observed. Bodin reveals himself to be something of an early modern reformer in matters concerning punishment. He is deeply critical of criminal justice organized on principles of arithmetic justice, where the law defining a punishment is indifferent to the status of the criminal offender.

One notable example of harmonic punishment was the *ordonnance* of Philip IV ("the Fair") on apparel and "superfluities of banquets."[53] Unlike the harsh and indifferent law of Charles IX, referenced earlier and enacted during Bodin's lifetime, his medieval predecessor, Philip IV, promulgated a sumptuary law on apparel which Bodin regarded as "approaching harmonic justice." Philip's *ordonnance*

[50] Cf. Livy 34.54.3–8.

[51] *République* 1018 [VI, 6]; *De Republica* 750 mentions the 558 years since the founding of Rome, citing Livy 34. It is likely that Grotius, whose famous chapter on the origins of private property in *De Jure Belli ac Pacis* II, 2, §2 compares the original possession of property in the earliest stages of humanity to the unregulated seating of the Roman theater, was thinking of Scipio. He cites Cicero, *De Finibus*, 288–89 [III, xx, §§67–68], and connects the claim that *theatrum commune sit* to Seneca, *De Beneficiis* 484–85 [VII, xii, §§3–4]. Cicero is likely imagining the theater ante Scipionem.

[52] *République* 338 [II, 7], 1050 [VI, 6].

[53] Bodin, at *République* 1032 [VI, 6], cites an *ordonnance* of 1294 enregistered in the Chambre des Comptes, "*au livre in titulé sancti Ludovi fol. 44.*" *De Republica* 759. *République* 1033 discusses the *loix somptuaires des Rommains.*

instituted varying punishments for transgressors of differing social ranks. Thus, while the nobility were liable to be fined one hundred *livres*, the clergy with dignities and endowed benefices were liable for only twenty-five *livres*.[54] But in his treatment of other laymen [*autres laiz*], regardless of estate or rank, the penalty reflected the value of their estate. So, those transgressors worth one thousand *livres* paid twenty-five, while those worth less, including clergy without dignities or benefices, were required to pay a lesser fine of one-hundred *sols*. Philip's differentiated schedule of penalties, thus, was neither based on arithmetic equality nor on mere geometric proportionality.

Bodin's discussion on crime and punishment was not exclusive to France. It included also a short commentary on the Roman *iudicia publica*, specifically the *lex Cornelia* on assassinations, one of several pieces of legislation promulgated during the later Republic establishing something like a Roman criminal code. Whereas the Early Roman Republic of the XII Tables favored criminal justice according to the principle of arithmetic equality, justice in the Empire gradually adopted harmonics when considering the rank of the transgressor. He cited one notable case related to the *lex Cornelia* which stated that anyone, regardless of rank, may be prosecuted and punished for the crimes of assassination and poisoning.[55] Bodin, however, recalls a rescript of the Emperor Antoninus Pius, centuries after the original promulgation of the *lex Cornelia*, which differentiated penalties according to the social rank of the transgressor:

> **D.48.8.1.5**: *Sed et in eum, qui uxorem deprehensam in adulterio occidit, divus Pius leviorem poenam irrogandam esse scripsit, et humiliore loco positum in exilium perpetuum dari iussit, in aliqua dignitate positum ad tempus relegari.*
>
> "With regard to a husband who kills his wife surprised in the act of adultery, the Divine Pius stated in a rescript that a lighter penalty should be inflicted upon him. And he ordered that anyone of inferior rank should be sent into perpetual exile, while a person of distinguished rank should be banished only for a limited time."

Bodin observes that this appeal to the Emperor Antoninus originated in a Roman provincial court that sentenced a patrician indifferently according to the *lex Cornelia* without regard to the defendant's rank. The Emperor eventually commuted the capital penalty imposed, to reflect the transgressor's rank. In doing so, penalties were differentiated in later Roman legal history: Whereas those of an honorable station were simply deported [*in honore aliquo positi deportari solent*],

[54] By contrast, clergy without dignities or preferments were liable for a fine of only one hundred *sols* (or about five *livres*).

[55] *République* 1033; *De Republica* 760.

those of "secondary rank were punished by death" [*qui secondo gradu sunt capite puniuntur*].[56]

One final example concerns the *actio de dolo malo*, the Roman remedy for delictal fraud.[57] Ulpian, referencing Labeo, observes the remedy cannot be claimed when the actor is attempting to sue a person of higher rank—for example, a plebeian against a person of consular rank, or a licentious person [*luxurioso*] or spendthrift [*prodigo*] or any other vile person [*alias vili*] against a man of irreproachable life.[58] But Bodin regards the immunity enjoyed by those of higher rank as just and proper.

To summarize, then, Bodin opposed the injustice of treating everyone alike on a principle of strict equality. He also rejected the principle of geometric proportionality which distributed rewards and penalties in accordance with worth and merit. Harmonic justice, for Bodin, superseded both principles by situating justice primarily as a matter about recognizing and mixing social rank and status.[59] Maintenance of such ranks will become essential to his vision of a well-ordered government—*gouvernement harmonique*.

Harmonic Government

Bodin's innovative analysis of the three forms of justice—arithmetic, geometric, harmonic—had a further application, beyond the subject of law. That concerned the question of which form of political rule was the most just. This is, of course, the original question that inaugurated Western political philosophy in Plato's *Republic*. And, even for Bodin, the Platonic principle that the political form of the state was a matter of justice would remain an enduring monument of Western political philosophy.

Bodin's own answer to this question was that only the state which was governed according to the principle of harmonic justice—what he calls "harmonic government"—can be regarded as just. Like the voices of a choir "gently intermingling" [*entremestant doucement*] and sounding a "very sweet and pleasant harmony" [*une harmonie fort douce & plaisante*] together, a state too can achieve a political

[56] D.48.8.16.

[57] D.4.3.11, referenced at *République* 1034 [VI, 6].

[58] Bodin, however, omits Ulpian's point that another remedy, the *actio in factum*, is available to such persons.

[59] There are times where Bodin seems to confuse merit (in geometric justice) with rank (in harmonic justice), especially in his use of Roman legal history. Sometimes, the difference between the patres and the plebs is treated simply as a matter of geometric, rather than harmonic, justice. The difference is explained in Roman histories. Whereas the early divisions of the orders accurately represented differences in merit, where the worthier patres held ranks of honor for their valor and service to the Republic, these orders hardened and were corrupted in later generations so that the divisions between patres and plebs did not correspond to merit. A different logic, thus, was necessary for a system of justice where class divisions were hardened, yet they were not differences in worthiness or merit.

harmony when the different classes and orders constituting the state intermingle and govern in tune with each other.[60] In order to achieve this civic harmony, the state requires a maestro. Bodin's ideal vision of state, as he discloses at the end of the *République*, is a monarchy, though a monarchy—the sovereignty of one person—coupled with the moderating influence of elite and popular forms of government. But harmonic government is not a strictly monarchical concept. Any sovereign state can, in theory, be governed harmonically.

This vision of harmonic rule relies on a critical distinction in Bodin's theory of state. That is the distinction between the constitutional form of a state's sovereignty and its mode of government [*modus gubernandi*].[61] Bodin remains famous for his definition of sovereignty as the supreme authority—or the *summum imperium*, as he designates it in the *Distributio*—of a state. It is the state's absolute and perpetual power, manifested above all in the power to make and unmake law.

Perhaps most notable in Bodin's theory of sovereignty is the indifference shown toward the *form* of sovereignty.[62] Sovereignty can take one of three—and only one of these three—forms, either monarchy (the sovereignty of one), aristocracy (the sovereignty of the few or numerical minority), and democracy (the popular sovereignty of the many or numerical majority of the people). Because he defines sovereignty as an indivisible bundle of sovereign rights, sovereignty cannot be distributed, shared, or mixed across different holders. "Mixed" states, where there are multiple competing sovereigns in one state, are theoretically impossible in Bodin's theory. Some sovereign must clearly stand above everyone else and even, in theory, above all laws. Hence, the sovereign alone is described as being *omnibus legibus solutus*.[63]

In practice, however, Bodin recognized that, despite holding all the rights of sovereignty, sovereigns, whether princely or popular, nevertheless cannot govern their states directly or personally and at all times. They need ministers and governments agents—whether "magistrates" or "commissioners"—entrusted to carry out the manifold functions of governing a state on behalf of their sovereign.

Yet, as we have already seen, sovereigns enjoy, in principle, a wide degree of latitude in deciding how to delegate and entrust the exercise of their public powers to other subordinates. A sovereign may, for example, choose to establish formally through legislation a public office with legally defined public powers and tenure of office (a "magistrate"). Or, by contrast, a sovereign may instead bestow powers extraordinarily on persons whose service continues only so long as it pleases the sovereign (a "commissioner"). Whereas the former is the basis for *droit gouvernement*, the latter is the basis for the despotic *seigneurial gouvernement* of

[60] *République* 1054 [VI, 6].
[61] Lee, *Popular Sovereignty*, 193–200.
[62] The indifference is already expressed in the *Distributio* at fol. E, s.v. *summum* [*imperium*].
[63] *De Republica* 84, citing D.1.3.31: *Princeps legibus solutus*. Cf. Lee, *Right of Sovereignty*, 94–99, where I show that *legibus solutus* was simply a principle of legal exemption.

sultans and tsars.[64] Harmonic government, as Bodin calls it, depends partly on the constitutional choice between these two options.

There is another constitutional choice available to sovereigns, a matter sometimes overlooked in the literature on Bodin's political theory. This is the sovereign's choice concerning access and personnel—who actually gets to serve the sovereign in public capacities and wield some share of the state's public authority? This turns out to be another flexible question with multiple possibilities. Whereas some sovereigns may choose to reserve public power only to the restricted few elites (such as the *patres*, the *ottimati*, the *nobiles*), others may open access to the many (the *plebs*, the *popolari*, the *humiliores*).

Taken together, one key principle can be constructed from these pieces: Harmonic government has nothing to do with the form of a state's sovereignty. Monarchies and republics alike (where the latter encompass both democracies and aristocracies) can be governed harmonically.

Harmonic Democracy: Bodin defined the "popular state" [*l'estat populaire*]—or democracy—as that state in which sovereignty belonged to the people, or to the greater number of citizens.[65] The distinguishing characteristic of all popular states, in Bodin's political theory, was its commitment to a strict and indifferent "equality and rectitude in all laws" [*equalité & droiture en toutes loix*].[66]

Bodin was thinking chiefly of the principle of isonomia originating in the classical Greek political culture of democratic equality where persons were treated equally in the law, regardless of age, wealth, status, or any other differences in distinguishing qualities. The law in a democracy, as he put it, was "invariable" allowing no space for any "equitable interpretation" nor any tolerance of special "privilege or respect of persons."[67] In a popular state, the old and the young, the rich and the poor, the courageous and the cowardly, the diligent and the indolent, were treated indifferently by public institutions and were thus legally equal.

Yet, while the people were collectively and equally sovereign in democracies, popular states needn't be governed democratically [*gouverné populairement*].[68] The Roman Republic presents the most important historical case in point. Bodin is exceptional, among sixteenth-century commentators of Roman politics, in treating Rome as a pure democracy, rather than a "mixed" state or "mixed constitution" as most commentators, such as Polybius, Cicero, and Machiavelli, conventionally concluded. Sovereignty in classical Rome, Bodin thought, rested entirely and indivisibly with the *Populus Romanus*, after the expulsion of the Tarquins.

[64] I have already written at length about this distinction. Lee, *Popular Sovereignty*, 215–17; *Right of Sovereignty* 202.

[65] *République* 332 [II, 7]: *la forme de République, ou la pluspart du peuple ensemble commande en souveraineté au surplus en nom collectif, & à chacun de tout le peuple en particulier.*

[66] *République* 937 [VI, 4].

[67] *République* 1019 [VI, 6]: *par loix invariables, sans interpretation equitable, sans privilege ny acception de personne.*

[68] *République* 272 [II, 2].

But, despite Rome's popular sovereignty, Rome's government was in no way democratic. Instead, the politics of the Early Republic resembled more an exclusive aristocracy—a state "governed by the people only in appearance"—where access to the consulship (the most senior magistracy) was exclusive to patrician elites, while the plebs, prior to the creation of the tribunate and the assembly of the *concilium plebis*, were shut out entirely of any meaningful role in governing Rome.[69] Roman politics in this period might, according to Bodin, best be described as "geometrical" since, it was argued, eligibility for high office, particularly the consulship, was class-sensitive, reserved to the patrician order only and thus preserving "similitude" among the governing class.

In recounting the constitutional history of the Early Republic, Bodin reveals himself to be a rather astute reader of Machiavelli's *Discorsi*.[70] Observing that sovereignty in Rome immediately after the expulsion of the Tarquins [*apres que les Rois furent chassés*] belonged to the people, he nevertheless followed Machiavelli's critique of Livy that, despite their sovereignty, the Roman people initially had no active public role to play in governing the city, since "all magistracies, dignities, benefices, and honorable commissions were granted only to the nobility"—that is, to the patricians.[71] Only after the struggle of the orders and the establishment of the plebeian tribunate, the *provocatio ad populum*, and the plebeian assembly [the *concilium plebis*], did Rome "little by little" [*petit à petit*] begin to establish a *gouvernement harmonique* where democracy was "intermixed" [*entremêlé*] with aristocratic rule.[72]

This harmonic equilibrium would begin to erode in the Late Republic when, through the "ambition of the tribunes" and the redistributive policies of the Gracchi, the plebs effectively seized control of the principal functions of Roman government. As Bodin put it, the emergence of an unbridled popular politics in

[69] *République* 945 [VI, 4]: *gouvernées en apparence par le peuple.*

[70] We know from the *Methodus* that Bodin not only was familiar with Machiavelli's historical writing, both the *Discorsi* and the *Istorie Fiorentine*, but that he regarded Machiavelli's skill to be preeminent and comparable to Caesar. See also Eric MacPhail, "Jean Bodin's First Reading of Machiavelli," *Jus Cogens* 7, no. 1 (2025): 131–44. https://doi.org/10.1007/s42439-025-00099-6; Laurent Gerbier, "Une méthode pour interpreter les histoires: Machiavel et Jean Bodin," *Revue de Métaphysique et de Morale* 2, *Méthode et interprétation à l'âge Classique* (2009): 151–66.

[71] *République* 1050 [VI, 6]: *tout les Magistrats, dignités, benefices, & commissions honorables n'estoyent donnés sinon à la noblesse, & les nobles n'estoyent mariés sinon aux nobles, les routuriers à leurs semblables.*

[72] *République* 1050 [VI, 6]. Bodin cites several milestone moments in the Early Republic that were crucial for realizing harmonic government—the *lex Canuleia* of 445 BC (establishing *ius connubii* between plebs and patricians) referenced also at *République* 338 [II, 7]; the *lex Liciniae Sextiae* of 367 BC (reserving one of the annual consulships to a plebeian) referenced at *République* 376 [III, 2]; the *lex Hortensia* of 287 BC (recognizing plebiscites as equivalent to legislation promulgated by comitial assemblies binding on all citizens) referenced at the Latin *De Republica* 257 [III, 1]. One historian of the ancient world has called the resulting arrangement a "patricio-plebeian state," which was not so much the "mixed constitution" venerated by Polybius and Cicero, but rather two coexisting constitutions—a plebeian and a patrician—over one Roman Republic. Endre Ferenczy, *From the Patrician State to the Patricio-Plebeian State*, trans. G. Dedinszky (Budapest: Akadémiai Kiadó, 1976).

the Late Republic might be compared to "the counterweight of a scale" [*comme le contrepoids d'une balance*] weighing too heavily and tipping the political scale altogether. Redistribution and indifference to the class origin of their highest officeholders were the quintessential markers that Rome had finally slipped from a balanced harmonic government to a full-blown "popular" or "democratic government."

The most unusual and perplexing feature of Bodin's analysis was his application of proportions to explain how the Roman constitution evolved from a geometric aristocracy of patricians to a harmonic mixed government. He illustrated this class discord between the patrician and plebeian orders of the Early Republic with the following sequence:

2, 4, 9, 18

These numbers represented the Roman constitutional practice (prior to the *lex Liciniae Sextiae*) of reserving the consulate strictly for the patricians and the tribunate for the plebs. A sort of geometric proportion of similitude connecting class to office, while segregating the classes from each other, characterized the Early Republic. To wit: Just as a member of the plebeian order (2) could become a tribune (4), only a patrician (9) could become a consul (18). In musical terms, the Early Republic, in Bodin's view, was not unlike playing two dissonant octaves (i.e., the 4:2 and 18:9) which, when played together, produced an "intolerable" and "a most harsh discord," between the numbers 4 and 9—and, correspondingly, between plebs and patricians.[73]

The solution was adjusting these proportions so that Rome could move away from a harsh geometric discord and toward a well-tempered harmonic concord among the elements of Roman society. In practice, this required opening access to the consulship to plebs (which was achieved by the *lex Liciniae Sextiae*), while also allowing patricians who renounced their patrician status (such as Publius Clodius Pulcher) to stand for election to the tribunate.[74] Such intermingling across class boundaries, while not entirely eliminating those boundaries, was essential for harmonic government.

Bodin represented this harmonic government resulting from the *lex Liciniae Sextiae* and the *lex Hortensia* (the statute that officially recognized plebiscites as having the force of law) with the following sequence:

4, 6, 8, 12

[73] *République* 1053 [VI, 6].

[74] *République* 1053–54 [VI, 6]. *De Republica* 774 speaks of all the major senior magistracies, not just the consulship: *plebi Consulatus, Censura, Praetura summaque sacerdotia paucis quibusdam exceptis communicarentur.*

Unlike the discord of the Early Republic, civic harmony in this post-Hortensian Republic was captured in the *diapason*, or the Pythagorean octave, by the ratios of 8:4 and 12:6. The *diapente*, or the Pythagorean perfect fifth, was represented by the ratios 6:4 and 12:8. And the *diatessaron*, or the Pythagorean perfect fourth, was represented by the ratio 8:6. Together, the Roman Republic, governed harmonically, produced what Bodin called "a sweet and pleasant harmony," one that can last only so long as these proportions across class and offices are preserved.[75]

Harmonic Monarchy: While both popular and aristocratic states could be governed "harmonically," as in Rome and Venice, it was in monarchies where harmonic government achieved its ideal form. When governed *harmoniquement*, monarchy became, as Bodin put it, "the most beautiful, the happiest, and the most perfect" of all forms of state.[76]

Not all monarchies, however, can achieve this ideal harmonic form. While monarchies, in general, were formally defined by the assignment of sovereignty to one person, they nevertheless varied widely with respect to how a sovereign chose to entrust the exercise of his sovereignty and how he ruled his subjects. He specified that neither seigneurial monarchies (wherein a monarch rules his subjects, just as a *seigneur* or *dominus* rules his slaves) nor tyrannies (wherein the tyrant lacks even the seigneurial title of *dominus* under the *ius gentium*) were fit for harmonic rule.[77] Harmonic monarchies could only be found in a *monarchie royal*, a monarchy where a lawful king [*roy legitime*] not only governs through the law but has sworn an oath to do so.[78]

Harmonic monarchies also needed to be differentiated from two contrasting models of monarchical rule—a monarchy governed "democratically" [*populairement*], on the one hand, and a monarchy governed "aristocratically" [*aristocratiquement*], on the other hand.[79] The former, in which all public offices were distributed by a strict arithmetic proportion [*par proportion égale*] without regard to rank or merit (especially when distributed by lottery), were extremely rare and even non-existent. The latter, by contrast, where offices were distributed by a scheme of geometric proportion [*par proportion geometrique*] favoring "the

[75] *République* 1054 [VI, 6]: *une harmonie sort douce & plaisante.*

[76] *République* 1051 [VI, 6].

[77] Cf. Lee, *Right of Sovereignty*, 202–12. The *monarchie seigneuriale* is distinct from tyranny and draws on the Bartolist distinction between those tyrants that lack a lawful title to rule and those tyrants that rule in a cruel or abusive manner. Seigneural rulership is his term to capture the oriental despotisms of the sultans and tsars.

[78] At *République* 273 [II, 2] and 393 [III, 3], Bodin explains that the first kings were all seigneurial, establishing their title to rule through war and conquest, and therefore ruled their subjects initially through their arbitrary will. Only after the invention of law—for which Bodin credits Moses—was it possible for kings to rule through law, *droit gouvernement*. The famous chapter on sovereignty, *République* I, 8, also includes a lengthy discussion of the coronation oaths of sovereigns. While his main purpose was to show that oaths typically do not require sovereigns to maintain and preserve the laws of their predecessors, they nevertheless swear to "reign well and righteously according to the laws of the land." *République* 135 [I, 8].

[79] *République* 1051–52 [VI, 6].

nobility of some" [*de la noblesse des uns*] and "the wealth of others" [*de la richesse des autres*] without regard to their merit or virtue, were regarded as being especially "pernicious."[80]

Having considerably narrowed the field of possibilities, Bodin described harmonic monarchy as that monarchy where the sovereign prince governed his kingdom "harmonically" [*harmoniquement*], through the use of harmonic proportions in the distribution of offices, honors, rewards, and punishments. In practice, Bodin's vision signaled a meritocratic politics of diversity, wherein a sovereign proportionally "grants [*communiquant*] offices, estates, dignities, and benefices to all men who are deserving [*qui le meritent*; *pro meritis*] of them," even if that meant traversing traditional class lines to join together "a nobleman with a commoner, the rich with the poor, the young with the old," in the inner sanctum of government.[81]

What a sovereign prince must avoid, above all, is the ruinous politics of exclusion, reserving the highest places of honor and power only to the virtuous, the wealthy, or the noble-born.[82] Such a policy will only alienate and antagonize those who are excluded from politics and lead to the state's own downfall. Exclusion itself can become a dangerously potent reason to oppose a sovereign. This is why, for Bodin, it is a much more prudent maxim of princely government to include "a few fools among the wise, a few men unworthy of their office among the experienced, and a few men of vice among the virtuous."[83]

There is a quasi-Rawlsian logic in Bodin's reasoning concerning the distribution of public offices. While offices should ideally be rewarded to the meritorious, the concept of merit itself was variable [*divers*], possibly even undeserved, and thus an unreliable marker for just distribution of offices. As a result, Bodin expressed some uncertainty and skepticism of the righteous demand that the meritorious and worthy claim to public offices of government, just as if it were an entitlement due to them. He is willing to allow that perhaps including the unmeritorious or unworthy

[80] *République* 1052 [VI, 6].

[81] *République* 1055 [VI, 6]; cf. *De Republica* 775: *pro meritis ac virtute*. Bodin supplies two examples of such social mobility in a harmonic monarchy—the son of a lowly physician [*le fils d'un poure medecin*] becoming the Chancellor of France (Michel de l'Hôpital) and the son of a poor soldier [*un poure soldat*] becoming the Constable of France (Bertrand du Guesclin). It is inaccurate to describe these men as *poure*. Du Guesclin's family were petty nobility and held the minor Breton seigneurie of Broons, while de l'Hôpital's father served as a personal physician to the Constable de Bourbon.

[82] His reasoning is numerical: "Men of virtue are always few in number and easily driven out by the many who lack virtue."

[83] *République* 1058 [VI, 6]. Not only does this function as a principle of government but also an aesthetic principle of contrast. Good music, for example, is only possible when there is an occasional dissonance [*quelque discord*] in a piece in order to "give even more grace" [*donner plus de grace aux bons accords*] to the harmony of fourths, fifths, and octaves. He is perhaps thinking of compositional techniques involving suspensions and the use of cross-relations in Renaissance polyphony. The "keen cook" [*les friands cuisiniers*], too, will improve their fine meats by adding certain "sharp and unsavory sauces" [*plats des sausses aspres et mal-plaisantes*] to it. And so too will "the learned painter" [*le docte peinte*] who can skillfully contrast bright and dark colors. Most notably, it is also a principle of theodicy. The *République* ends with the thesis that evil in the world makes possible a better good. This was, as Bodin puts it, the harmony in the divine plan.

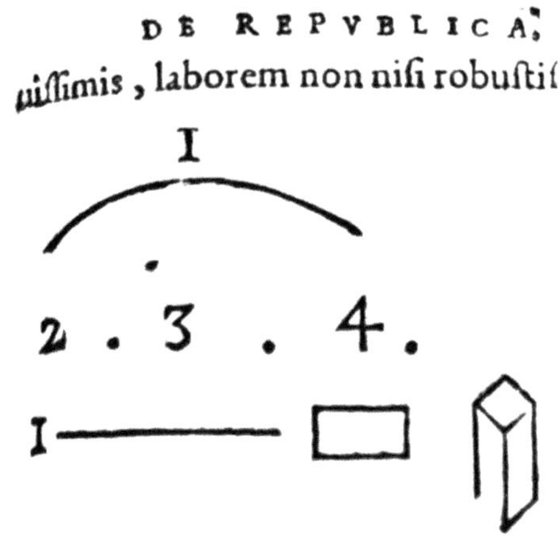

Figure 3.5 Schematic representation of harmonic monarchy in the numbers 1, 2, 3, and 4.

in a place of honor might achieve a better justice, since the perceived lack of merit itself might be undeserved.

The reasoning for harmonic monarchy was also straightforwardly utilitarian. The common people will "feel totally honored" [*se sentent tous honnorés*] to be entrusted with a public charge alongside the nobility, just as the wealthy will "themselves feel honored" [*se feutiront honnorés*] to share in a public duty with the poor though virtuous.[84] Such "gentle intermingling" [*entremestant doucement*] between the nobility with the commons, of the rich with the poor, unveils the most important reason of all for harmonic government, which is that it ties the members of a state together into a quiet harmony—peace.[85]

France, not surprisingly, becomes Bodin's model for the possibilities of harmonic monarchy, which he represents numerically (see Figure 3.5).

It is patterned after the harmonious rulership of the "Great God of Nature" [*grand Dieu de nature a compose harmoniquement le monde*] over the created world.[86] Whereas the sovereign prince (1) is "raised above all subjects" [*éslevé par dessus tous les subjects*] and "whose majesty allows no more division than unity itself" [*non plus division que l'unité*] like a single point, the other numbers represent the Three Estates of the realm—the ecclesiastical First Estate (2), the military

[84] *République* 1055 [VI, 6]. Bodin's recognition of the need and desire to be honored reciprocally anticipates a major theme of French and Scottish Enlightenment political thought, especially Montesquieu and Smith.

[85] *République* 1054 [VI, 6].

[86] *République* 1059 [VI, 6], criticizing Plato's *Timaeus*.

Second Estate (3), and the Third Estate of the commons (4). And these four numbers, again, can be recombined to form the basic harmonies of justice.[87]

I once argued that, in Bodin's view, all democracies have a "constitutional choice" to make with respect to how they will choose to exercise their popular sovereignty in governing themselves.[88] The same point must be made again about monarchies. All sovereign princes, like peoples, must choose how they will govern. This is a conscious constitutional choice that sovereign princes must make. But it is not so much a matter of law, as it is a matter of a sovereign's prudence.

Conclusion: The Politics of Harmony

Bodin's musically inspired vision of a "harmonic monarchy" resonated with later generations, who appealed similarly to harmony and concord as musical metaphors to illustrate a well-ordered political society under the rule of a sovereign, a wise symposiarch, blending the contrasting elements of society together, like trebles and basses connected by the inner voices of a choir.[89] Most notable among later commentators was the German mathematician and astronomer, Johannes Kepler (1571–1630), whose work, *Harmonice Mundi* (1619), included a "Political Digression on the Three Means," a critical essay on Bodin's theory of harmonic justice.

Remembered now in the history of science chiefly for his laws of planetary motion, Kepler turns out to be a careful and critical reader of Bodin's *République* and his attempt to apply harmonic principles to law and politics.[90] Kepler is particularly critical of Bodin's mathematical skill, observing that harmonic proportions cannot be derived simply as a mixture of arithmetic and geometric ratios. Describing Bodin's writing as "very profuse," Kepler responds that "this definition [of harmonic justice] is not true" and simply "drags in mere combinations of arithmetic and geometrical proportions."[91] Kepler even assails Bodin's ability as a political theorist, suggesting that "Bodin would have learned from this *Harmony* of mine ... how to be a better political philosopher."[92] But despite these attacks and

[87] In addition to unisons, the diapasons (2:1, 4:2), the diapente (3:2), and the diatessaron (4:3), this sequence also allows for additional harmonies in the twelfth (3:1) and the double octave (4:1).

[88] Lee, *Popular Sovereignty*, 215–23.

[89] Some prominent examples include Leibniz and Pufendorf.

[90] Johannes Kepler, *The Harmony of the World*, trans. E. J. Aiton et al. (Philadelphia: American Philosophical Society, 1997). The "Political Digression on the Three Means" begins at 255 and is largely a critical reading of Bodin's *République* VI, 6. Kepler's topics and examples follow Bodin, beginning with the three forms of justice, assignment of tunics in Xenophon's *Cyropaedia*, and the application of the three forms of justice in marriage, seating at a theater and a banquet, crime and punishment, and sumptuary laws.

[91] Kepler, *Harmony*, 257. Kepler later objects, at 275, to Bodin's "mistaken" harmonic sequence of 4, 6, 8, 12.

[92] Kepler, *Harmony*, 275.

misgivings regarding Bodin's musico-mathematical analysis, Kepler nevertheless shows a deep admiration for Bodin's vision of a politics of harmony and ultimately "recommends harmonic proportions" to all sovereigns.[93]

It is sometimes thought that Jean Bodin, the quintessential theorist of sovereignty and the public law jurisprudence of the early modern state, had no normative vision of politics to offer. That is, however, a profoundly misleading assessment. As we have now seen in this chapter, Bodin's normative ideal was a politics of harmony, an ideal which Bodin, writing during the most violent and disharmonious periods of the French Wars of Religion, probably thought to be unattainable in his lifetime.[94]

Unattainable perhaps, but it was not impossible. All that was needed, in Bodin's analysis, was a sovereign prince wise enough to recalibrate the constituent elements of society in proper harmonic proportion, so to achieve a stable order among the various parts of the state. Indeed, this is one major reason why Bodin prioritized the need for a sovereign prince: Only a sovereign, standing above and outside the fray of everyday politics, can realize the harmonic politics idealized by Bodin and, like a skilled musician, extract a harmony from natural dissonances.[95]

The challenge for the sovereign is finding that right balance, a point Bodin explored in his last work, the *Colloquium Heptaplomeres*, a dialogue between representatives of different religions and philosophical traditions on religious toleration. A main observation of Book IV was that such balance was near impossible in a religiously divided society such as sixteenth-century France, where Catholics and Huguenots were violently trying to overpower each other (just as dissonant tones "conquer each other" [*uter utrum vincat*]).[96] Curtius, the Calvinist interlocutor in the *Colloquium*, explains why:

> Nothing is more destructive [*perniciosius*] in a state than for citizens to be split into two factions [*cives in duas factiones*], whether the conflict is about laws, honors, or religion. If, however, there are many factions, there is no danger of civil war, since the groups, each acting as a check on the other [*alii aliis quasi mediis vocibus intercedentibus*], protect the stability and harmony of the state.[97]

Harmony, whether in music or in politics, requires a *media vox*—a "middle voice." Fridericus, the Lutheran, explores that principle, first, in Pythagorean music theory:

[93] Kepler, *Harmony*, 276.

[94] While Bodin gestures toward this politics of harmony in *République* VI, it is the *Colloquium*, Bodin's last and most controversial work on religious pluralism, which investigates this ideal of a harmonious society.

[95] A recurring theme in Bodin's discussion of harmony is the value of dissonance, in order to reinforce the melodious qualities of consonance by way of contrast.

[96] *Colloquium* 112.

[97] *Colloquium* 117. Kuntz's translation of this passage, at *Colloquium of the Seven About Secrets of the Sublime*, trans. Marion Leathers Kuntz (Princeton, NJ: Princeton University Press, 1975), 151, obscures the logic of the *media vox* or "middle voice" in explaining political stability as harmony among plural voices.

> In musical modulations that contrariety does not seem to be destroyed, but extreme opposites are brought together by intermingling [*interiectis*] of the middle tones [*mediis*]. For the simple sound of the υπατων ["hypaton," the lowest-pitched tetrachord] produces a sweet harmony with the highest sound of the υπερβολαιων ["hyperbolaion," the highest-pitched tetrachord] or the διαπασῶν ["diapason," the perfect octave] since from opposites it is united in the whole diameter. If you shall join the middle voice to these, with one it will produce a diapason [octave], with another a diapente [perfect fifth], from which comes the most pleasing harmony of all modulation from the proper union of opposites.[98]

The same principle could be applied to the conflicting schools of ancient philosophy. Toralba, the natural philosopher, observes that, despite the philosophical divisions and principled conflicts between the ancient Stoics and Epicurians, harmony continued to be preserved among the ancient schools because they were joined "as if by certain bonds, midway [*mediis ordinibus*] by the Academics and Peripatetics."[99]

The task of a harmony-seeking sovereign should likewise be to identify that *media vox* in politics, not unlike Aristotle's "middle part" of the constitution. Coronaeus, the Catholic host of the colloquium, illustrates with a Roman example:

> A third party [*tertius*] forces two opposing factions toward harmony ... As long as Marcus Crassus lived there was no disagreement of will between Pompey and Caesar, since Crassus, a middle voice [*quasi media vox*] as it were, easily reconciled Caesar to Pompey; however, when Crassus was killed in Chaldaea, the other two rushed to arms.[100]

Even the mixed constitution of the Roman Republic, which Bodin had described in the *République* as a harmonic government, was a harmony produced by the tribunate, which functioned as Rome's *media vox* between the ongoing strife between the patrician and plebeian orders.[101]

Seeing, then, that faulty harmonies and dissonances lead to the downfall of states, Bodin saw the aim of his harmonic politics to be one of inclusion. More voices—"middle voices"—have a lasting stabilizing effect that can forestall political disaster. It is a lesson that France tragically failed to learn during Bodin's lifetime.

[98] *Colloquium* 113–14; Kuntz, *Colloquium of the Seven*, 146.
[99] *Colloquium* 116; Kuntz, *Colloquium of the Seven*, 148.
[100] *Colloquium* 116; Kuntz, *Colloquium of the Seven*, 149.
[101] *Colloquium* 116. Machiavelli may likely have been a source of Bodin's reasoning when, speaking through Curtius, he explains that *singulorum civium inimicitiae universorum concordiam alunt.*

Epilogue

The Origins of Modern Legal Science

Jean Bodin's *Iuris Universi Distributio* was a product of the most transformative period in the history of Western jurisprudence. What was once primarily an exegetical field of interpreting and applying rules of Roman law in a post-Roman medieval world, made up of kingdoms, principalities, feudalities, free cities, all united by one Church universal, became an autonomous legal science aimed at elucidating the universal logic of all legal systems.

We can now view Bodin as a pioneer in taking one of the first steps in an intellectual trajectory that will culminate centuries later in the monumental work of the great German Pandectists of the nineteenth century, such as Friedrich Karl von Savigny, Gustav Hugo, and Bernhard Windschied.[1] While I am not suggesting any line of direct influence from Bodin to the Pandectists, I do wish to highlight in this Epilogue the origins of a modern legal science, united by a shared concept of *ius universum.*

Modern legal science owes a great debt to the critical academic achievements of humanist jurisprudence in the sixteenth century. By treating Roman law with some degree of academic skepticism, as the artifact of a foreign ancient legal culture, those jurists drove a wedge, a substantial critical distance separating the inherited Justinianic text of the *Corpus Iuris Civilis* studied in the law schools, on the one hand, and legal modernity, on the other. It became possible, not only to document and represent the logic and reasoning in the structure of classical Roman law but also to imagine a juridical logic transcending Roman law entirely.

A golden age of legal science unfolds in the generations following Bodin. Doneau [Donellus], in his *Commentaria* on the civil law (later published in full in the eighteenth century), perhaps the most influential of the French Ramist systematists of civil law, set the standard for what such a legal science might look like.[2] A professor of law at Leiden, one of his most important students and influences was the young Hugo Grotius, who would publish his own system of the emerging Roman–Dutch

[1] Peter Stein, *Roman Law in European History* (Cambridge: Cambridge University Press, 1999), 115–23.

[2] André-Jean Arnaud, *Les origines doctrinales du Code civil français*, Bibliothèque du philosophie du droit IX (Paris: Librairie Générale de droit et de jurisprudence, 1969), 121. Donellus's work, in fact, would also serve as a model for von Savigny's Pandect-Science. Stein, *Roman Law in European History*, 119.

law in the form of a Ramist-inspired visual table, in his *Inleiding tot de Hollandsche Rechts-geleertheyd* ("Introduction to the Jurisprudence of Holland," 1631).[3]

What these later generations, continuing into the *usus modernus Pandectarum* of the Enlightenment, accomplished was what Bodin had hoped to achieve—an orderly system of jurisprudence divorced from Roman law and based on rational divisions of legal concepts and principles. From them, we have numerous examples, some of which attempt to codify a rational, even "natural," legal system for emerging nation-states. These include James Dalrymple, the Viscount Stair's (1619–95) *Institutes of the Law of Scotland*, Jean Domat's (1625–96) *Les Lois Civiles Dans Leur Ordre Naturel*, Johann Gottlieb Heineccius's (1681–1741) *Elementa Juris Civilis Secundum Ordinem Pandectarum*, Robert Joseph Pothier's (1699–1772) *Pandectae Justinianae in Novum Ordinem Digestae* and *Traité Des Obligations*, as well as many others.[4] This literature of an emerging legal science also includes works by some of the most prominent figures in modern political thought and philosophy as well, notably the works of Grotius, Samuel Pufendorf's (1632–94) *Elementorum Jurisprudentiae Universalis Libri Duo*, and Gottfried Wilhelm Leibniz's (1646–1716) *Nova Methodus Discendae Docendaeque Jurisprudentiae*.[5]

What we lack in the modern Anglophone scholarship is a proper historical treatment of Western legal science. In part, this is due to the common law bias in legal history. But I believe the more important reason is due to the tendency to confuse the history of law with the history of jurisprudence. Just as understanding the history of any "normal science" requires an understanding of accepted scientific conventions, vocabulary, and styles of reasoning, a history of legal science likewise requires those features that make jurisprudence an autonomous normal science.[6] We might see Bodin's *Distributio* as one of the first steps in this direction, but this history of legal science remains yet to be written in full.

[3] The tables of law are reproduced in the 1926 Oxford edition of Grotius's *Jurisprudence of Holland*, trans. R. W. Lee (Oxford: Clarendon Press, 1926).

[4] Even in the common law world of England, the aspiration for a systematic "universal" jurisprudence influenced the work of academic jurists, particularly the English Civilians, such as John Cowell and Richard Zouche, and English jurists increasingly influenced by the theoretical influence of the Natural Law school, such as John Selden. On the English Civilians, one of the best studies is Brian Levack, *The Civil Lawyers in England, 1603–1641: A Political Study* (Oxford: Clarendon Press, 1973).

[5] The latter was the subject of a book by Patrick Riley, *Leibniz's Universal Jurisprudence: Justice as the Charity of the Wise* (Cambridge, MA: Harvard University Press, 1996).

[6] Thomas Kuhn, *The Structure of Scientific Revolution* (Chicago, IL: University of Chicago Press, 1962).

APPENDIX 1

Jean Bodin, *Iuris Universi Distributio* Translator's Preface

Introduction

The *Iuris Universi Distributio* was published three times during the life of its author. The first edition, Paris 1578, sets out the *Distributio* in tabular form, preceded by the dedication and with Bodin's running commentary located in the right margin. The second edition, Köln 1580, disposes the *Distributio* instead as continuous prose in roman type, with Bodin's marginal commentary interspersed in italic type. A third edition, Prague 1581, was edited by Jean Kocin and transforms the *Distributio* into a dialogue between Jean Bodin and the dedicatee, Jean Nicolai. Kocin gave this work the title *Nova distributio iuris universi … dialogo explicata a Ioanne Cocino*. I have consulted all three, but we believe that the 1578 tabular edition is the best representation of Bodin's vision for the *Distributio*, which we aim to restore in this book. The tabular layout of that edition is a great aid to understanding Bodin's thought and method in the *Distributio*; it makes his division of jurisprudence and law far more intelligible than prose alone. As such, before the English translation, we have included high-quality photos of the 1578 table.

Method of the Translation

To lay a solid foundation for the translation herein, I began by preparing an edition of the original Latin text of the *Distributio*. My goal was to establish a Latin text which reflected the intention of the author as accurately as possible. I began with an exact transcription of the 1580 edition. I used the 1580 text because in it, Bodin writes out in full sentences certain things which are only expressed visually in the 1578 table, such as how many parts something is divided into. However, the 1580 edition has occasional typographical and grammatical errors which are not present in the 1578 edition. Moreover, as mentioned a moment ago, the tabular format of the 1578 edition clarifies or solves some difficulties presented by the 1580 text. For example, on p. 14 of the 1580 edition, the words *aut magistratus edictum vel interdictum* ("either an edict or an interdict of a magistrate") are erroneously printed in italics as though they are part of the commentary and belong with the set of Roman law citations in italics which immediately precede them, while the 1578 edition shows that these words should be in roman type, and that they introduce a new division of *sanctio seu iussum* ("sanction or command"). I have emended the text in seven places where I judge both the 1578 and 1580 editions to contain an error which obstructs the meaning intended by the author. A good example can be found in the discussion of onerous transactions (*mercenarium*), where I explain what the original editions said in a footnote. I have flagged all of my editorial interventions in footnotes providing both the original Latin and my revision.

In my translation I aim at producing readable English which is faithful to the original Latin. My highest priority has been to communicate the sense intended by the author according to our best understanding of it. In some cases the sense intended by the author is not entirely clear to me; I have tried to stay close enough to the original Latin that readers of the English translation can make their own intelligent guesses about how to interpret Bodin's thought. A caveat is in order here, however, about Roman legal terminology, which I will return to.

Modern Editions and Translations of the *Iuris Universi Distributio*

Witold Wolodkiewicz helpfully published a reproduction of the three first editions of the *Distributio* in 1985. With the advent of digitization, it is now also possible to access scans of the three editions online. There are three translations of the *Distributio* into modern languages of which I am aware, each including a Latin text: Pierre Mesnard's French translation (1951), Lucien Jerphagnon's French translation (1985), and Cecilia Pedrazza Gorlero's Italian translation (1999). A. London Fell also translates some extracts into English in his *Bodin's Humanistic Legal System* (1987). I have compared my translation to the French translations by Mesnard and Jerphagnon for help interpreting the Latin. Mesnard's work is particularly illuminating.

Jean Bodin's Latin Style

Throughout this work, Jean Bodin writes fluent humanistic Latin. A few humanistic characteristics stand out; for example, the use of *id genus* for *eius generis* "of the same sort," the incorporation of Greek words and quotations (including coining a Greek neologism, *epieikonomia* [ἐπιεικονομία]), and the restoration of *ae*- diphthongs in place of the *e*- of medieval Latin.[1] However, Jean Bodin employs quite different Latin styles in his dedication and in the body of the *Distributio* proper, and therefore I will discuss them separately.

In the elegant dedication to Jean Nicolai, Jean Bodin writes a fine Ciceronian Latin. The vocabulary is thoroughly classical and presents no special difficulties, apart from the incorporation of Greek terminology and quotations—as is common in humanist writers.[2] Dedications of medieval and Renaissance works tend to be written in a higher register than the work itself, at least for prose works, and Bodin's dedication of the *Distributio* is no exception. The register is raised, here, principally by the adoption of a quasi-oratorical "periodic" style, which gives the dedication a particularly Ciceronian flavor.[3] The very first sentence of Bodin's dedication exhibits this style perfectly. It opens with a concessive clause introduced

[1] See Terence O. Tunberg, "Humanistic Latin," in *Medieval Latin: An Introduction and Bibliographical Guide*, ed. F. A. C. Mantello and A. G. Rigg (Washington, DC: Catholic University of America 1996), 131.

[2] In dealing with Bodin's Greek I relied on the assistance of Dan Russell, then an honors student in Classics at the University of Winnipeg, to whom I am very grateful. Any errors, however, are my responsibility.

[3] On Cicero's "periodic" style, and Latin rhetoric more broadly, see J. G. F. Powell, "Cicero's Style," in *The Cambridge Companion to Cicero*, ed. Catherine Steel (Cambridge: Cambridge University Press, 2013), 41–72.

by *etsi* "though, although," exactly as Cicero's first political speech to the Roman people opens with *quamquam* "though, although." This sentence runs to six lines in length, interrupted by frequent parentheses (e.g., *quicquid est* "such as it is") and relative clauses (*qui … queruntur* "those who complain that … ," *quod a me exquiritur* "which is sought from me," *ea quae … leguntur* "those materials which are read … ," etc.), but with the main clause carefully signposted by means of *etsi* "even though," *non tamen* "nevertheless … not," and *ante … quam* "before"; the final four lines all depend on *quam*, completed elegantly with the verb *conclusissem* "I had included" in final position. The use of relatively long, grammatically intricate sentences continues through the whole dedication. Bodin likewise makes fluent use of classical word order, for instance in his placement of verbs and genitives (e.g., *hanc legitimae artis distributionem* "this division of legal art," *in infinita librorum multitudine* "in an infinite multitude of books"). Some of his sentences make striking use of balance and symmetry (e.g., *respondeant extrema primis, media utrisque omnia omnibus* "that the last things respond to the first, the middle to either, and each to all"), and occasionally contrastive asyndeton ("two phrases placed in parallel without any expressed conjuction, showing that they contrast with one another,"[4] as in *quid antecedat, quid sequatur* "what is antecedent and what is consequent"). Bodin uses Greek more frequently in the dedication than in the *Distributio* itself; there is at least one Greek word on every page of the dedication, including learned allusions to Aristotle and to Stoicism. The oratorical style is heightened further in the final sentences of the dedication through directly addressing the dedicatee (*ineunte aetate facile emendabis …* "you shall amend it with ease as you come of age …"). On the whole, the dedication is not a remarkable specimen of humanistic Latin, but an admirable one.

In the *Distributio* itself a much plainer and syntactically simpler style is employed. This style could well be described as Scholastic. It is the sort of utilitarian style employed for teaching and debate in the university faculties of law, arts, and theology since their inception in the twelfth and thirteenth centuries. It is terse, concise, and straightforward; it is repetitive, typically employing parallel constructions rather than variation; and it is marked by a large amount of technical terminology and formulae from one or another branch of academic learning. In the *Distributio*, there is a small amount of terminology from philosophy (e.g., *forma, materia, efficiens, finis* "form, matter, efficient cause, end") and mathematics (*proportio arithmetica, geometrica, harmonica* "arithmetic, geometric, and harmonic proportion").[5] The majority, however, of technical terminology, by a wide margin, is drawn from the discipline of law.

Legal Terminology

As just discussed, Bodin's Latin syntax in the *Distributio* is not especially difficult. What creates difficulties for the reader, however, and for the translator, is the use of a very large stock of legal vocabulary and technical formulae, drawing on the *ius commune* ("common law") of medieval and early modern Europe, including Roman civil law and the Catholic Church's canon law. Kenneth Pennington warned that a translator of medieval legal texts "must not assume that a familiar word is not also a technical term in law," and this warning applies to

[4] Powell, "Cicero's Style," 63.

[5] For background on philosophical terminology I have often consulted Roy J. Deferrari and M. Inviolata Barry, *A Lexicon of St. Thomas Aquinas based on the Summa Theologica and selected passages of his other works* (Washington, DC: Catholic University of America, 1948).

the *Distributio* as well.[6] For example, in the *Distributio* under the heading *Facta* ("Deeds"), one reaches a division of *negotium* "transaction" into the three categories *mercenarium, gratuitum, et mistum* ("onerous, gratuitous, and mixed"). While these terms in themselves are fairly straightforward, Bodin's explanation of each category employs an extensive set of terms and formulae whose technical meanings were known well to jurists in medieval and early modern Europe, but are not at all evident to the reader who knows Latin but is not experienced with texts of the European *ius commune*. Such terms and formulae as *permutatio, foenus, reditus, locatio, conductio, do ut facias, societas, fideiussio, expromissio, mandatum, negotiorum gestio, curatio, procuratio, tutela*, etc., refer to specific institutions and concepts from civil law, each with a well-developed apparatus of jurisprudential analysis associated with it.[7] I have translated legal terms like these into English, but we also included the original Latin terms, which specialists in Roman and canon law will readily recognize, within square brackets in the translation.

In similar vein, there are certain terms which are so unique to Roman and canon law that we have decided it is better not to translate them. The outstanding instance is the long list of types of suit under the heading *Actio* within Bodin's discussion of the efficient cause of jurisprudence. The meaning of lawsuits like the *condictio, actio quanti minoris, actio ex stipulatu incerta, actio de eo quod certo loco, actio damni infecti vel dati*, etc., cannot really be captured by a translation; but they can be looked up using the Latin, for even today in the literature they are usually discussed with reference to their Latin names.

Although he uses a huge stock of Roman legal terms, Bodin's stated intention in the *Distributio* is not to deal with the Roman "civil law" specifically, but to deal with "law as a whole":

> And those who profess to teach the "art of civil law" [*artem iuris civilis*] are greatly in error, since the civil law [*ius civile*] is particular to a single state [*unius civitatis proprium*]. Art, however, belongs to universal things, not particulars. This is the reason why we should disregard the partition of civil law, treating it as a single indivisible thing [*quasi unius individui*], and we should apply the law of nations or the "common law" [*ius gentium seu commune*] to the art which we are seeking.

The most formidable source of complexity in interpreting the *Distributio* has been identifying the normal juristic significance of the legal terminology employed, and then balancing this with the recognition that Bodin intended each concept to be, in principle, of universal validity. Hence, for each technical term, it has been necessary both to examine carefully the way it is used in the Roman legal sources (and sometimes in medieval commentaries on them), and also to take stock of the term's location within the context of Bodin's division of law as a whole. We have done this meticulously in preparing this translation, and it underlies what may appear to the casual reader to be some surprising translation choices. For example, under the heading of *Delictum* ("Delict"), at one point in the 1578 edition we find *furtum* ("theft") divided into *manifestum, non manifestum, conceptum, oblatum, suspecti crimen*.[8] The first two are straightforward—"manifest, non-manifest"—but each

[6] Kenneth Pennington, "Roman and Secular Law," in *Medieval Latin: An Introduction and Bibliographical Guide*, ed. F. A. C. Mantello and A. G. Rigg (Washington, DC: Catholic University of America, 1996), 262–63.

[7] See Adolf Berger, *Encyclopedic Dictionary of Roman Law*, Transactions of the American Philosophical Society, n.s., 43, pt. 2 (Philadelphia: American Philosophical Society, 1953), s.v.

[8] In the 1580 edition *suspecti crimen* "embezzlement" is treated as a separate delict from theft, and I have followed this arrangement in the text below.

of the latter three is a technical term employed in civil law, denoting "theft by receiving, theft by planting, and embezzlement"—I have translated them as such.[9] As noted a moment ago, however, I have also included the original Latin in square brackets. On the other hand, Bodin's use of the term *Senatusconsulta*—which in civil law refers to resolutions made by the Roman Senate—highlights Bodin's intention of speaking about universal concepts, not specifically Roman ones. Bodin himself states that "in every state [*republica*] the Senate is accustomed to make resolutions [*Senatus decernere ... solet*], but the ruler to command [*princips vero iubere*]," indicating that, with the term *Senatusconsulta*, he is not referring solely to the Roman institution. Bodin's use of the term *legis actio* is another example of this sort of complexity. In the earliest recorded stage of Roman civil procedure, *legis actio* referred to a set of ritual methods for initiating lawsuits. Classically, it referred to the action of an individual suing in a trial (or to the whole trial proceedings).[10] Bodin, however, has a more universal concept in mind; indeed, Bodin seems to give the term *legis actio* an extremely wide sense—including extrajudicial action—which I have tried to reflect with "action of law."

In some cases, chiefly for terms that are used frequently throughout the *Distributio*, it has not seemed appropriate to adopt a single formulaic translation, but to translate differently depending on context. The outstanding example is the word *lex* (pl. *leges*). Throughout the dedication, Bodin seems to use *lex*, *leges* simply to mean "the law, laws" in the sense of positive law. In the rest of the *Distributio*, Bodin sometimes uses *lex* in the same way, but he also very commonly uses it with the clear sense of "legislation" or "statute." Hence he says in one place that "even if the Roman Senate had in very distant times the power to make law, even so this law was not statute" [*non tamen ius illud lex erat*]. For the more ultimate sense of law, "a ray of divine benevolence and prudence granted to men, and applied by them for the advantage of human society" [*ad utilitatem humanae societatis*], Bodin uses *ius*. In my translation of the *Distributio*, the word "law" usually translates Latin *ius*, but to make it clear to the reader which term Bodin is using, we have often included the original Latin in square brackets.

Citations of Roman Law

Throughout the *Distributio* there are a large number of references to the *Corpus Iuris Civilis*—the texts of Roman (civil) law compiled by the Emperor Justinian in the sixth century AD, that is, the *Digest* (*Pandects*), *Code*, *Institutes*, and *Novels*. Bodin cites these texts using the standard formulae employed by jurists of the *ius commune* since the "resurrection of Roman law" in the eleventh and twelfth centuries.[11] I have modernized Bodin's citations following the standard method employed by scholars of legal history. I looked up these citations using the indices of the *Corpus Iuris Civilis* published by Ochoa and Diez and by Nicolini and d'Amico.[12] Parentheses in my modernized citations indicate where the

[9] In translating these and some other terms, I have followed the English–Latin Word List contained in Ernest Metzger, ed., *A Companion to Justinian's Institutes* (Ithaca, NY: Cornell University Press, 1998), 256–59.

[10] See Celsus, D.45.1.51; Berger, *Encyclopedic Dictionary of Roman Law*, s.v. *actio*.

[11] Pennington, "Roman and Secular Law," 254. Pennington's article includes an explanation of medieval and early modern citation methods. See also Stephan Kuttner, "Notes on the Presentation of Text and Apparatus in Editing Works of the Decretists and Decretalists," *Traditio* 15 (1959): 452–64.

[12] Xaviero Ochoa and Aloisio Diez, *Index canonum et legum totius Corporis iuris canonici et civilis*, Universa bibliotheca iuris: subsidia 2, 2 vols (Rome: Institutum iuridicum Claretanum, 1964–65); H. Nicolini and F. S. d'Amico, *Indices corporis iuris civilis iuxta vetustiores editiones cum criticis collatas*, 5 vols (Milan: Typis Giuffre, 1964–67).

medieval and early printed "vulgate" text of the *Corpus Iuris Civilis* differs from the critical edition by Mommsen et al. In some cases I have included in a footnote a quotation from the text cited, to give the reader a sense of its relevance to Bodin's argument. In other cases I have indicated that the text cited does not seem to answer. However, this should not be taken as a certain judgment that Bodin has cited the wrong text. It is possible that Bodin has in mind not so much the text itself as the jurists' commentaries which grew up around that text.[13]

Acknowledgements

I would like, first of all, to thank Daniel Lee, who initiated this project when I was a graduate student at the University of Toronto by inviting me to translate the *Iuris Universi Distributio*, and then developed it into a book proposal for Oxford University Press. Moreover, Dan has invested a great deal of time and thought into interpreting the *Distributio* and figuring out how best to present it, all of which has greatly improved the translation. I also thank Dan Russell, who helped me by preparing an exacting study of the Greek terms and allusions in the *Distributio*. I did most of my work editing and translating the *Distributio* while I was a sessional instructor in Classics at the University of Winnipeg, and I'm pleased to have the chance to acknowledge my colleagues there: Melissa Funke, Tyson Sukava, Matt Gibbs, Peter Miller, Conor Whately, Pauline Ripat, Michael MacKinnon, Victoria Austen, and Keith Collins, as well as (from other departments) Chris Araujo and Heather Patrick. Their warmth and friendliness made me feel very welcome at the university, and I always enjoyed discussing our work and ideas together. Lawrin Armstrong read a draft of this preface as well as parts of the translation and provided incisive comments. Finally, I would like to express my gratitude to my family, especially my children Rosalie, Gabrielle, Elisabeth, Michaël, and Catherine, and my wife Jacqueline, who gave me up for hours or days at a time while I locked myself away in the office or disappeared to the library to finish this.

I dedicate this translation to my late professor Joe Goering (1947–2023), one of the great medievalists of our time and a beloved mentor to me and a host of others who studied at the Centre for Medieval Studies. We miss him dearly.

Jason Brown
3 May 2025
Winnipeg, Manitoba

Dedicated to Joe Goering †2023
Ricordare non me ne posso sanza lagrime, vedendo me et la dolcie patria privati di tanto padre.
—Baldovino Baldovini, *Vita di S. Antonino* (circa 1480)

[13] For deciphering Bodin's occasional references to these jurists, see William H. Bryson, *Dictionary of Sigla and Abbreviations to and in Law Books before 1607* (Charlottesville, VA: University Press of Virginia, 1975); Kenneth Pennington et al., *Bio-Bibliographical Guide to Medieval and Early Modern Jurists* (Online: Harvard University and the Ames Foundation, 2011–17), last updated online 27 May 2017.

APPENDIX 2

Iuris Universi Distributio (Paris, 1578)

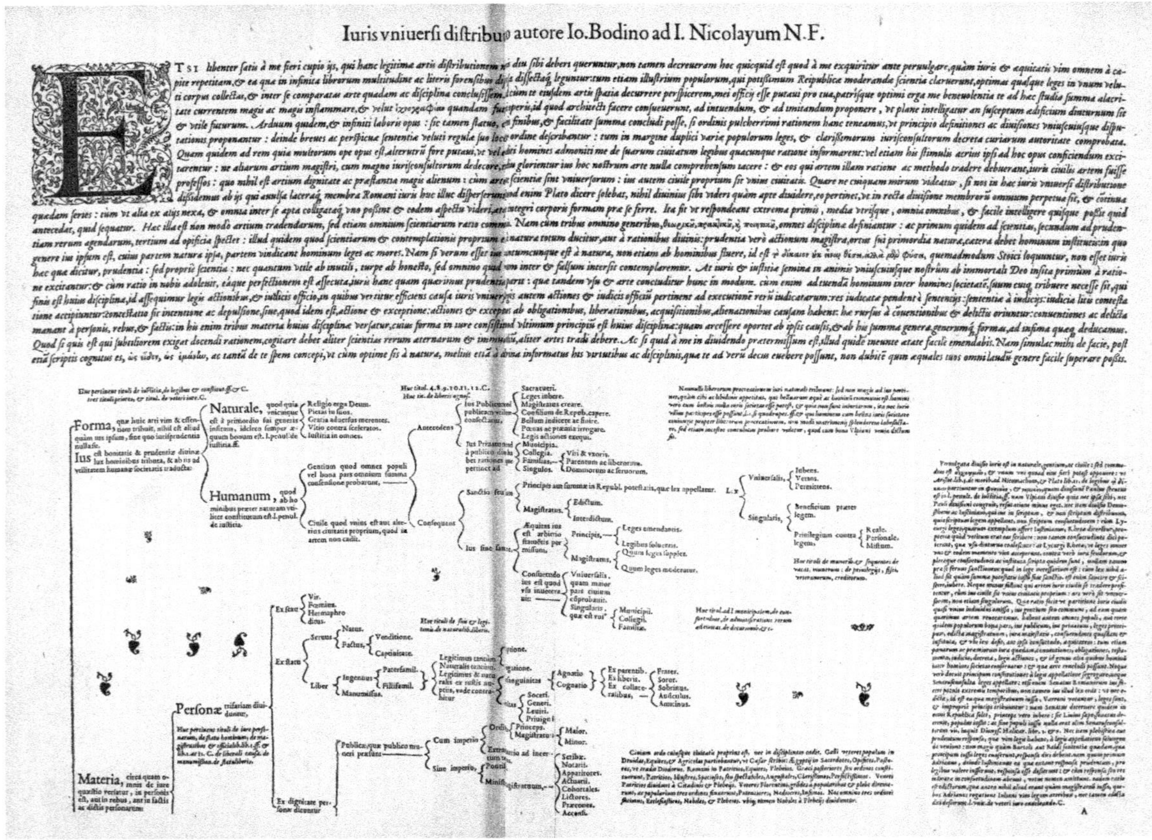

Figure A Folio A of Bodin's *Iuris Universi Distributio*

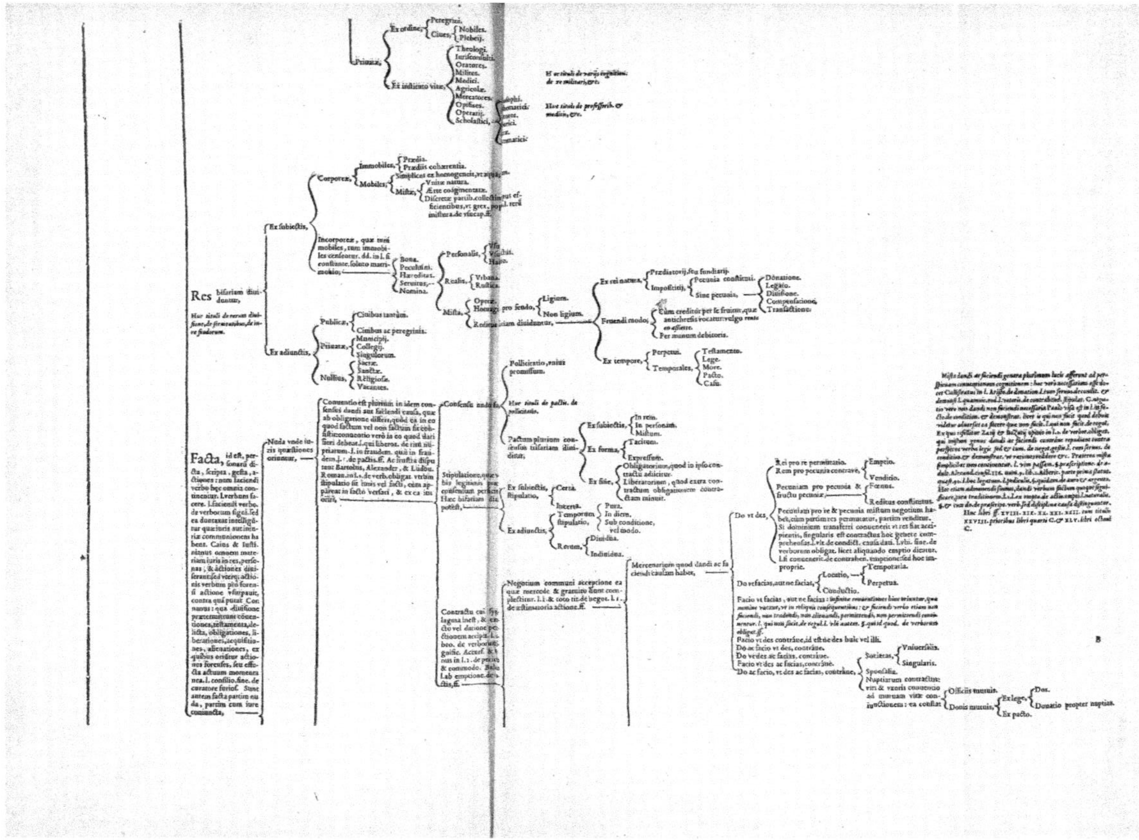

Figure B Folio B of Bodin's *Iuris Universi Distributio*

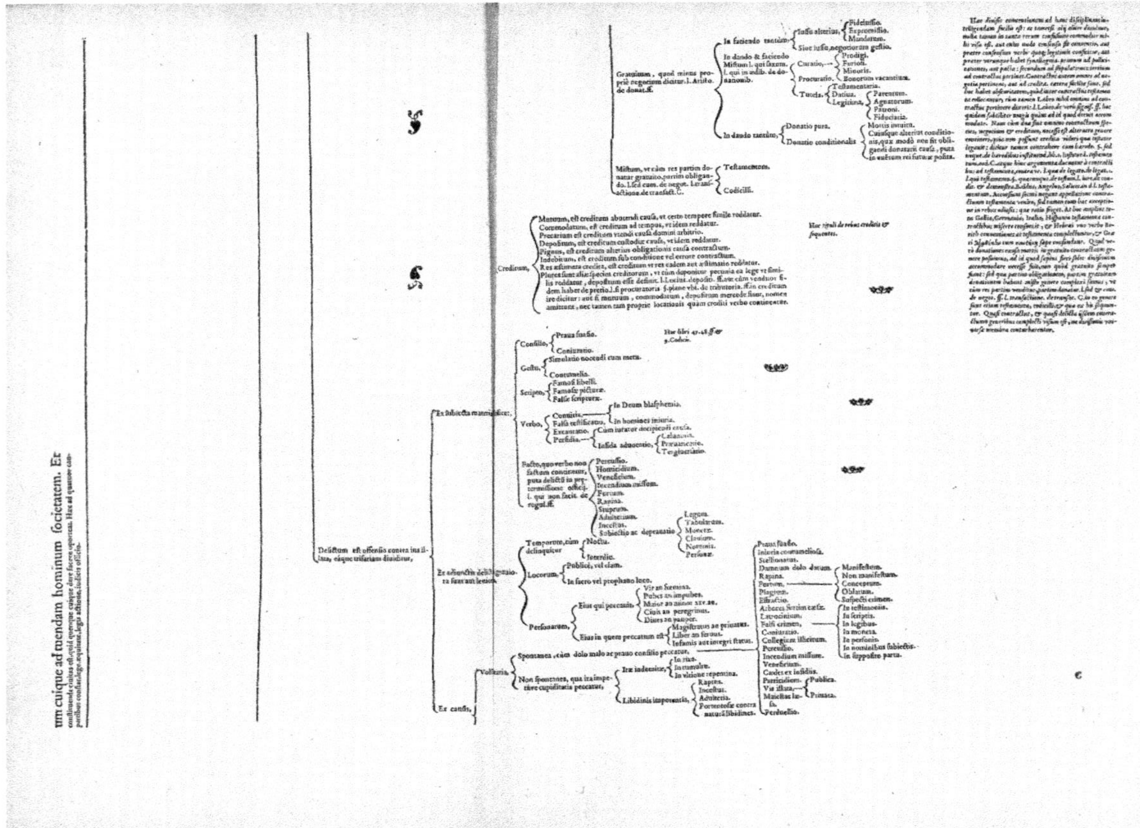

Figure C Folio C of Bodin's *Iuris Universi Distributio*

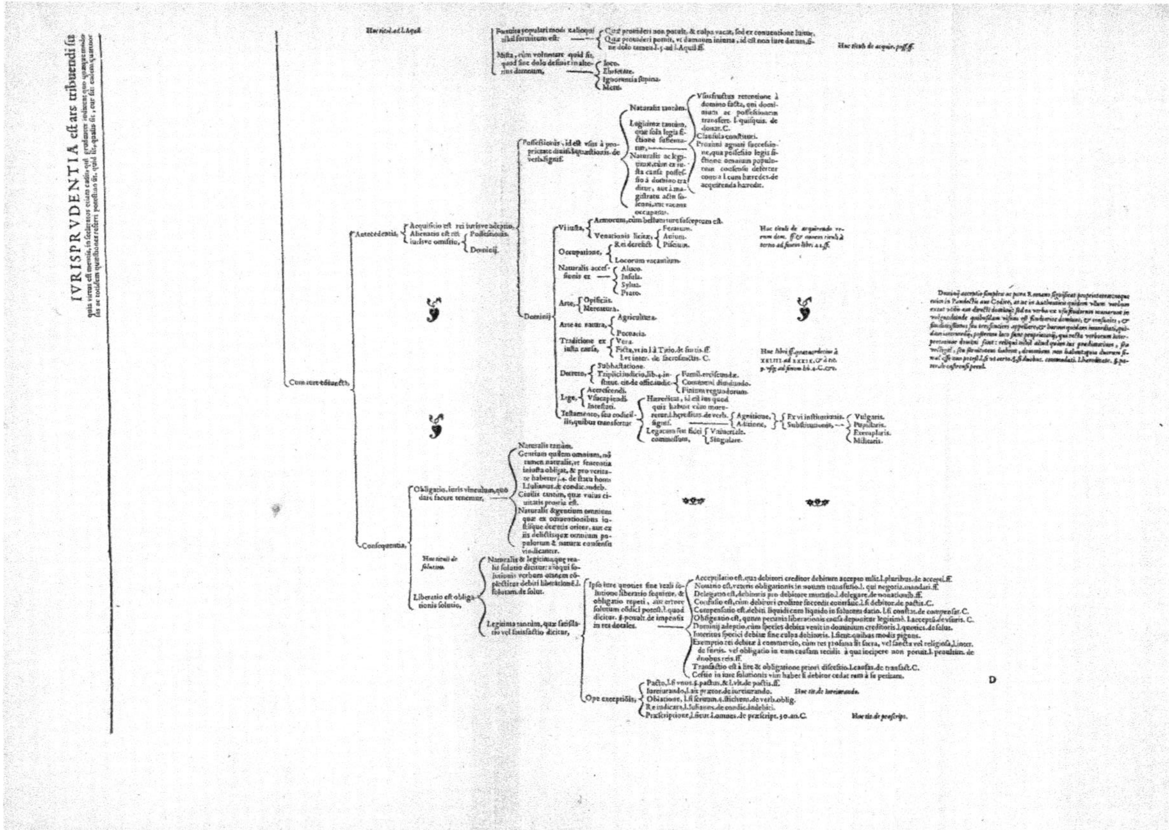

Figure D Folio D of Bodin's *Iuris Universi Distributio*

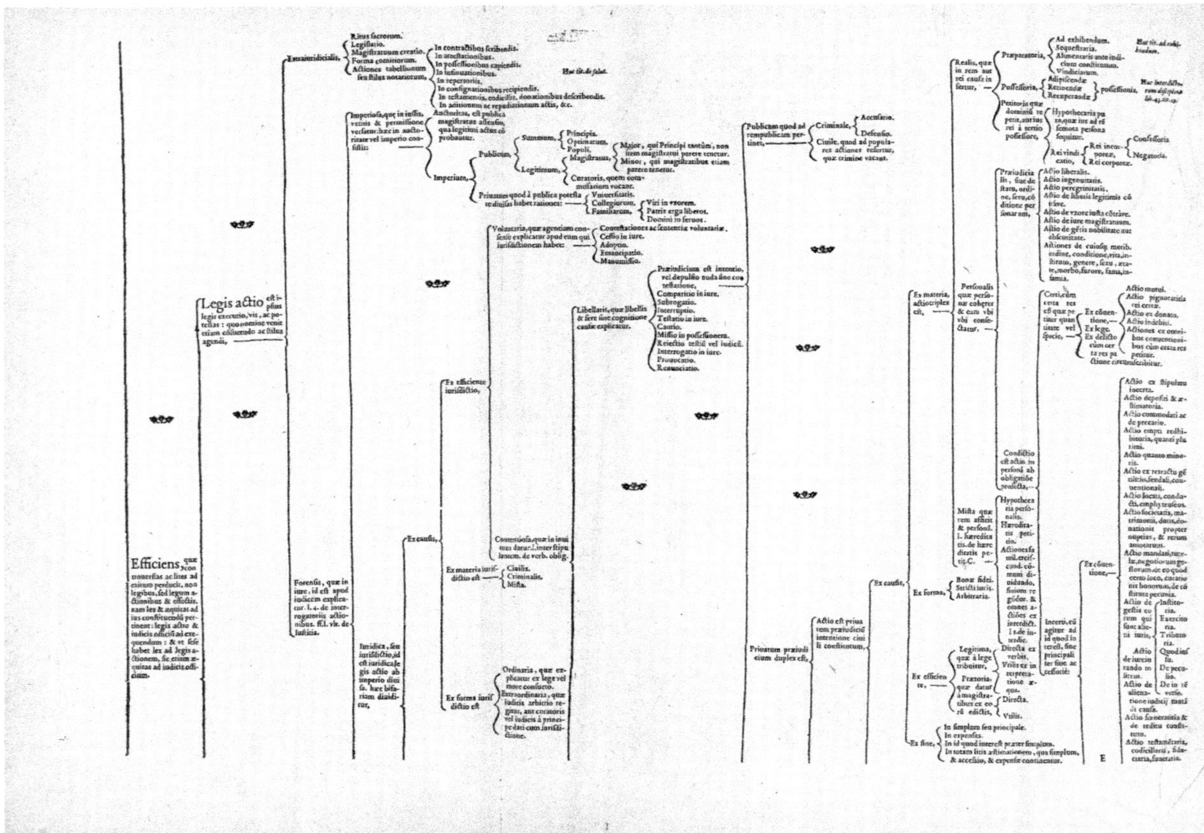

Figure E Folio E of Bodin's *Iuris Universi Distributio*

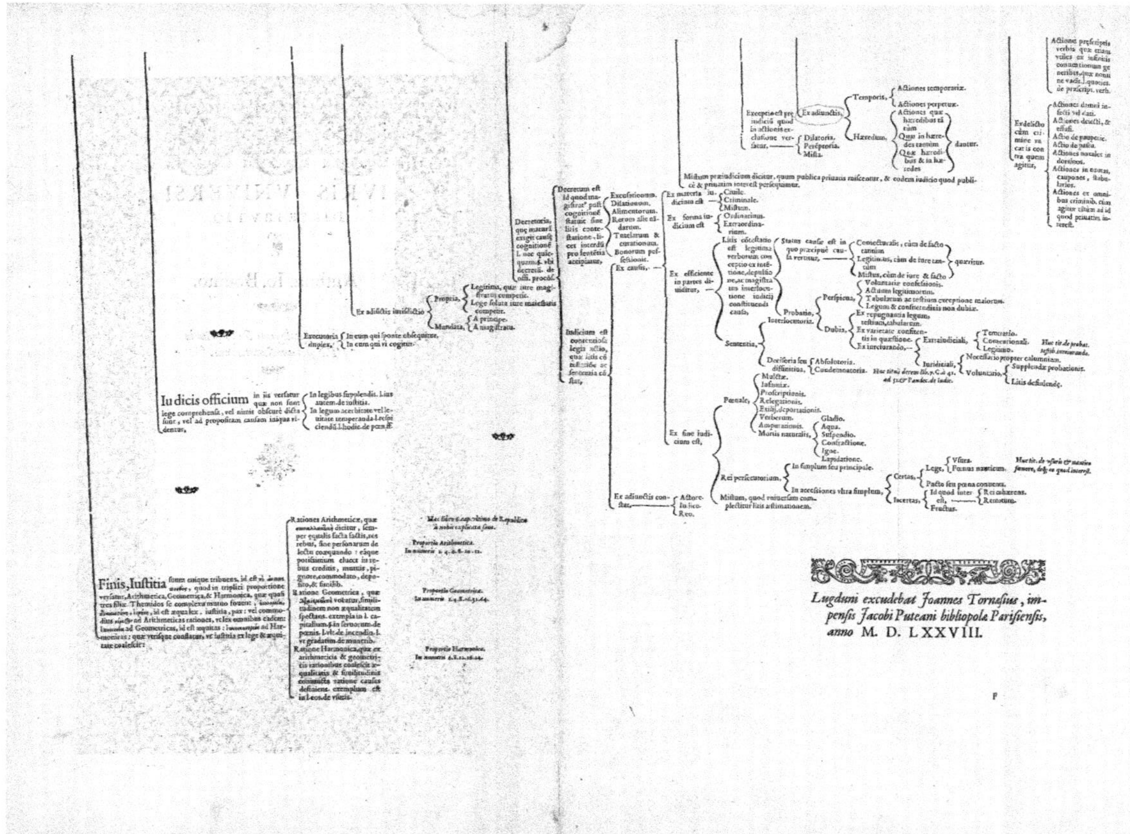

Figure F Folio F of Bodin's *Iuris Universi Distributio*

APPENDIX 3

A Division of Law as a Whole

By the author Jean Bodin to Jean Nicolai N.F.

Even though I willingly desire to satisfy those who complain that this division of legal art has been owed to them for far too long, I had nevertheless decided not to publish this thing (such as it is) which is sought from me, before I had included all the force of law and equity [*iuris et aequitatis vim*] traced back from the beginning, and those materials which are read scattered and piecemeal in an infinite multitude of books and forensic literature, as well as every one of the best laws [*leges*] of the illustrious nations who have distinguished themselves above all in the science of governing the state, collected into one body, so to speak, and compared amongst themselves according to some manner of art and discipline. But when I observed that you were pursuing the same art, I thought it belonged to my duty, in view of your kindness and the kindness of your most excellent father towards me,[1] to enkindle you more and more as you race to these studies with the most intense alacrity; and to set out, as a kind of *ground-plan* [ἰχνογραφίαν][2] of a future work, such a thing as architects have been in the habit of making to be inspected and modeled, so that one may clearly grasp whether the edifice under construction will be long-enduring and useful.

An arduous work indeed, and of infinite labour. In spite of this, I judge that the work may be concluded within fixed boundaries and with the greatest facility, if we hold fast to this design of exquisite order—namely, that, at the beginning, the definitions and divisions of each argument be proposed; then, brief and perspicuous statements be set out as rules in their proper place and order; and after that, in either margin, various laws [*leges*] of the nations and the most brilliant jurists' decisions [*iurisconsultorum decreta*] which have been approved by the authority of courts. Since the help of many is certainly essential for this task, I thought that either of these would be the case—namely, that erudite men, being prompted, would instruct me by some method about the laws of their own states [*suarum civitatum legibus*], or else they would be provoked sharply enough by these proddings to accomplish the work themselves, lest the masters of other arts, to the great shame of jurists, should boast overlong that this our law [*ius*] lies prostrate, comprehended by no art; and that those whose duty it was to hand on that art according to a system and method, practised the art of "civil law" [*iuris civilis artem*].

Nothing is more foreign to the dignity and excellence of the arts than this, since the arts and sciences concern universals, but civil law [*ius civile*] is specific to a single state [*proprium sit unius civitatis*]. With this in mind, it should not seem extraordinary to anyone if, in this *Division of Law as a Whole*, we have dissented from those who scattered hither and thither the uprooted and mutilated members of Roman law. For what Plato was accustomed to say—"nothing seemed to him more divine than to divide fittingly"—is pertinent here,[3]

[1] Jean Nicolai, the dedicatee of the *Distributio*, was appointed *conseiller* in the Parlement of Paris. His father, Antoine de Nicolai was the *premier président* of the Chambre des Comptes since 1553. Lloyd, *Jean Bodin*, 56–57.

[2] *ichnographian.*

[3] See Plato, *Phaedrus* 266 in Plato, *Euthyphro, Apology, Crito, Phaedo, Phaedrus*, trans. Harold North Fowler, Loeb Classical Library 36 (Cambridge: Harvard University Press, 1914), 535: "Now I myself,

inasmuch as in a right division, there is an unbroken and continuous sort of sequence of all the elements. Furthermore, the different elements, being linked one to another, and all fitted and composed among themselves, may be taken in at a single glance and exhibit the form of an entire body. It is prepared such that the last things respond to the first, the middle to either, and each to all, and anyone can readily recognize what is antecedent and what is consequent.

This is the very method common not only to the teaching of the arts, but also to all sciences. Now, whereas all disciplines are defined according to three classes in all, theoretical, practical, and productive [θεωρικοῦ, πρακτικοῦ, καὶ ποιητικοῦ],[4] and the first has regard to the sciences, the second to prudence in carrying out affairs, and the third to the crafts, what is indeed proper to the sciences and contemplation is derived entirely from nature or from divine principles.

But prudence, mistress of our actions, owes the first stages of her birth to nature, and the remainder to human institutions.[5] Law itself is of this kind [*in quo genere ius ipsum est*], one part of which nature claims, and the laws and customs of men [*hominum leges ac mores*] the other. For if it were true that law [*ius*], to the extent that it is of nature, does not also derive from mankind, i.e., that justice arises not from institution but rather from nature [τὸ δίκαιον οὐκ εἶναι θέσει, ἀλλὰ μὲν φύσει],[6] as the Stoics have it, then there would not be that which we call a "prudence" of law (jurisprudence), but, strictly speaking, a "science" of law. Nor could our consideration extend to distinguishing useful from useless, dishonourable from honourable, but only to the difference between true and false.[7] But the seeds of law and justice, planted in each of our souls by immortal God, are first awakened by reason. And, when reason has matured in us, and has attained its fulness [*perfectionem*], it gives birth to this legal wisdom [*iuris ... prudentiam*] which we seek, which by long usage and art is fitted into the following system.

Because it is necessary for the preservation of human society among men to render to each his due [*suum cuique tribuere*], which is the end [*finis*] of this discipline, we achieve it by means of actions of the law [*legis actionibus*] and the duty of the judge [*iudicis officio*], in which is implicated the efficient cause of law as a whole [*efficiens causa iuris universi*]. The actions of the law and the duty of the judge pertain to the execution of judicial decisions [*executionem rerum iudicatarum*]. Judicial decisions [*res iudicatae*] derive from sentences

Phaedrus, am a lover of these processes of division and bringing together, as aids to speech and thought; and if I think any other man is able to see things that can naturally be collected into one and divided into many, him I follow after and walk in his footsteps as if he were a god."; 571: "A man must know the truth about all the particular things of which he speaks or writes, and must be able to define everything separately; then when he has defined them, he must know how to divide them by classes until further division is impossible."

[4] *theōricou, praktikou, kai poiētikou.* See Aristotle, *Metaphysics* in *The Complete Works of Aristotle: The Revised Oxford Edition*, trans. W. D. Ross, ed. Jonathan Barnes (Princeton: Princeton University Press, 1984), 2:1619–20 [VI, 1, 1025^{b}25]: "Therefore, if all thought is either practical or productive or theoretical, natural science must be theoretical"; Aristotle, *Topics* in *Complete Works of Aristotle*, trans. W. A. Pickard-Cambridge, ed. Jonathan Barnes (Princeton: Princeton University Press, 1984), 1:244 [VI, 6, 145^{a}15–16]: "[Knowledge] is classed as speculative, practical, and productive; and each of these denotes a relation; for it speculates upon something, and produces something, and does something."

[5] This sentence is related to Aristotle's discussion of the intellectual virtues: *Nicomachean Ethics* 330–33 [VI, ii, §6-VI, iii, §2, 1139^{b}15–25]; 334–35 [VI, iv, §§1–5, 1140^{a}1–20]; 336–37 [VI, v, §1, 1140^{a}25–1140^{b}30]; 344–45 [VI, vii, §7, 1141^{b}15].

[6] *to dikaion ouk einai thesei, alla men phusei.* Alternatives for "institution": "art," "convention," "legislation," "ordinance." Compare Plato, *Laws*, 10: 889^δ–890^α.

[7] See Aristotle, *Nicomachean Ethics* 328–29 [VI, ii, §§2–3, 1139^{a}26–28].

[*sententiis*]; sentences from trials [*iudiciis*]; trials are taken up through joinder of issue [*litis contestatione*]; joinder of issue is carried out by means of pleading and reply [*intentione ac depulsione*], or what is the same thing, by action and exception [*actione et exceptione*].

Actions and exceptions have their grounds in obligations [*obligationibus*], discharges [*liberationibus*], acquisitions [*acquisitionibus*], alienations [*alienationibus*]. These, again, originate from agreements [*conventionibus*] and delicts [*delictis*]. Agreements and delicts derive from persons, things, and deeds [*personis, rebus, et factis*]. In these three is implicated the material cause [*materia*] of this discipline. Its formal cause [*forma*] consists in law [*in iure consistit*], which is the ultimate foundation of the discipline.

It is necessary to derive this discipline from these four causes, and to deduce from them the highest categories, and their contours, down to the lowest. But if there is anyone who demands a subtler method of exposition, he ought to consider that the sciences of eternal and unchangeable things need to be taught in one way, and the arts in another. And if anything has been overlooked by me in my division, you shall certainly amend it with ease as you come of age. For, as soon as I became acquainted with you in person, and afterwards also in writing, "one look, and I was mad [ὡς εἶδον, ὡς ἐμάνην],"[8] and I conceived such great hope about you that, because you are perfectly trained by nature and still more by learning in those virtues and disciplines which can exalt you to true glory, I do not doubt but that you can easily surpass your contemporaries in every kind of merit.

Jurisprudence

Jurisprudence is the art of rendering to each his due [*ars tribuendi suum cuique*],[9] for the preservation of human society [*hominum societatem*]. And as it is a faculty of mind, one finds it even among criminals, who prudently judge with what method they should establish their community [*civitas*], and what is necessary for each member to give and do for each. This can be referred to four causes or four questions:

Whether it exists [*An sit*]?
In what does it consist [*Quid sit*]?
In what way does it manifest itself [*Qualis sit*]?
Why does it exist [*Cur sit*]?

It Consists of Four Parts

Jurisprudence consists of four parts:
Legislation [*lex*]
Equity [*aequitas*]
Action of the law [*legis actio*]
Duty of the judge [*iudicis officium*]

[8] *hōs eidon, hōs emanēn*. See Theocritus, *Idylls*, trans. Anthony Verity (Oxford: Oxford University Press, 2002), 9: "One look, and I was mad; my helpless heart caught fire."
[9] D.1.1.1.pr, D.1.1.10.pr.

I. The Form [*Forma*] of Jurisprudence

The form [*forma*] which gives to this art its force and essence is none other than the law itself [*ius ipsum*], without which jurisprudence would be nothing.

To this pertain the titles "On justice" [*De iustitia*, D.1.1], *"On legislation"* [*De legibus*, D.1.3], *"On imperial decrees"* [*De constitutionibus*, D.1.4] *in the Digest, and the first three titles* [C.1.1–3] *and the title "On explaining the ancient law"* [*De veteri iur. enuclean.*, C.1.17] *in the Code.*

What Is Law [*ius*]

Law [*ius*] is a ray of divine benevolence and prudence granted to men, and applied by them for the advantage of human society [*ad utilitatem humanae societatis*].[10]

The Division of Law [*eius divisio*]

There are two kinds of law, natural law and human law.[11]

The well-known division of law [*pervulgata divisio iuris*] *distinguishes natural law* [*naturale*], *the law of nations* [*gentium*], *and civil law* [*civile*]. *But a* dichotomy [διχοτομεῖν][12] *is more convenient, and, as far as possible, one-to-one distinctions. Thus, Aristotle, in Book V of the Nicomachean Ethics,*[13] *and Plato, in Book II of the Laws,*[14] *divide* justice [τὸ δίκαιον] *into* "natural" [φυσικὸν] *and* "legal" [νομικὸν],[15] *which is the division Paul followed in l.penult.de iustitia.ff.* [D.1.1.11].

For Ulpian's division, which does not even agree with itself, let alone with Paul's division, hardly needs refutation, nor do the divisions of Demosthenes[16] *and Justinian,*[17] *who divide law into written and unwritten*[18] [*ius in scriptum et non scriptum distribuunt*]*—for they*

10 Cf. D.1.1.10.2.

11 This sentence is added in the second edition.

12 *dichotomein*, "to divide in two."

13 Aristotle, *Nicomachean Ethics* 294–97 [V, vii, §§1–5, 1134^{b}18–1135^{b}7].

14 I have not found the precise passage to which Bodin refers in Plato, *Laws*; but compare Plato, *Gorgias*, 488^{b}2–3, 488^{e}4.

15 *to dikaion* ("the just thing"); *physicon* ("that which pertains to nature"); *nomikon* ("that which pertains to law").

16 See possibly Demosthenes, oration 23 "Against Aristocrates," in *Demosthenes: Orations*, Vol. 3, *Orations 21–26*, trans. A. T. Murray, Loeb Classical Library 299 (Cambridge: Harvard University Press, 1935), 253–55: "Is it not monstrous, is it not manifestly contrary to law—I do not mean merely to the statute law but to the unwritten law of our common humanity—that I should not be permitted to defend myself against one who violently seizes my goods as though I were an enemy?"

17 D.1.1.1.2–4: Ulpian first divides public [*ius publicum*] from private law [*ius privatum*], then subdivides private law into natural law [*ius naturale*], law of nations [*ius gentium*], and civil law [*ius civile*]. In a famous passage at D.1.1.4, often referenced as *lex Manumissiones*, he contrasts, by way of example, human freedom as originating in natural law from slavery and manumission as deriving from the law of nations. He divides civil law into written and unwritten in D.1.1.6. At Inst.1.1.4, Justinian initially follows Ulpian's tripartite division. However, further on, at Inst.1.2.11, Justinian seems to follow Gaius by dividing law into natural law and civil law.

18 Inst.1.2.pr–2.

call written law "legislation" [legem] and unwritten "custom" [consuetudinem]. Although the laws [leges] of Lycurgus, whose example Justinian cites,[19] *were called* Rhetras[20] *because it was forbidden to write them, nevertheless they could not have been described as customs which grow from longstanding use [quae usu diuturno coalescunt], for in fact the* Rhetras *of Lycurgus, like all legislation [leges], took force at one and the same instant. But on the other hand, feudal rights [iura feudorum] and a great many customs and institutions [instituta] are indeed written down; nevertheless they exhibit no sanction [nullam tamen prae se ferunt sanctionem], which is necessary for legislation, since legislation is none other than the command or the sanction of sovereign authority [cum lex nihil aliud sit quam summae potestatis iussum sive sanctio]. For to command [iubere] is to forbid [sancire] and to approve [sciscere].*

And those who profess to teach the "art of civil law" [artem iuris civilis] are greatly in error, since the civil law [ius civile] is particular to a single state [unius civitatis proprium]. Art, however, belongs to universal things, not particulars. This is the reason why we should disregard the partition of civil law, treating it as a single indivisible thing [quasi unius individui], and we should apply the law of nations or the "common law" [ius gentium seu commune] to the art which we are seeking.

All peoples [omnes populi], indeed, or certainly a good part of them, have public law [ius publicum], private law [ius privatum], rulers' legislation [leges principum], magistrates' edicts [edicta magistratuum], rights of sovereignty [iura maiestatis], certain customs and institutions, and where the law [lex] or even custom is wanting, equity [aequitatem]; then also certain laws of penalty and reward [poenarum ac praemiorum iura], agreements, obligations, wills, trials, decrees, actions of law [legis actiones], and other things of the same sort[21] *by which human society is maintained among men; and these may be included in the art.*

Nor indeed was it fitting to separate the enactments of rulers [principum constitutiones] from the category of legislation [legis], any more than to call resolutions of the Senate [Senatusconsulta] by the name legislation [leges]. For even if the Roman Senate had in very distant times the power to make law [ius facere potuit], even so this law was not legislation [non tamen ius illud lex erat]; just as the edicts [edicta], i.e. those things which are called commands of magistrates [magistratuum iussa] by Varro,[22] *are not legislation [non ... leges sunt], and are improperly attributed to the emperor [improprie principi tribuuntur]. For in every state [Republica] the Senate is accustomed to make resolutions [Senatus decernere ... solet], but the ruler to command [princeps vero iubere]. Thus Livy often says, "the Senate decided and the people commanded [senatus decrevit, populus iussit],"*[23] *and Dionysius of Halicarnassus*[24] *says in books 2 and 7 that in the old days the resolutions of the Senate had no force [nulla ... vis] without the command of the people*

[19] Inst.1.2.10.

[20] *Rhetra* was the Spartan word for law; see Plutarch, *Lycurgus*; Alberto Maffi and Joe Jackson, "Sparta," in Stanley Katz, ed., *Oxford International Encyclopedia of Legal History* (Oxford: Oxford University Press, 2009).

[21] The Latin reads *id genus* instead of *eius generis*, a common usage in humanistic Latin; see Tunberg, "Humanistic Latin," 131.

[22] I have not identified this reference to Varro. However, compare Bodin, *De Republica*, 151 [I, 10]: *verbis igitur abutuntur, qui edicta, quae propria sunt magistratuum, leges appellant.*

[23] There are many examples throughout Livy; for instance, Livy, *History of Rome, Books VIII–X*, ed. Benjamin Foster, Loeb Classical Library 191 (Cambridge, MA: Harvard University Press, 1926), 4:401 [X, 12, 3]: "When these things were known at Rome, the senate advised and the people voted a declaration of war against the Samnites."

[24] Dionysius of Halicarnassus, *Roman Antiquities* II, 14; VII, 18; and especially VII, 38.

[populi iussu]. Again, neither plebiscites [plebiscita] nor the replies of jurists [prudentum responsa] which have the force of law [quae vim legis habent] should be excluded from the category of legislation, any more than certain opinions [sententiae] of Bartolus or Baldus, which by order of the emperors have turned into laws [quae principum iussu leges evaserunt], should be called "responses" [responsa]. For when first Hadrian and thereafter Justinian commanded that the recorded responses of jurists should have the force of laws [pro legibus valere iusserunt], they ceased to be responses [responsa esse desierunt]. And when responses or judicial decisions [res iudicatae] pass into custom, they lose their old names. The same principle applies to edicts—which formerly were nothing other than orders of magistrates [magistratuum iussa] and to which Hadrian, at the proposal of Julian, imputed the force of legislation [vim legum attribuit]. Even so they did not cease to be called edicts, l.unic. de veteri iure enucleando. C. [C.1.17.1].

Natural law [*naturale*], because it is innate in each from the beginning of its kind, is therefore always equitable and good [*aequum bonum*], *l.penul.de iustit.ff.* [D.1.1.11], as in worship for God, piety for one's relatives, gratitude for the deserving, vengeance for criminals, justice for all.

Some attribute the procreation of children to the natural law. But this does not pertain to law [ius] any more than the appetite for food or sex, which is equally common to beasts and men. But there can be no society of law [iuris societas] among men and beasts. Because they are not capable of participating in crimes, so neither can they participate in any law. l.1.Si quadrupes.ff [D.9.1.1.3].[25] *Whoever unites man with beast in a society of law by reason of procreation of children, not only seems to undermine the splendor of matrimony, but even to approve impure kinds of copulation. This is the dictum that finds Ulpian's good favor. To this pertain the titles 4, 8, 9, 10, 11, and 12 of the Code and the title "On the recognition of freeborn children"* [*De liberis agnoscendis*, D.25.3].

Human law [*humanum ius*] is what is decreed by men beyond natural law for their advantage, *l.penul.de iustitia* [D.1.1.11]

The Division of Human Law

Furthermore, human law is divided into the law of nations [*ius gentium*] and civil law [*ius civile*].

Law of nations

Law of nations [*ius gentium*] is what all peoples [*omnes populi*], or a good part of them, have unanimously approved. It is of two kinds, the antecedent and the consequent.

Antecedent law of nations: The antecedent law of nations is subdivided into public law and private law.

Public law [*ius publicum*] is what aims at public advantage [*publicam utilitatem*]. Things of this kind are upholding sacred things [*sacra tueri*], enacting legislation [*leges iubere*], creating magistrates [*magistratus creare*], taking advice concerning matters of state [*consilium de republica capere*], declaring and ending war [*bellum indicere ac finire*], establishing punishments and rewards [*poenas ac praemia irrogare*], executing actions of law [*legis actiones exequi*].

[25] D.9.1.1.3.

Private law [*ius privatum*] is that law which considers interests other than public. It pertains to towns [*municipia*], private associations [*collegia*], and families [*familias*], such as matters involving husband and wife, parents and children, masters and slaves, and individuals [*singulos*].

Consequent law of nations: The consequent law of nations [*consequens ius*] is called either sanction [*sanctio*], or law without sanction [*ius sine sanctione*].

Sanction [*sanctio*] or the command of the prince [*iussum principis*] or of the sovereign authority in a state [*summae in republica potestatis*] is called legislation [*lex*]. Legislation is either general [*universalis*]—commanding, prohibiting, or permitting something [*iubens aliquid, vetans, aut permittens*]—or particular [*singularis*], which is divided in turn into benefit beyond legislation [*beneficium praeter legem*] and privilege contrary to legislation [*privilegium contra legem*].[26] This, in turn, is either real, personal, or mixed.

To this pertain the titles in the Digest, "On public employments" [*De muner.*, D.50.4] *and the following titles, "On exemption from public employments"* [*De vacat. munerum*, D.50.5], *"On fiscal privileges"* [*De privilegiis fisci*, C.7.73], *"On veterans"* [*De vetanorum*, D.38.12, D.49.18, C.12.46], *"On whether a creditor ought not to evict a pledge"* [*De creditorum*, C.8.45].

The sanction or command of a magistrate is either an edict [*edictum*] or an interdict [*interdictum*].[27]

Law without sanction is likewise of two kinds, equity and custom.

Equity [*aequitas*] is law [*ius*] entrusted to the judgment of the one deciding [*arbitrio statuentis permissum*], whether of the sovereign when he emends legislation or releases subjects from legislation [*legibus solventis*], or of the magistrate when he supplements or moderates legislation [*leges supplet... moderatur*].[28]

Custom [*consuetudo*] is law [*ius*] which has become established by use. It is either universal, which the greater part of the citizens have recognized [*maior pars civium comprobavit*], or particular, which belongs to one town, private association, or family.

To this pertain the titles "On *municipes* and foreign residents" [*l.municipalem*, D.50.1], "On statutes, *senatus consulta*, and long-established custom" [*De consuetudine*, D.1.3], *"On*

[26] The manifold functions of legislation—commanding, prohibiting, permitting—originate in Modestinus, D.1.3.7: *Legis virtus haec est imperare, vetare, permittere, punire.* Cf. Brian Tierney, *Liberty and Law: The Idea of Permissive Natural Law, 1100–1800* (Washington, DC: The Catholic University of America Press, 2014). The distinction of privileges, *praeter legem* or *contra legem*, appears also in the *Methodus* 263 [VI], where Bodin discusses the authority of judges who may be empowered to decide sometimes *praeter legem* or even *contra legem* in creating exceptions in specific cases for reasons of equity. The terms originate in nominalist literature. Lee, *Right of Sovereignty*, 93–94.

[27] Cf. *De Republica* 150–51 [I, 10]. In Roman law, these are the principal sources of praetorian legislation, or *ius honorarium*, referenced at D.1.1.7.1, such as the possessory interdicts and the edicts that introduced new equitable remedies that would later be collected in the *Edicta Perpetua*.

[28] Cf. *De Republica* 155 [I, 10] and D.1.1.7.1, which describes the function of the praetor to "supplement or correct the civil law" [*supplendi vel corrigenda iuris civilis*] for public advantage. On the significance of the sovereign's "absolute power" to release subjects from legislation and the principle of *legibus solutus* in D.1.3.31, see Lee, *Right of Sovereignty*, 159–63.

the administration of property belonging to cities" [*De administratione rerum ad civitatem pertinentium*, D.50.8], *"On decurions"* [*De decurionibus*, D.50.2, C.10.31], *et cetera.*

Civil law

Civil law [*ius civile*], which is specific to one state or another, does not belong to this science.

II. The Matter [*Materia*] of Jurisprudence

The Matter of Jurisprudence

The[29] matter around which every question of law [*iure*] revolves consists in persons [*in personis*], or in things [*in rebus*], or in the deeds and words of persons [*in factis ac dictis personarum*].[30]

Persons and their division

Persons are divided in three ways—by sex, by status, and by dignity.

To this pertain the titles "On the law of persons" [*De iure personarum*, Inst.1.3], *"On the status of men"* [*De statu hominum*, D.1.5], *"On magistrates and officials" in Book 1 of the Digest* [*De magistratibus & officialib. lib. 1 ff.*],[31] *and Book 1 and Book 12 of the Code, and the titles "On the suit for freedom"* [*De liberali causa*, D.40.12, C.7.16], *"On manumissions"* [*De manumissionibus*, D.40.1], *"On statuliberi"* [*De statuliberis*, D.40.7].

According to **sex** [*ex sexu*], a person is called either a man, woman, or hermaphrodite.

According to **status** [*ex statu*], one is either a slave or free. A slave, in turn, is either born [*natus*] a slave, or is made [*factus*] a slave by being sold or captured [*aut venditione, aut captivitate*].[32] A free person is either born free [*ingenuus*], or manumitted [*manumissus*]. A freeborn man is either the head of a family [*paterfamilias*], or a son under the power [*filiusfamilias*]. A son, again, is only a legal son [*legitimus*], either by adoption or adrogation, or only a natural son; or he may be both a legal and natural son, born from a lawful marriage [ex *iustis nuptiis*]. From this one contracts consanguinity, consisting of agnatic and cognatic relationships, which each flow from ascendants, from descendants, and from collateral relatives (such as brother, sister, nephew uncle, cousin), and also affinity, from which come fathers-in-law, sons-in-law, brothers-in-law, and stepsons.

According to dignity [*ex dignitate*], persons are called either public or private.

[29] The 1580 edition (Köln) of the *Distributio* has a marginal heading beside this paragraph which says *materia iuris* ("the matter of law") rather than *materia iurisprudentiae* ("the matter of jurisprudence"). This heading is an error. As Bodin made clear in the dedication, the structure of the *Distributio* is based on the four causes of jurisprudence, not of law. Moreover, in the tabular layout of the 1578 edition it is clearly jurisprudence, not law, that is divided into four causes. The same error appears in the marginal headings beside "The Efficient Cause of Jurisprudence" and "The Final Cause of Jurisprudence."

[30] Cf. D.1.5.1.

[31] This is not a title in the *Digest*. Bodin is likely referring to the titles in Book I of the *Digest* on the *officia*, or "duties," of senior magistrates, such as the consuls (D.1.10, *De officio consulis*), the praetorian prefects (D.1.11, *De officio praefecti praetorio*), the quaestors (D.1.13, *De officio quaestoris*), and the proconsuls (D.1.16, *De officio proconsulis et legati*).

[32] Cf. Inst.1.3.4.

Public persons [*publicae*] are those who are in charge of a public duty [*publico muneri praesunt*]. Those with authority [*cum imperio*] either have ordinary authority [*ordinario*], such as the sovereign and greater and lesser magistrates, or extraordinary [*extraordinario*], for an uncertain time [*ad incertum tempus*].[33] Those without authority [*sine imperio*] include pontiffs and delegates of magistrates [*ministri magistratuum*], such as clerks, notaries, lictors [*apparitores*], recordkeepers, military attendants [*cohortales*], magisterial attendants [*lictores*], heralds, or minor attendants [*accensi*].[34]

Private persons [*privatae personae*] are considered in two ways—either according to class [*ex ordine*], such as foreigners [*peregrini*] or citizens [*cives*], of whom some are noble [*nobiles*], others are plebeian [*plebeii*]; or according to occupation [*ex instituto vitae*], such as theologians, jurists, physicians, orators, soldiers, peasants, merchants, workmen, laborers, and scholars. These last are subdivided into philosophers, mathematicians, rhetors, historians, poets, and grammarians.

To this pertain the titles "On various examinations" [De variis cognition., D.50.13], *"On military law" [De re militari,* D.49.16 & C.12.36], *et cetera. Also the title "On teachers and physicians" [De professorib. et medicis,* C.10.53(52)], *et cetera.*

The order of citizens [civium ordo] is particular to each state [civitatis proprius est], and does not pertain to our discipline. The ancient Gauls divided the people into druids [druidas], knights [equites], and farmers [agricolas], as Caesar writes;[35] the Egyptians, as Diodorus relates, into priests [sacerdotes], workmen [opifices], and shepherds [pastores];[36] the Romans into patricians [patricios], equestrians [equites], and plebeians [plebeios]. The later Greeks[37] [Graeci posteriores] established six classes: patricians [patritios], illustrious [illustres], magnificents or respectables [speciosos seu spectabiles], augusts [augustales], most distinguisheds [clarissimos], and most perfects [perfectissimos]. The Venetians divided patricians [patricios] from citizens [citadinis] and plebeians [plebeiis]. The ancient Florentines separated the greats [grandes] from the people [popularibus] and the plebs [plebe], and arranged three classes of the people, the more powerful [potentiores], the ordinary [mediocres], and the lowest [infimos]. As for ourselves, we distinguish three orders [tres ordines] in all: clergy [ecclesiasticos], nobles [nobiles], and commoners [plebeios], although nobles are divided from commoners everywhere.[38]

[33] Cf. *De Republica* 259 [III, 2]. In *De Republica*, Bodin distinguishes between officers of state whose duty is established and defined by law [*lege*] and commissioners whose extraordinary charge is dependent on the goodwill [*arbitrio*] and pleasure of the sovereign. At *De Republica* III, 3, Bodin explains that all magistrates are officers, although not all officers are magistrates. The difference rests on whether or not they hold *imperium*. Bodin uses the phrase *ad breve tempus* at *De Republica* 79 [I, 8].

[34] Cf. *De Republica* 284 [III, 3]; 303 [III, 5]: *munera quaedam publica sine Imperio.*

[35] Caesar, *Gallic Wars* VI, 13.

[36] Diodorus, *Library of History*, 1.28; but the division of Diodorus is into priests, workmen, and soldiers. Cf. *Methodus* 6, where he has not *pastores* "shepherds" but *milites* "soldiers."

[37] I.e., those of the Byzantine Empire.

[38] Compare Bodin, *Methodus*, 244: *Neque solum in Republica Rom. sed ubique discrimen illud civium reperiemus. Romae quidem in iisdem moenibus fuerunt patricii, equites, plebei. apud veteres Aegyptios sacerdotes, milites, opifices, ut scribit Diodorus: apud maiores nostros, Druidae, equites, agricolae: nunc sacerdotes, nobiles, plebei. apud Venetos nobiles, citadini plebei. apud Florentinos olim grandes, populares, plebei. et popularium tres ordines; potentiores, mediocres, infimi. Plato quoque.*

Things and their division

Things [*res*], as the matter around which law [*ius*] revolves, are divided into two, according to subjects [*ex subiectis*] and adjuncts [*ex adiunctis*].[39]

> *To this pertain the titles "On the division of things"* [*De rerum divisione*, Inst.2.1, D.1.8], "On servitudes" [*De servitutibus*, Inst.2.3, D.8.1, D.8.2, D.8.3] and "On the law of fiefs" [*De iure feudorum*].

According to subjects [*ex subiectis*], some things are corporeal [*corporeae*], some incorporeal [*incorporeae*].

> **Corporeal things** [*corporeae*] are either immovables [*immobiles*], such as land [*praedia*] and things attached to land, or movables [*mobiles*]. The latter, again, are either simple, made up of homogeneous things, such as water and wine, or mixed things, of which some are made of components united by nature, others of components conjoined by art, others made of separate components with parts collectively forming one body, such as a herd [*grex*] or a people [*populus*]. *l.rerummistura.De usucap.ff.* [D.41.3.30].
>
> **Incorporeal things** [*incorporeae*] are reckoned first movables, then immovables. *DD. in l.si constante.soluto matrimonio.* [the doctors on D.24.3.24]. These include *bona, peculium, haereditas, nomina, servitus.*
>
> **Servitudes** are of three kinds [*triplex*]—personal, such as the right of use [*usus*], usufruct [*usufructus*], habitation [*habitatio*]; real, either urban or rustic; or mixed, such as services [*operae*], homage for a fief [*homagium pro feudo*], which is either liege [*ligium*] or not, and revenues [*reditus*].
>
> **Revenues** are divided in three ways.
>
> In revenues divided **according to the nature of the property** [*ex rei natura*], some are related to properties [*praediatorii*] or land [*fundiarii*], others are charges [*impositiii*], which again are either fixed in money [*pecunia constituti*] or without money, such as in a gift [*donatione*], legacy [*legato*], division of common property [*divisione*], compensation [*compensatione*], or negotiated settlement [*transactione*].
>
> In revenues divided **according to how proceeds are taken** [*fruendi modo*], either the creditor takes the proceeds directly, which is called "antichresis" or, in French, *rente en assiette*, or through the hand of a debtor [*per manum debitoris*].
>
> In revenues divided **according to time** [*ex tempore*], some are called perpetual, others temporary, such as for the duration of a will [*testamento*], legislation [*lege*], custom [*more*], pact [*pacto*], or circumstance [*casu*].

According to adjuncts [*ex adiunctis*], some things are public [*publicae*], and these can be public for citizens only, or for citizens and foreigners alike. Other things are private [*privatae*], belonging to towns [*municipii*], private associations [*collegii*], or individuals

39 "Thing" is the standard translation for the Latin *res*. It carries a special meaning in Roman law, indicating an asset, anything of value that could potentially by the object of a legal dispute. This included all those things that one owns (property) as well as all those things that one owes another (obligations).

[*singulorum*]. Still others belong to no one [*nullius*] such as things sacred [*sacrae*], sanctified [*sanctae*], religious, or vacant.

Deeds

Deeds [*facta*] encompass the words, writings, achievements, and actions of persons—for all these are contained by the word "doing" [*faciendi*]. *l.verbum facere. l.faciendi verbo. De verborum significatione* [D.50.16.175; D.50.16.218]. But it is understood that it includes only those deeds which are associated with law or injury [*iuris aut iniuriae communionem habet*]. Gaius and Justinian had divided all matter of law into things, persons, and actions [*in res, personas, et actiones*]. But both of them exploited [*usurpavit*] the word "action" [*actionis verbum*] to mean "forensic action" [*pro forensic actione*], against which Connan argued. And by this division, they overlook agreements [*conventiones*], wills [*testamenta*], delicts [*delicta*], obligations [*obligationes*], discharges [*liberationes*], acquisitions [*acquisitiones*], alienations [*alienationes*], from which forensic actions, or the consequential effects of acts, arise.

Some deeds are bare deeds [*partim nuda*], and some are conjoined with law [*partim cum iure coniuncta*].

Bare deeds [*nuda*], from which questions of law arise, revolve either around agreement [*conventionem*] or delict [*delictum*].

An **agreement** [*conventio*] is the consensus of several people into one engagement to give or to do something [*plurium in idem consensus dandi aut faciendi causa*]. It differs from an obligation, because that consists in what has been done or not done [*factum vel non factum*]. But an agreement really consists in what ought to be given or done [*quod dari fieri debeat*]. *l.qui liberos. de rit. nupt.* [D.23.2.19] *l.in fraudem. quae in fraud. creditorum.* [D.42.8.4] *l.1. de pactis. ff.* [D.2.14.1]. But Bartolus, Alexander [Tartagnus Imolensis], and Ludovicus Romanus [Pontanus] dispute in vain, at *l.1.de verborum obligatione* [D.45.1.1], whether a *stipulatio* belongs to law or fact [*iuris vel facti*], since it is evident that it is implicated in fact, and law arises from it [*ex ea ius oriri*].

Some agreements are concluded by bare consent [*nudo consensu*], some by verbal obligation [*stipulatione*], and others by a contract involving bilateral obligation [*contractu cui synallagma inest*].

> An **agreement by bare consent** can be either a pollicitation [*pollicitatio*], which is a promise made by a single person [*unius promissum*], or a pact [*pactum*], which is consent among several people and which can be divided in three ways—according to subjects [*ex subiectis*], such as *in rem, in personam*, or mixed; according to form [*ex forma*], whether tacit or express; and according to end [*ex fine*], in which one is obligatory [*obligatorium*], which is added in the contract itself, and the other is liberatory [*liberatorium*], which subtracts a contracted obligation outside a contract.
>
> *To this pertain the titles "On pacts"* [*De pactis*, D.2.14] *and "On pollicitations"* [*De pollicitationib.*, D.50.12].
>
> An **agreement concluded by verbal obligation** [*stipulatione*] is executed by legal words [*verbis legitimis*] in addition to consent. This may be divided in two ways. According to subjects [*ex subiectis*], a verbal obligation is certain or uncertain. According to adjuncts [*ex adiunctis*], one concerns time [*temporum stipulatio*] and is concluded either pure, or limited to a fixed date [*in diem*] or condition or extent [*sub conditione aut modo*]. The other concerns things [*rerum*] and is either divisible or indivisible.
>
> An **agreement concluded by contract involving bilateral obligation** [*contractu facta cui synallagma inest*] is completed by a thing being done or given [*ex facto vel datione*].

l.Labeo.de verborum significatione [D.50.16.19]. Accursius and Cinus da Pistoia on *l.1.de periculo et commodo rei venditae* [D.18.6.1]. Baldus de Ubaldis on *l.ab emptione. de pactis.ff.* [2.14.58]. It comprehends transaction [*negotium*] and loan [*creditum*].

"**Transaction**" [*negotium*], as the word is commonly received, embraces those things which are done in return for payment [*mercede*] and those which are gratuitous [*gratuito*]. *l.1. & toto tit.de negot. gest. l.1.de aestimatoria actione.ff* [D.3.5.1–48(49); C.2.18(19).1–24; D.19.3.1]. And this category of *negotium* is divided into onerous [*mercenarium*], gratuitous [*gratuitum*], and mixed [*mistum*].

Onerous transactions [*mercenarium*], which have their cause in giving or doing something [*dandi ac faciendi causam habet*], are examined according to nominate and innominate contracts.[40]

"I give so that you give" [*Do ut des*]. This includes barter, the exchange of a thing for another thing [*rei pro re permutatio*];[41] the contract of sale [*emptio venditio*], the exchange of something for money and vice-versa [*rem pro pecunia contrave*]; money-exchange and the earnings of money [*pecuniam pro pecunia & fructu pecuniae*], whether in the form of interest [*foenus*] or a fixed income [*reditus constitutus*]; and a mixed transaction, when something[42] is exchanged, partly for another thing, and partly sold for money [*partim res permutatur: partim venditur*]. If it is arranged that ownership is transferred [*dominium transferri*], so that the thing becomes the property of the recipient, this is the unique contract included in this genus. *l.ult. de condict. caus. dati.* [D.12.4.16], *l.ubi, in fine de verb. oblig.* [D.41.1.75]. Granted, this is sometimes called a sale. *l.si convenerit. de contrahen. empt.*[43] But this is wrong.

"I give so that you do, or do not do" [*Do ut facias, aut ne facias*], such as in the contract of hire [*locatio conductio*], whether temporary or perpetual.

"I do so that you do, or do not do" [*Facio ut facias, aut ne facias*]. Infinite agreements proceed from this, which are unnamed, such as the rest that follow. And the word "doing" [*faciendi verbo*] also includes "not doing" [*non faciendi*], "not transferring" [*non tradendi*], "not selling" [*non alienandi*], "permitting" [*permittendi*], "not permitting" [*non permittendi*]. *l.qui non facit. de regul. iur.* [D.50.17.121], *l.ubi autem.§. qui id quod. de verborum obligat.ff.* [D.45.1.75.7].

"I do so that you give," or vice-versa [*facio ut des, contrave*], that is, so that you do not give to someone or other [*ne des huic vel illi*].

"I give and do so that you give," or vice-versa [*Do ac facio ut des, contrave*].

"I give so that you give and do," or vice-versa [*Do ut des ac facias, contrave*].

"I do so that you give and do," or vice-versa [*Facio ut des ac facias, contrave*].

"I give and do, so that you give and do," or vice-versa [*Do ac facio, ut des ac facias, contrave*], from which flow contracts of partnership [*societas*], whether universal or particular, betrothals [*sponsalia*], and contract of marriage [*nuptiarum contractus*], which is an agreement of husband and wife for the mutual union of life [*viri & uxoris conventio ad mutuam vitae coniunctionem*]. The nuptial contract is based on mutual

40 Cf. Grotius, *De Jure Belli ac Pacis* 229 [II, 12, §3]: *Jus naturae ignorat haec discrimina.*

41 The 1578 edition says *rei pro re permutatio*, while the 1580 edition says *rem pro re, et est permutatio*, in parallel with the rest of the paragraph.

42 The 1578 and 1580 editions both say *pecuniam* "money," which should be read as *rem* "something."

43 This citation does not seem to be correct. The title *De contrahenda emptione et de pactis inter emptorem et venditorem compositis* [D.18.1] does not have a *lex* beginning with the incipit, *Si convenerit.*

duties as well as mutual gifts, which arise either from law [*ex lege*], such as dowry [*dos*] and marriage gift [*donatio propter nuptias*], or else from pact [*ex pacto*].[44]

A **gratuitous transaction** [*gratuitum negotium*], which is less properly called a *negotium*, consists in the following. *l.Aristo. de donationib.ff.* [D.39.5.18].

In doing only [*faciendo tantum*], and that either at the bidding of another, such as in a surety [*fideiussio*], novation [*expromissio*] or a mandate [*mandatum*]; or without his bidding, such as in[45] the unauthorized management of someone else's affairs [*negotiorum gestio*].[46]

In a mixed giving-and-doing [*dando & faciendo mistum*]. *l.qui saxum.* [D.39.5.6], *l.qui in aedibus. de donationib.* [D.39.5.9]. These can be found in the supervision of a spendthrift [*curatio prodigi*], a madman [*furiosi*], a minor [*minoris*], or exposed goods [*bonorum vacatium*]; general agency [*procuratio*]; and guardianship [*tutela*], whether testamentary [*testamentaria*], appointed [*dativa*], or statutory [*legitima*], by a parent, an agnate, a patron, or fiduciary.

In giving only [*in dando tantum*], as in pure gift [*donatio pura*], or conditional gift [*conditionalis*], which be made either in anticipation of death [*mortis intuitu*], or whatever other condition, as long as it is not purely established in order to constrain the will of the beneficiary [*donatarii*] supposing the occurrence of a future event.[47]

A transaction is called **mixed** [*mistum*], when a thing is partly given gratuitously [*partim donator gratuito*], and partly in order to create an obligation [*partim obligando*], such as in wills or codicils. *l.sed et cum, de nego.* [D.3.5.15], *l.transactione. de transact. C.* [most likely C.2.4.35].

The mixed kinds of giving and doing [*mista dandi ac faciendi genera*] *shed much light for the clear understanding of agreements. Callistratus indeed teaches that this is necessary. l.Aristo.de donation.* [D.39.5.18, not from Callistratus but a fragment from Ulpian citing Aristo], *l.cum servus. de condit. & demonstr.* [D.35.1.82], *l.quamvis. eod.* [D.35.1.32], *l.veteris. de contrahend. stip. C.* [C.8.37(38).13]. *The negative, of not giving or doing, appeared necessary to Paul. l.in facto. de condit. & demonstr.* [D.35.1.60] *granted that he who does not do what he ought to have done seems to act against those things which he does not do. l.qui non facit.de regul.iur.* [D.50.17.121]. *Whence the opinion of Zasius and Bezutius*[48] *in l.2.de verb.oblig.* [Ulrich Zasius and Bezutius on D.45.1.2] *is refuted, who reject the mixed category of giving and doing and vice-versa, against the clear words of the law* [*contra perspicua verba legis*] *l.sed & cum de negot. gestis.* [D.3.5.15], *l.cum servus. de condition. & demonstra. ut rationes reddere &c.* [D.35.1.82, beginning with the words *ut rationes reddere*].[49] *Moreover, the mixed categories are not contained in the simple ones. l.vim passam. §.praescriptione. de adult.* [D.48.5.40(39).5], *Alexand.*

[44] Cf. *De Republica* 82 [I, 8], where Bodin uses the law of gifts to explain the irreversible nature of the *lex regia* transaction whereby sovereignty is transferred permanently from people to prince.

[45] The 1580 edition says *vel sine iussu vel negotiorum gestio*, while the 1578 edition says *sine iussu, negotiorum gestio*.

[46] *Negotiorum gestio* is one example of the anomalous category in Roman law designated by Justinian as "quasi-contract," so called because they approximate a recognized contractual obligation, like the contract of mandate, though lacking in one key element. Quasi-contracts are actionable through a *condictio*, although it is debatable whether they should count as a true contract. Bodin avoids this debate entirely, choosing to classify them as a species of a gratuitous contractual engagement.

[47] Berger, *Encyclopedic Dictionary of Roman Law*, s.v. "donatio sub modo."

[48] Ulrich Zasius (1461–1535) and one "Bezutius" or "Bozutius" whom I have not identified.

[49] Bodin refers to the words cited repeatedly in this fragment, *si rationes reddiderit* "if he render accounts").

Consil.116. num.9. lib.2. [Alexander Tartagnus de Imola, book 2, *Consilium* 116, §9], *Alberic. parte prima statut. quaest.90.* [Alberic on the first part of the *Statutes*, question 90], *l.hoc legatum.* [D.32.1.45(43)], *l.pediculis. §.quidam. de auro & argento* [D.34.2.32.3].[50] *Let us also be warned, that the word "giving" [dandi verbum] equally well signifies a deed [factum], as for example a transfer [traditionem]. l.1.* [D.19.1.1], *l.ex empto. de actio. empt.* [D.19.1.11], *l.naturalis. §.&cum do. de praescript.verb* [D.19.5.5.2].[51] *But the two terms have been distinguished for the sake of discipline. To this pertain Books 18, 19, 20, 21, and 22 of the Digest with the first 28 titles of Book 4 and the first 45 titles of Book 8 of the Code.*

Loan [*creditum*], which we have said is the second half of this kind of agreement, has a great many species.

Mutuum is a loan for consumption [*creditum abutendi causa*], requiring that its equivalent be paid back at a set time [*certo tempore simile reddatur*].

Commodatum is a loan for use for a fixed time [*creditum ad tempus*], requiring that the borrowed thing be returned.[52]

Precarium is a precarious grant for use by the permissive will of the owner [*domini arbitrio*].[53]

Depositum is a loan for safekeeping [*creditum custodiae causa*], requiring that the thing itself be returned.[54]

Pignus is a loan contracted in view of another obligation.

Indebitum is a loan contracted conditionally or by mistake.[55]

Res aestimata credita[56] is a loan requiring that the thing itself or its appraised value be paid back.

There are many other species of loan, such as when money is initially deposited with a clause that its equivalent should be paid back; it then ceases to be a contract of *depositum. l.Lucius. depositi.ff.* [D.16.3.24]. Or, when a seller accepts delayed payment of the price, which is said to be done "on credit" [*in creditum*]. *l.si procuratoris. §.plane ubi. de tributo. actio. ff* [D.14.4.5.17].[57] If a *mutuum*, a *commodatum*, or a *depositum*

[50] Alberic is probably Albericus de Rosate (d.1360) or Albericus de Maletis (fl. 1431–33).

[51] The incipit of D.19.5.5.2 is not *et cum do*, but *at cum do*.

[52] Bodin uses the contract of *commodatum* to explain the legal obligation of officeholders to "return" the powers of office to the sovereign at the expiry of their term in office, just like a lessee. *De Republica* 263 [III, 2]. Cf. Lee, *Popular Sovereignty*, 208–15.

[53] *Arbitrio*, literally "at the judgement of the owner." *Precarium* lasts as long as the grantor permits. Bodin uses the *precarium* to explain the "precarious" legal position of commissioners in despotic or "seigneurial" regimes. Lacking any legal right of office, commissioners serve entirely at the arbitrary goodwill and pleasure of the sovereign. *De Republica* 263 [III, 2]. A recurring observation in Bodin's discussion of the French legal system in the sixteenth century is the sudden transformation of judicial appointments into "commissions," so that judges, once enjoying judicial independence in their tenure of office (since Louis XI, according to Bodin), now became mere "precarious" servants dependent on the goodwill and pleasure of the prince. Lee, *Right of Sovereignty*, 128, n.60.

[54] Cf. *De Republica* 81 [I, 8], 304 [III, 5].

[55] The *indebitum* was a quasi-contract, approximating the *mutuum*. It arises when one party pays another party in error, mistakenly believing there is an outstanding debt, when, in reality, no payment is due. The recipient of the mistaken payment, who is unjustly enriched, is legally obliged to return the payment. The obligation is actionable by the *condictio indebiti*.

[56] Could be translated, "loan of an appraised thing."

[57] The incipit is *procuratoris*, not *si procuratoris*. However, the text does not answer to Bodin's point.

is done for remuneration, they lose their specific name. Nevertheless, these are less properly described by the word "lease" [*locationis*], than they are by the word "credit" [*crediti verbo*].

To this pertain the titles "On things lent" [*De rebus creditis*, C.4.1; D.12.1] *and the ones that follow.*

This division of agreements [*divisio conventionum*] *facilitates the easy comprehension of our discipline. And although some make the division differently, none seemed to me more apt in the extreme confusion of the material. For an agreement is concluded either by bare consent* [*nudo consensu*], *executed also by legal words* [*verbis legitimis*] *in addition to consent, or in addition to these two, it contains a bilateral obligation* [*synallagma*].

The first category pertains to pollicitations and pacts [*ad pollicitationes, aut pacta*]*; the second to verbal obligations* [*ad stipulationes*]*; and the third to contracts. Now all contracts pertain to transactions* [*negotia*] *and loans* [*credita*]. *The rest is easy.*

But this has the obscurity that wills are positioned among contracts, whereas Labeo said that they do not pertain to contracts at all. l.Labeo. de verb. sign. ff. [D.50.16.19]. *This is, to tell the truth, a subtlety rather than answering what is required. For since there are two overall species of contracts, transaction* [*negotium*] *and loan* [*creditum*], *it must necessarily be counted in the first* [*alterutro*][58] *category, because what the testator bequeathed cannot be considered a loan. And yet, he is said to make a contract with the heir. §.sed neque, de haeredibus instituend. lib. 1. inst.* [Inst.2.10.10], *l.testamentum. eod. C.* [C.6.23.17].[59]

From here arguments are also drawn from contracts to wills, and vice versa. l.quae de legato. de legat. 1. [D.30.[1].46], *l.qui testamento. §.quaecunque. de testa.* [D.28.1.20.3], *l.iure. de cond. & demonstra.* [D.35.1.24]. *Baldus* [Baldus de Ubaldis], *Angelus* [Angelus de Ubaldis], *and Salicet, in d.l. testamentum,*[60] *following Accursius, deny that wills come from the category of contracts, with one exception for odious clauses* [*in rebus odiosis*]. *But this account is not compelling. And, what is more, all of France, Germany, Italy, and Spain are accustomed to mix wills in with contracts. The Hebrews also use the same word* Berith[61] *for agreements and wills, and the Greeks often confound* will [διαθήκην] *with* agreement [συνθήκῃ].[62]

It was necessary that we arrange gifts in anticipation of death [*donationes causa mortis*] *in the gratuitous kind of contracts, in order to accommodate our division to what is more often done, even though they are not always done gratuitously. But we have included in the "mixed" category things which are partly an obligation* [*partim obligationem*] *and partly a gratuitous gift* [*partim gratuitam donationem*], *such as when a thing is partly sold and partly given* [*partim venditur, partim donatur*]. *l.sed & cum. De negot. ff.* [D.3.5.15], *l.transactione. de transact. C.*[63] *Wills, codicils, and those things that follow from them are also in the same*

[58] *Alteruter*, more usually "either," but here context requires "the first" or "the former."

[59] This citation seems garbled. The best candidate would seem to be Inst.2.10.10. The citation to the *Code* would seem to be C.6.23.17, but this does not appear to answer.

[60] Commenting on the law beginning *testamentum* (in the Digests?). This could be: Dig. 26. 2. 3, 17, 21; Dig. 28. 3. 1; Dig.28. 1. 1; Cod. 6. 23. 17; Cod. 3. 28. 24; Inst.2. 10. pr; Inst.2. 17. pr.

For Angelus, see William Bryson, *Dictionary of Sigla and Abbreviations to and in Law Books before 1607* (University Press of Virginia, 1975), s.v. Angel. etc.; either Angelus de Ambilionibus de Aretio (fl. 1422–51), Angelus de Ubaldis (d.1407), Angelus de Periglis (d.1446), or Angelus Carletus de Clavasio (d.1495). Salicet is Bartholomaeus de Saliceto (d.1412).

[61] *Berith* [ברית] is often translated "covenant."

[62] *diathēkēn cum sunthēkēi.*

[63] Cod. 2.4.26 or 30 match the *incipit* but do not answer; see Cod. 2. 4. 21 ("When it is stated in writing that the things which are agreed to be given or retained on account of a compromise are received by the person who was to receive them under the agreement, as though he were a purchaser,

category. Finally, it seems sensible to include quasi-contracts and quasi-delicts in the same categories of contracts, so that the elements of the division of the whole [divisionis universae membra] are not disturbed.[64]

Delict [*delictum*] constitutes the other half of the category, deeds [*altera pars factorum*]. A delict is an offense inflicted against law [*offensio contra ius*], and it is divided in three ways—according to its material subject [*ex subiecta materia*], according to adjuncts [*ex adiunctis*], and according to causes [*ex causis*].

> According to material subject [*ex subiecta materia*], some delicts are committed **by counsel** [*consilio*], such as evil persuasion [*prava suasio*] and conspiracy [*coniuratio*]; others **by gesture** [*gestu*], such as frightening simulation of injury [*simulatio nocendi cum metu*] or outrage [*contumelia*]; others **by writing** [*scripto*], such as malicious publications [*famosi libelli*], malicious paintings [*famosae picturae*], or false documents [*falsae scripturae*]; others **by word** [*verbo*], such as verbal offenses [*convitia*]—which are of two kinds, either blasphemies against God [*in Deum blasphemia*] or contumely against men [*in homines iniuria*]—false witness [*falsa testificatio*], sorcery [*excantatio*], perfidy which is committed either when one swears in order to deceive, or when a dishonest plea is entered, which consists in trickery [*calumnia*], collusion [*praevaricatio*], or deserting an accusation [*tergiversatio*]; other delicts are committed **by action** [*facto*] which includes also inaction [*non factum continetur*], as in the delict for neglect of duty [*delictum in praetermissione officii*]. *l.qui non facit. ff. de reg. iur.* [D.50.17.121]. These are battery, homicide, poisoning, arson, theft [*furtum*], robbery [*rapina*], criminal fornication [*stuprum*], adultery, incest, and counterfeiting or subversion [*subiectio ac depravatio*] of legislation [*legum*], records, money, keys, claims, and personal reputations.[65]
>
> *To this pertain Books 47 and 48 of the Digest and Book 9 of the Code.*
>
> According to adjuncts [*ex adiunctis*], delicts are graver [*graviora*] or lighter [*leviora*]. These may be measured according to **the circumstances of time** [*quod metimur ex circumstantiis temporum*], when an offense is committed by night or by day [*cum noctu delinquitur, aut interdiu*]; of **place** [*locorum*], when it is done publicly or secretly [*publice vel clam*], or in a sacred or profane place [*in sacro vel prophano*]; or of **persons** [*personarum*], considering both the condition of the perpetrator [*qualitate eius qui peccavit*]—man or woman, pubescent or prepubescent, major or minor of twenty-five years, citizen or foreigner, rich or poor—and likewise, the condition of the one injured [*eius in quem peccatum est*]—magistrate or private person, free or slave, infamous or of intact status [*infamis aut integri status*].[66]

then, since fictitious transactions are regarded as void, payment of the fictitious price will be demanded in vain").

64 Unlike Justinian, Gaius does not identify separate categories of "quasi-contract" or "quasi-delict," although he acknowledges the obligations arising from *indebitum* and *negotiorum gestio*. Bodin's division, thus, might be interpreted as a reaffirmation of Gaius.

65 Compare Bodin's list with the moral theologians' traditional mnemonic for cooperation in evil: *iussio, consilium, consensus, palpo, recursus, participans, mutus, non obstans, non manifestans*; "by command, by counsel, by consent, by flattery, by receiving, by participation, by silence, by not preventing, by not denouncing." Thomas Aquinas, *Summa theologiae*, II^{a}–II^{ae} 62. 7. *re*; Dominic Prümmer, *Handbook of Moral Theology*, trans. Gerald Shelton (Mercier, 1957), 123–25.

66 Compare the classic "seven circumstances of a human act": "Tully, in his *Rhetoric*, gives seven circumstances, which are contained in this verse: *Quis, quid, ubi, quibus auxiliis, cur, quomodo, quando*—who, what, where, by what aids, why, how, and when." Thomas Aquinas, *Summa Theologiae* I^{a}-II^{ae}, 7, 3, *co*; Prümmer, *Handbook of Moral Theology*, 21–22.

According to causes [*ex causis*], delicts are intentional [*voluntaria*], accidental [*fortuita*], or mixed [*mista*].[67]

Intentional [*voluntaria*] delicts are twofold.

They are **deliberate** [*spontanea*] when one offends with malice [*dolo malo*] or evil intention [*pravo consilio*]. From their number are evil persuasion [*prava suasio*], contumelious slander [*iniuria contumeliosa*], swindling [*stellionatus*], loss maliciously inflicted [*damnum dolo datum*], robbery [*rapina*], theft [*furtum*]—which is of four kinds, manifest [*manifestum*], non-manifest [*non manifestum*], theft by receiving [*conceptum*], and theft by planting [*oblatum*]—embezzlement [*suspecti crimen*],[68] kidnapping [*plagium*], burglary [*effractio*], secretly felling trees [*arbores furtim caesae*], highway robbery [*latrocinium*], misrepresentation [*falsi crimen*]—which reckons about seven kinds, in testimony, writing, laws [*legibus*], money, persons, false claims [*in nominibus subiectis*], and substitution of a newborn [*in suppositio partu*]—conspiracy [*coniuratio*], illicit association [*collegium illicitum*], battery [*percussio*], arson [*incendium missum*], poisoning [*veneficium*], covert felling [*caedes ex insidiis*], parricide [*parricidium*], infliction of violence [*vis illata*], either public or private, high treason [*maiestas laesa*], betrayal to an enemy [*perduellio*].

Delicts are **not deliberate** [*non spontanea delicta*] when committed in a rage or a fit of passion [*ira impetuve cupiditatis peccatur*], which happens in two ways, either from fierce anger [*irae indomitae*], such as in a fight [*in rixa*], a riot [*in tumultu*], or rash vengeance [*in ultione repentina*]; or else from violent lust [*libidinis impotentia*], such as abduction, incest, adultery, and perversions against nature.

Delicts popularly called **accidental** [*fortuita*], although nothing is really an accident, are of two kinds. Some could not be foreseen [*praevideri*], and no one is at fault [*culpa vacant*], but by convention they are compensated. Some could have been foreseen, as in unlawful injury [*damnum iniuria*], that is, an injury caused wrongfully [*non iure datum*], but without malice [*sine dolo*]. *l.5. ad l.Aquil.ff.* [D.9.2.5].

To this pertains the title "On the Lex Aquilia" [*Ad l.Aquil.*, D.9.2].

Delicts are called **mixed** [*mista delicta*], when something that ends in another's injury [*in alterius damnum*] is done intentionally but without malice [*sine dolo*], such as in a joke [*ioco*], drunkenness [*ebrietate*], crass ignorance [*ignorantia supina*], or duress [*metu*].

Deeds conjoined with law

So far, we have considered bare deeds [*de factis nudis*]. Now let us see those which must be considered **conjoined with law** [*de iis quae cum iure coniuncta*]. These are distributed into antecedents and consequents.

Antecedents [*antecedentia*] include acquisition [*acquisitio*], which is the obtaining of a thing or a right [*rei iurisve adoptio*], and alienation [*alienatio*], which is the laying aside of a thing or a right [*rei iurisve omissio*].

[67] Cf. D.48.19.11.2.

[68] *Suspecti crimen*, "embezzlement," is set out as a fifth category of theft in the 1578 Paris *editio princeps*. But this is inadmissable in the 1580 Köln edition, which describes theft as *quadruplex*.

Now, **acquisition** is either of possession or of ownership [*vel possessionis vel dominii*]. **Alienation** similarly is either of possession or of ownership [*aut possessionis aut dominii*].

Possession [*possessio*] is use separated from ownership [*usus a proprietate divisi*], *l.quaestionis. de verb. signif.* [D.50.16.115]. Possession can be **natural only** [*naturalis tantum*]. It can be **legal only** [*legitimae tantum*], which is sustained by a mere legal fiction, under which are included usufruct [*ususfructus*] when the owner who transfers both ownership and possession [*dominium ac possessionem transfert*] retains the usufruct, *l.quisquis. de donat. C* [C.8.53(54).28], and likewise a clause of detention [*clasula constituti*] and the succession of the nearest agnate [*proximi agnati successio*] by which possession is conferred by a legal fiction [*legis fictione*] with the agreement of all peoples [*omnium populorum consensu*], against the rule of *l.cum haeredes. de acquirenda haeredit.* [D.29.2.52]. Possession can also be **both natural and legal** [*naturalis ac legitimae simul*], when possession is transferred by the owner for a just cause [*iusta causa*], or by a magistrate's solemn act, or when a vacant property is occupied.

To this pertain the titles "On acquiring possession" [*De acquir. poss. ff.* D.41.2ff.], *in the Digest.*

Acquisition of ownership [*domini acquisitio*] is done in, more or less, nine ways:

By **just force** [*vi iusta*], namely, of arms, when engaged in lawful war [*armorum cum bellum iure susceptum est*], or in licit hunting of wild animals, birds, and fish [*veneationis licitae, ferarum, avium, piscium*];

By **occupation** of abandoned property or unoccupied places [*occupatione rei derelictae, aut locorum vacantium*];[69]

By **natural accession** [*naturali accessione*] which happens in the case of riverbeds, islands, forests, and meadows;

By **art** [*arte*], such as crafts or commerce;

By **art and nature** [*arte et natura*], such as agriculture or livestock;

By **transfer with a just cause** [*traditione ex iusta causa*], and this is either real or fictive [*vel vera, vel ficta*], such as in *l.a Titio. de furt. ff.* [D.47.2.65.(64)], *l.ut inter. de sacrosanctis. eccles. C.* [C.1.2.23];

By **order** [*decreto*], such as in a public auction [*subhastione*] or the three proceedings [*triplici iudicio*] referenced in *lib.4. Instit. tit. de off.iud.* [Inst.4.17.4–6], the *familiae erciscundae iudicium*, the *communi dividundo*, and the *finium regundorum*;

By **legislation** [*lege*], of which there are three: annexation [*accrescendi*], usucaption [*usucapiendi*], and intestacy [*intestati*].

To this pertain the titles "On acquisition of ownership of things" [*De acquir. rer. dom. ff.*, D.41.1] *in the Digest and the nine titles from the third to the end in the Digest Book 41.*

By **will or codicils** [*testamento seu codicillis*], by which a transfer is made of either an estate [*haereditas*] or a legacy or trust [*legatum seu fidei commissum*]. An **estate** [*haereditas*] is the right [*ius*] which one has at the time of death. *l. haereditas, de verb. signif.* [D.50.16.119]. This is accomplished either by request or acceptance of the inheritance [*agnitione vel aditione*], either on the strength of appointment [*ex vi institutione*] or of substitution [*substitione*], and substitution is either ordinary [*vulgaris*], for a child [*pupillaris*], for the

[69] Cf. Inst.2.1.12.

insane [*exemplaris*], or military substitution [*militaris*]. A **legacy or trust** [*legatum seu fidei commissum*] is either universal or particular [*universale vel singulare*].

To this pertain fourteen books of the Digest, from 24 to 39 and from title 9 to the end of Book 6 in the Code, etc.

The pure and simple sense of the word "ownership" [dominii] for the Roman signifies full ownership [propretatem].[70] *For neither in the Pandects nor the Code, nor indeed in the Authentics, does any word exist of "dominium utile" or "dominium directum." But these terms have spread from feudal custom into general usage. And then, to some people, it seems good to describe "fonciers" [fundiarios], census-tenants [censuales], and "tresfonciers" [fundiarissimos] as owners [dominos], and, of these, some as immediate [immediati], some intermediate [intermedia], and some, finally, as proprietary owners [proprietarii].*[71] *But by a right interpretation of words, these last are the owners. The others have nothing other than a mortgage-right [ius praediatorium], a rent [vectigal], or a servitude [servitutem], but they do not have ownership, because ownership cannot belong to two people at the same time [duorum simul esse non potest]. l.si ut certo. §.si duobus. commodati.* [D.13.6.5.15], *l.haereditate. §.pater. de castrensi pecul.* [D.49.17.19.3].

Consequent deeds [*consequentia facta*] bound up with law are obligation [*obligatio*] and release [*liberatio*].

Obligation is a bond of law by which we are required to give or to do something [*iuris vinculum quo dare facere tenemur*].[72] It is of four kinds [*quadruplex*]:

Natural obligation [*naturalis*];

Obligation of the law of all peoples [*gentium omnium*], but nevertheless not of natural law [*non tamen naturalis*], such as an unjust verdict which is nevertheless held to be true, *l.4.de statu hom.* [D.1.5.4], *l.Iulianus. de condic. indeb.* [D.12.6.60];

Civil obligation only [*civilis*], which is specific to one state [*unius civitatis propria*];

Obligation of both natural law and the law of all peoples [*naturalis et gentium omnium*], which arises from agreements and lawful orders [*conventionibus iustisque decretis oritur*], or from those delicts [*ex iis delictis*] which are censured by the agreement of all peoples and nature [*omnium populorum et naturae consensu vindicantur*].

Release [*liberatio*] is the performance of an obligation [*obligationis solutio*], of which there are two kinds.

To this pertains the title "On performances" [*De solutionibus*, D.46.3].

Natural and legal [*naturalis et legitima*], which is called "real performance" [*realis solutio*]. Otherwise, the word "performance" [*solutionis verbum*], embraces every release from debt [*omnem debiti liberationem*], *l.solutam. de solut.* [D.46.3.49].

[70] *Dominium* and *proprietas* are treated as synonyms in Roman law (D.50.16.115). We lack an ideally adequate synonym for "ownership" in English.

[71] French *fonciers*, "having to do with real estate." There appears to be no standard English translation of the Latin *fundiarius, fundiarissimus*, nor of the French *foncier, trèsfoncier*; see, for example, Frederic W. Maitland, *The Collected Papers of Frederic William Maitland*, ed. Herbert Fisher, 3 vols. (Cambridge: Cambridge University Press, 1911), 2:255–56.

[72] Cf. Inst.3.13.pr: D.44.7.3.pr.

Legal only [*legitima tantum*], which is called security [*satisdatio*] or satisfaction [*satisfactio*]. This is done either by the force of law [*ipso iure*] or through an exception [*ope exceptionis*].

By the **force of law**, whenever a discharge obtains without real performance [*sine reali solutione liberatio sequitur*], and the obligation may be reclaimed [*repeti*], or what was paid by mistake may be reclaimed [*errore solutum condici potest*], *l.quod dicitur. §.penult. de impensis. in res dotales* [D.25.1.5.3]. Its kinds are:

Verbal release [*acceptilatio*], where the creditor declares to the debtor his acceptance of the debt. *l.pluribus. de accepti.ff.* [D.46.4.6].

Novation [*novatio*] is the transformation of an old obligation into a new one, *l.qui negotia, mandati.ff.* [D.17.1.34].

Delegation [*delegatio*] is the replacement of one debtor by another, *l.delegare. de novationib.ff.* [D.46.2.11].

Confusion [*confusio*] is when the creditor succeeds to the debtor, or vice-versa, *l.si debitor. de pactis. C.* [C.2.3.7].

Set-off [*compensatio*] is the discharge of a liquid debt [*debiti liquidi datio*] as payment for another liquid debt [*cum liquido in solutum*], *l.si constat. de compensat. C.* [C.4.31.4].[73]

Seal and deposit [*obsignatio*] is when money is legally deposited to discharge a debt [*pecunia liberationis causa deponitur legitime*], *l.acceptum. de usuris. C.* [C.4.32.19].

Obtaining of ownership [*domini adeptio*], when the thing owed comes into the creditor's ownership, *l.quoties. de solut.* [D.46.3.61 or 1 or 37].

The **destruction of the thing owed** through no fault of the debtor, *l.sicut. quibus modis pignus* [D.20.6.8].

The **exemption from commerce of the thing owed** [*exemptio rei debitae a commercio*], when a profane thing is made sacred, or sanctified, or religious [*sacra, vel sancta, vel religiosa*]. *l.inter. de furtis* [D.47.2.46].[74] Or when the obligation reverts into a cause such as could not suffice to initiate it. *l.penultim. de duob. reis.ff.* [D.45.2.18].

Compromise [*transactio*] is withdrawal [*discessio*] from a prior suit and obligation. *l.causas. de transact.* C. [C.2.4.16].

Cessio in iure has the force of performance, if the debtor cedes the thing sought from him.

Release from obligation through an exception [*ope exceptionis*] is introduced in these ways:

By a **pact** [*pacto*], *l.si unus. §.pactus.* [D.2.14.27.2] *&* *l.ult. de pactis.ff.* [D.2.14.62].

By an **oath** [*iureiurando*], *l.ait praetor. de iureiurando* [D.12.2.3 or 7].

To this pertains the title "On oaths" [*De iureiurando*, D.12.2].

By an **obligation** [*obligatione*], *l.si servum. §.Stichum. De verb. oblig.* [D.45.1.91].[75]

[73] Cf. D.16.2.1.
[74] The text does not appear to answer.
[75] This text lacks a section beginning *Stichum*, but it is possible that it answers.

By a **judicial decision** [*re iudicata*], *l.Iulianus. de condic. indebiti* [D.12.6.60].[76]

By **prescription** [*praescriptione*], *l.sicut.* [C.7.39.3] *l.omnes. de praescript. 30. anno. C.* [C.7.39.4].

To this pertain the titles "On prescriptions" [*De praescriptionib*, C.7.33, C.7.39].

III. The Efficient [*efficiens*] Cause of Jurisprudence

The **efficient cause** brings disputes and lawsuits [*controversias ac lites*] to a close, not by means of laws [*non legibus*], but by their actions and effects [*legum actionibus & effectis*].[77] For legislation and equity pertain to the creation of law [*lex & aequitas ad ius constituendum pertinent*], whereas the action of law and the duty of the judge pertain to its execution [*legis actio & iudicis officium ad exequendum*]. Just as legislation is to the action of the law, so also is equity to the duty of the judge.

The efficient cause of jurisprudence therefore consists in *legis actio* and *officium iudicis.*

Legis Actio

Legis actio is the law's [*legis*] very execution, force, and power. This term also covers custom [*consuetudo*] and procedure [*stilus agendi*]. It is of two kinds—namely, extrajudicial and forensic.

Extrajudicial action [*extraiudicialis*], such as sacred rites [*ritus sacrorum*], legislation [*legislatio*], the appointment of magistrates [*magistratuum creatio*], the form of assemblies [*forma comitiorum*], acts of legal clerks or the practice of notaries [*actiones tabellionum, seu stilus notariorum*], which consist in writing contracts, attestations, taking possessions, notifications, registrations, taking signatures,[78] making copies of wills, codicils, and donations, in acts of acceptance and refusal, etc.

Forensic action [*forensis*] is deployed in court [*iure*], i.e., in the presence of a judge [*apud iudicem*], *l.4. de interrogator. actionibus.ff.* [D.11.1.4], *l.ult. de iustit.* [D.1.1.11–12]. It is subdivided into authoritative [*imperiosam*], judicial [*iuridicam*], and executive [*executoriam*] action.

Authoritative *Legis Actio*

Authoritative action [*imperiosa*] is involved in commands, prohibitions, and permission [*in iussis, vetitis, & permissione*]. It consists in either *auctoritas* or *imperium.*

Auctoritas is the public assent of a magistrate [*publica magistratus assensio*] by which legal acts are approved [*legitimi actus comprobantur*].

Imperium is either public or private.

Public *imperium*, in turn, is either sovereign [*summum*], such as the sovereign *imperium* of a monarch [*principis*], of an aristocracy [*optimatuum*], or of the people [*populi*]. Or it can be legal [*legitimum*]—such as the *imperium* of a magistrate

[76] It is not clear how this text answers.

[77] A marginal heading in the 1580 Köln edition erroneously says *causa efficiens iuris* instead of *iurisprudentiae.* See the note on "The Matter of Jurisprudence."

[78] Or "seals."

[*magistratus*], whether a higher magistrate [*maioris*], who is bound to obey only the sovereign but not other magistrates, or a lesser magistrate [*minoris*], who is bound also to obey superior magistrates—or the *imperium* of a curator, which they call a "commissioner" [*commissarium*].

Private *imperium* is that which has origins separate from public *imperium*, such as in corporations [*universitatis*], associations [*collegiorum*], and families [*familiorum*], within which the husband has *imperium* over the wife [*in uxorem*], the father over his children [*erga liberos*], and the master over slaves [*in servos*].

Jurisdiction

Judicial [*iuridica*] *legis actio*, or **jurisdiction**, is separate from *imperium*. This is divided in two ways—according to causes [*ex causis*] and according to adjuncts [*ex adiunctis*].

According to causes, it is again divided in three ways—regarding efficient [*ex efficiente*], material [*ex materia*], and formal [*ex forma*] cause.

According to **efficient cause**, some jurisdiction is voluntary [*voluntaria*], some contentious [*contentiosa*].

Voluntary jurisdiction is that which unfolds from the consent of the actors [*agentium consensu*], in the presence of the one who has jurisdiction. In this class are contestations and judgments [*contestationes ac sententiae voluntariae*], *cessio in iure*, adoption, emancipation, and manumission.

Contentious jurisdiction is applied against someone unwillingly [*invitum*], *l.inter stipulantem. de verb. oblig.* [D.45.1.83]. This is divided into libellary [*libellarem*] and decisive [*decretoriam*].

A **libellary action** [*libellaris*] is carried out by written submissions [*libellis*] and almost without a judicial examination of the case [*fere sine cognitionem causae*].[79]

One kind of libellary action is **preliminary** [*praeiudicium*], which includes mere pleading [*intentio*] or reply without contest [*depulsio nuda sine contestatione*], appearance in court [*comparitio in iure*], substitution [*subrogatio*], interruption, testimony in court [*testatio in iure*], pledge of security [*cautio*], sending to take possession [*missio in possessionem*], rejection of witnesses or judges, interrogation in court, appeal [*provocatio*], renunciation.

From these, there are three kinds of preliminary action in all—public, private, and mixed.

A **public preliminary action** is that which pertains to the state [*quod ad rempublicam pertinet*]. One such category of preliminary action is criminal, such as accusation or defense. The other is civil, which refers to popular actions [*populares actiones*] not involving crime.

There are two kinds of **private preliminary action**, action and exception [*actio & exceptio*].

[79] See Berger, *Encyclopedic Dictionary of Roman Law*, s.v. *libellus contradictionis, libellus conventionis*.

Actio

An ***actio*** is a private preliminary action brought about by entering a civil plea [*intentione civili constitutum*]. It is divided according to causes [*ex causis*] and according to adjuncts [*ex adiunctis*].

According to causes, an *actio* is divided fourfold, namely, according to its matter [*materia*], formal [*forma*], efficient [*efficiente*], and final [*fine*] cause.

According to their **matter** [*ex materia*], there are three kinds of *action*—real, personal, and mixed.

A **real *actio*** [*realis*] proceeds in pursuit of a thing [*in rem*], or for the sake of a thing [*rei causa*]. These are, again, of three kinds:

preparatory [*praeparatoria*], such as the actions *ad exhibendum*; *sequestraria*;[80] *alimentaris ante iudicium constitutum*; *vindiciarum*;

To this pertains the title "On the action ad exhibendum" [*Ad exhibendum*, D.10.4].

possessory [*possessoria*], of acquiring [*adipiscendae*], retaining [*retinendae*], or recuperating [*recuperandae*] possession;[81]

To this pertains the study of interdicts [*interdictorum disciplina*], *lib.43. ff. tit.29* [D.43.29].[82]

petitionary [*petitoria*], which reclaims ownership [*dominium*] or the right to a thing [*ius rei*] from a third party possessor [*a tertio possessore*]. These include the pure hypothecary action [*hypothecaria pura*], which pursues the right to a thing [*ius ad rem*] without consideration of person, and the *rei vindicatio*, just as much for a corporeal thing [*corporae rei*] as for an incorporeal thing [*incorporae*]. The latter is of two kinds, *actio confessoria* and *actio negatoria.*

A **personal *actio*** [*personalis*], which attaches to a person and pursues that person anywhere [*personae cohaeret & eam ubi ubi consectatur*], is of two kinds: preliminary and *condictio.*

A **preliminary personal *actio*** [*praeiudicialis*][83] is that by which a dispute is carried out concerning the status [*statu*], rank [*ordine*], sex [*sexu*], or condition [*conditione*] of persons:

Actio liberalis

Actio ingenuitatis

Actio peregrinitatis

Actio de liberis legitimis, and vice-versa

[80] See Berger, *Encyclopedic Dictionary of Roman Law*, s.v. *sequester.*

[81] These refer to the interdicts known as *adipiscendae, retinendae possessionis*, and *recuperandae possessionis.*

[82] Bodin is referring here to the possessory interdicts, the most important of which are the interdicts known as *quorum bonorum, uti possidetis*, and *utrubi*. See also D.43.1, *De interdictis sive extraordinariis actionibus, quae pro his competent.*

[83] See Berger, *Encyclopedic Dictionary of Roman Law*, s.v. *actiones praeiudiciales, formulae praeiudiciales, praeiudicia, intentio.*

Actio de uxore iusta, and vice-versa

Actio de iure magistratuum

Actio de gentis nobilitate aut obscuritate

Actio concerning anyone's character, rank, condition, occupation,[84] ancestry, sex, age, illness, insanity, reputation, or infamy.

A ***condictio*** is an *actio in personam* founded on an obligation. These are of two kinds, certain and uncertain claims [*certi & incerti*].[85]

A *condictio* is certain [*certi*] when what is sought is certain [*certa res*] in quantity or *specie*. A claim is certain by agreement [*ex conventione*], by legislation [*ex lege*], or by delict [*ex delicto*] when a certain thing is defrauded in a transaction [*certa res pactione circumscribitur*]. From agreement arise the following actions:

Actio mutui

Actio pignoratitia rei certae

Actio ex donato

Actio indebiti

Actions on all agreements where a certain thing is claimed.

A *condictio* is uncertain [*incerti*] when the suit claims one's expected gain on an obligation [*agitur ad id quod interest*], whether principally or secondarily [*sive principaliter, sive accessorie*].[86]

These arise from agreement [*ex conventione*], such as:

Actio ex stipulatu incerta

Actio depositi and *aestimatoria*

Actio commodati and *de precario*

Actio empti, redhibitoria, quanti plurimi

Actio quanto minoris[87]

Actio ex retractu gentilicio, feudali, conventionali

Actio locati, conducti, emphyteuseos

Actio societatis, matrimonii, dotis, donationis propter nuptias, and *rerum amotarum*

Actio mandati, tutelae, negotiorum gestorum, de eo quod certo loco, curationis bonorum, de constituta pecunia

Actio de gestis eorum qui sunt alieni iuris, of which there are six kinds:

Institoria
Exercitoria

[84] The 1578 and 1580 editions both say *vita, instituto*, which should be read as *vitae instituto*.
[85] Cf. D.45.1.74.
[86] Cf. D.46.8.13.pr.
[87] Although Bodin wrote *quanto minoris* in both the 1578 and 1580 editions, this lawsuit is better known by the name *actio quanti minoris*.

Tributoria
Quod iussu
De peculio
De in rem verso

Actio de iureiurando in litem

Actio de alienatione iudicii mutandi causa facta

Actio foeneratitia and *de reditu constituto*

Actio testamentaria, condicillaris, fiduciaria, funeraria

Actiones praescriptis verbis, as well as[88] those *actiones utiles* on the infinite sorts of innominate agreements. *l.quoties. de praescript. verb.* [D.19.5.21].

They also arise from delict [*ex delicto*], when the one who is sued has committed no crime:

Actiones damni infecti or *dati*

Actiones deiecti and *effusi*

Actio de pauperie

Actio de pastu

Actiones noxales in dominos

Actiones in nautas, caupones, stabularios

Actions on every sort of crime [*ex omnibus criminibus*] wherein the suit concerns only one's private interest [*ad quod privatim interest*]

An *actio* is said to be mixed [*mista actio*] which affects both a thing and a person [*rem afficit & personam*]. *l.haereditatis. de haereditatis petit. C.* [C.3.31.7]. Of such kind are personal hypothecary action [*hypothecaria personalis*], claim for an inheritance [*haereditatis petitio*], *actiones familiae erciscundae, communi dividundo, finium regundorum*, and all actions arising from interdicts. *l.1. de interdict.* [D.43.1.1].

According to **form** [*ex forma*], some actions are *bonae fidei*, some *stricti iuris*, some *arbitraria*.

According to **efficient cause** [*ex efficiente*], some actions are statutory [*legitima*], which are granted by legislation [*a lege tribuitur*], some are praetorian [*praetoria*], which are granted by magistrates from their edicts [*a magistratibus ex eorum edictis*]. Both of these can be either *directa*, on the basis of wording [*ex verbis*], or *utilis*, on the basis of a fair interpretation [*ex interpretatione aequa*].

According to **end** [*ex fine*], an action is given for a simple claim or principal [*in simplum seu principale*]; for expenses [*in expensas*]; for one's interest beyond the simple claim [*in id quod interest praeter simplum*]; for the total value of the suit [*in totam litis aestimationem*], which includes the simple claim [*simplum*], additional value [*accessio*], and expenses [*expensae*].

88 The 1578 and 1580 editions say *quae etiam utiles* but this should be read quin *etiam utiles*.

According to adjuncts [*ex adiunctis*], which we set out as the second portion into which actions are divided (p. 161), *actio* is twofold. In relation to time [*temporis*], some are called temporary [*actiones temporariae*], and others perpetual [*actiones perpetuae*]. And in relation to an heir [*haeredum*], some are in favor of heirs [*actiones quae haeredibus tantum*], some against heirs [*actiones quae in haeredes tantum*], and some both in favor of, and against, heirs [*actiones quae haeredibus & in haeredes dantur*].

Exceptio

An ***exceptio*** (which we have established as the second part of a private preliminary action) is a preliminary action exercised in exclusion of an *actio*. There are three kinds of *exceptio*—dilatory, peremptory, and mixed.

A **preliminary** [*praeiudicium*] is called mixed [*mistum*], when public and private things are mingled, and when in the same trial we pursue what is of both public and private interest [*eodem iudicio quod publice & privatim interest persequimur*].

Decisive jurisdiction [*decretoria iurisdictio*], the second part of contentious jurisdiction, reckons up a mature examination of the case [*maturam exigit cognitionem*]. *l.nec quicquam. §.ubi decretum. de offic. procons.* [D.1.16.9.1]. And it consists of two parts, order [*decretum*] and trial [*iudicium*].

An **order** [*decretum*] is what a magistrate decides after an examination [*quod magistratus post cognitionem statuit*] without joinder of issue [*sine litis contestatione*], although sometimes it is accepted as a sentence. It revolves around excuses, adjournments, maintenances, things to be alienated, guardianships and curatorships, and estate possession [*bonorum possessiones*[89]].

A **trial** [*iudicium*] is a contentious *legis actio*, which consists in the joinder of issue [*litis contestatione*] and the sentence. And likewise, it is divided according to causes [*ex causis*] or according to adjuncts [*ex adiunctis*].

According to **causes** [*ex causis*], there are four—material [*ex materia*], formal [*ex forma*], efficient [*ex efficiente*], and final cause [*ex fine*].

According to **matter** [*ex materia*], a trial is civil, criminal, or mixed.

According to **form** [*ex forma*], some trials are ordinary, others extraordinary.

According to **efficient cause** [*ex efficiente*], a trial is divided into two parts, the joinder of issue and the sentence.

Joinder of issue [*litis contestatio*] is the legal formulation of words [*legitima verborum conceptio*], based on pleading, rebuttal, and also magistrate's intervention, in order to complete a trial [*iudicii constituendi causa*]. Its parts are situation [*status causae*] and proof [*probatio*].

The **situation of the case** [*status causae*] is the matter with which the case is chiefly concerned. It is of three kinds—conjectural, when the question is only of fact [*de facto*]; legal [*legitimus*], when the question is only of law [*de iure*]; mixed, when it is of both law and fact [*de utroque iure & facto*].

[89] The 1578 and 1580 editions say *bonorum possessionis* but this should be read *bonorum possessiones*.

Two kinds of proof

There are two kinds of proof [*probatio*].

Clear [*perspicua*], as in spontaneous confession [*voluntariae confessionis*], formal legal transactions [*actuum legitimorum*], documents or witnesses, with the exception of ascendants [*tabularum ac testium exceptione maiorum*], and settled law and custom [*legum & consuetudinis non dubiae*].

Doubtful [*dubia*], from conflict of laws, witnesses, or documents [*ex repugnantia legum, testium, tabularum*]; from the inconsistency of the one speaking to the question [*ex varietate consistentis in quaestione*]; from an oath [*ex iureiurando*].

Oaths are either extrajudicial [*extraiudiciali*], of which there are three kinds—temerary [*temerario*], conventional [*conventionali*], and legal [*legitimo*], or juridical [*iuridicali*]. These latter are either compulsory [*necessario*] because of deception [*propter calumniam*], or voluntary [*voluntario*] for the sake of supplying proof [*supplendae probationis*] or of defining the issue [*litis definiendae*].

To this pertain the titles "On proof" [*De probat* D. 22.3, C.4.19], *"On witnesses"* [*De testib*, D.22.5, C.4.20], *and "On oaths"* [*De iureiurando*, D.12.2].

Sentence

Some sentences are interlocutory [*interlocutoria*]. Some are decisive [*decisoria seu diffinitiva*], and the latter, in turn, are either absolutory [*absolutoria*] or condemnatory [*condemnatoria*].

To this pertain the ten titles in the Code Book 7 from title 42 to 51 [C.7.42–51], *and the title "On trials"* [*De iudic*, D.5.1], *in the Pandects.*

According to final cause [*ex fine*], some trials are penal [*poenale*], some suing for a thing [*rei persecutorium*], some mixed.

Penal, such as a penalty of fine [*mulctae*], infamy [*infamiae*], outlaw [*proscriptionis*], relegation [*relegationis*], exile [*exilii*], banishment [*deportationis*], lashing [*verberum*], amputation [*amputationis*], physical death [*mortis naturalis*] inflicted by sword [*gladio*], water [*aqua*], hanging [*suspendio*], breaking [*confractione*], fire [*igne*], or stoning [*lapidatione*].

Suit for a thing [*rei persecutorium*] is of two kinds, either for the simple value or principal [*in simplum seu principale*], or for accessions beyond the simple value [*in accessiones ultra simplum*]. These latter are either certain [*certas*] or uncertain [*incertas*].

Certain suits for a thing are either by legislation [*lege*], such as interest [*usura*] and maritime loan [*foenus nauticum*], or else by pact or agreed penalty [*pacto seu poena conventa*].

To this pertains the titles "On interest" [*De usuris*, C.4.32], *"On transmarine loans"* [*De nautico foenore*, D.22.2], *and "*Verdicts given for indemnification of one's interest" [*De eo quod interest*, C.7.47].

Uncertain suits for a thing are either for one's interest [*id quod interest*], whether attached to [*rei cohaerens*] or detached from [*remotum*] the thing, or else for profits [*fructus*].

Mixed, which embraces the entire appraisal of the claim [*universam complectitur litis aestimationem*].

According to adjuncts [*ex adiunctis*], a trial consists in a plaintiff [*actore*], a judge [*iudice*], and a defendant [*reo*].

According to **material cause** [*ex materia*], some jurisdiction is civil [*civilis*], some criminal [*criminalis*], some mixed [*mista*].

According to **formal cause** [*ex forma*], some jurisdiction is ordinary, which arises from legislation [*ex lege*] or custom [*more consueto*]; others are extraordinary, which are ruled by the decision of a judge [*iudicis arbitrio regitur*] or of a commissioner [*curatoris*], or a judge appointed with jurisdiction by the sovereign [*iudicis a principe dati cum iurisdictione*].

According to **adjuncts** [*ex adiunctis*], some jurisdiction is held as one's own [*propria*], which can be either lawful [*legitima*], pertaining to the right of a magistrate [*iure magistratus competit*], or exempt from the law [*lege soluta*], pertaining to the right of sovereignty [*iure maiestatis*]. Other forms of jurisdiction are delegated [*mandata*], either by the sovereign [*a principe*] or by a magistrate [*a magistratu*].

Executive *legis actio*

The last species of *legis actio* is executive [*executoria*], and there are two kinds—namely, against one who voluntarily complies [*in eum qui sponte obsequitur*], and against one who is compelled by force [*in eum qui vi cogitur*].

Officium Iudicis

The duty of the judge [*iudicis officium*] is involved with those things that are not comprehended by legislation [*quae non sunt lege comprehensa*], or are said too obscurely [*nimis obscure dicta*], or which seem unjust [*iniqua*] as applied to the case at hand [*ad propositam causam*]. It operates, above all, in supplementing the laws [*in legibus supplendis*], *l.ius autem. de iustitia* [D.1.1.7], and in moderating the severity or lenience of the laws [*in legum acerbitate vel lenitate temperanda*], *l.respiciendum.* [D.48.19.11], *l.hodie. de poenis. ff.* [D.48.19.13].

IV. The End [*finis*] of Jurisprudence

The **end** [*finis*] of jurisprudence is justice rendering to each his due [*iustitia suum cuique tribuens*], that is, *a requital* [τὸ ἀντιπεπονθὸς].[90] It is arranged in a triple proportion [*in triplici proportione*]: arithmetic, geometric, and harmonic. These support each other by a shared embrace like the three daughters of Themis, *Eunomia* [εὐνομία], *Dikaiosunē* [δικαιοσύνη], *Eirēnē* [εἰρήνη],[91] that is, good law, justice, and peace [*aequa lex, iustitia, pax*]. Or, more aptly, *nomos* [νόμος] applies to the arithmetic order [*arithmeticas rationes*], where law [*lex*] is the same for all; *epieikeia* [ἐπιεικεία] to the geometric [*ad*

[90] *to antipeponthos*, "requital, to be reciprocally proportional." See Aristotle, *Nicomachean Ethics*, 278–79 [V, v, §1, 1132^{b}21]. A marginal heading in the 1580 (Köln) edition erroneously says *finis iuris* instead of *iurisprudentiae* for the title of this final section. See the note on "The Matter of Jurisprudence" above.

[91] On Themis and these three daughters, see Christiane Sourvinou-Inwood, "Themis," in *Oxford Classical Dictionary*, ed. Simon Hornblower et al., 4th ed. (Oxford: Oxford University Press, 2012).

geometricas], that is, equity [*aequitas*]; *epieikonomia* [*ἐπιεικονομία*] to the harmonic [*ad harmonicas*], which is refined from both, as justice coalesces from law and equity [*ex lege et aequitate*].[92]

Arithmetic proportion in the numbers 2, 4, 6, 8, 10, 12

The arithmetical order,[93] which is called *commutative* [συναλλακτίκη],[94] always renders equivalent things equal [*aequalia*][95], deeds to deeds [*facta factis*], things to things [*res rebus*], without discrimination of persons. It shines forth above all in loans [*in rebus creditis*], such as loans for consumption [*mutuis*], pledge [*pignore*], loans for use [*commodato*], deposit [*deposito*], and the like.

Geometric proportion in the numbers 2, 4, 8, 16, 32, 64

The geometrical order, which is called *distributive* [διανεμητίκη],[96] regards analogy and not equality [*similitudinem non aequalitatem*]. Examples are in *l.capitalium. §.in servorum. de poenis* [D.48.19.10 or 28],[97] *l.ult. de incendio.* [D.47.9.12], *l.ut gradatim. de munerib.* [D.50.4.11].

Harmonic proportion in the numbers 6, 8, 12, 16, 24

The harmonic order, which coalesces from the arithmetical and geometrical orders, determines cases by the married order of equality and analogy [*aequalitatis et similitudinis coniuncta ratione*]. An example is in *l.eos. de usuris* [C.4.32.26].

These topics are explained by us in the final chapter of Book VI of *De Republica.*

Here ends the Division of Law as a Whole by Jean Bodin.

[92] *epieikonomia,* a combination of the two preceding Greek words; it does not appear in Greek dictionaries or lexicons. This appears to be a neologism invented by Bodin.

[93] The 1578 and 1580 editions say *ratione arithmeticae,* but this should be read as *ratione arithmetica* in parallel to *ratione geometrica* and *ratione harmonica* in the next two paragraphs

[94] *sūnallaktikē,* literally "for contracts," from *sūnallagē* "commerce, interchange."

[95] The 1578 and 1580 editions say *aequalis,* but this should be read aequalia.

[96] *dianemētikē,* from *dianemēsis,* "distribution."

[97] Pierre Mesnard proposes that this citation represents a contamination with D.48.19.28.11, forming a transition with D.47.9.12.

Bibliography

Works by Bodin

Bodin, Jean. *Colloquium Heptaplomeres de Rerum Sublimium Arcanis Abditis*, edited by Ludovicus Noack. Paris: Typis Friderici Guilelmi Baerensprung, 1857.

Bodin, Jean. *Colloquium of the Seven About Secrets of the Sublime*. Translated by Marion Leathers Kuntz. Princeton: Princeton University Press, 1975.

Bodin, Jean. *De Republica Libri VI*. Paris: Jacques Du Puys, 1586.

Bodin, Jean. *Exposé du droit universel: Juris universi distributio*. Translated by Lucien Jerphagnon, edited by Simone Goyard-Fabre. Paris: Presses Universitaires de France, 1985.

Bodin, Jean. *I sei libri dello stato*, edited by Margherita Isnardi Parente and Diego Quaglioini. Turin: UTET, 1964–67.

Bodin, Jean. *Iuris Universi Distributio*. Paris: Jacques Du Puys, 1578.

Bodin, Jean. *Iuris Universi Distributio*, edited by Witold Wolodkiewicz. Naples: Jovene, 1985.

Bodin, Jean. *Juris Universi Distributio*. Cologne: Apud Joannem Gymnicum, 1580.

Bodin, Jean. *La Iuris Universi Distributio di Jean Bodin*, edited by Cecilia Pedrazza Gorlero. Rovereto: Edizioni Osiride, 1999.

Bodin, Jean. *Les Six Livres de la République*. Paris: Jacques Du Puys, 1583.

Bodin, Jean. *Les Six Livres de la République/De Republica Libri Six*, edited by Mario Turchetti. Paris: Classiques Garnier, 2013.

Bodin, Jean. *Method for the Easy Comprehension of History*. Translated by Beatrice Reynolds. New York: Columbia University Press, 1945.

Bodin, Jean. *Methodus ad Facilem Historiarum Cognitionem*. Paris: Apud Martinum Iuvenem, 1572.

Bodin, Jean. *On Sovereignty*, edited by Julian Franklin. Cambridge: Cambridge University Press, 1992.

Bodin, Jean. *Oppiani de Venatione*. Paris: Apud Michaëlum Vascosanum, 1555.

Bodin, Jean. *Oratio de Instituenda in Republica Iuventute ad Senatum Populumque Tolosatem*. Toulouse: Ex Officina Petri Putei, 1559.

Bodin, Jean. *Six Books of the Commonwealth*. Translated by M. J. Tooley. Oxford: Basil Blackwell, 1955.

Bodin, Jean. "Tableau du droit universel." In *Oeuvres Philosophiques de Jean Bodin*, edited and translated by Pierre Mesnard. Paris: Presses Universitaires de France, 1951.

Bodin, Jean. *Universae Naturae Theatrum*. Lyon: Apud Iacobvm Rovssin, 1596.

[Knolles, Richard]. *Six Bookes of a Commonweale*. London: G. Bishop, 1606.

[Kocin, Jan]. *Nova Distribvtio Ivris Vniversi*. Prague: George Nigrinus, 1581.

Roman and Canon Law

Codicis Dn.Iustiniani. Editio Postrema. Venice: Apud Nicolaum Bevilaqua, 1574.

Codicis Iustiniani. Lyon: Apud Hugonem à Porta, 1560.

Decretales [*sive Liber Extra*] *D. Gregorii Papae IX*. Rome: In Aedibus Populi Romani, 1582.

Institutiones Divi Caesaris Iustiniani. Editio Postrema. Venice: Apud Nicolaum Bevilaqua, 1569.

Lex Duodecim Tabularum ["The Twelve Tables"]. In *Fontes iuris Romani antejustiniani*, edited by S. Riccobono, vol. 1. Florence, 1941.
Nicolini, H., and F. S. d'Amico. *Indices Corporis Iuris Civilis Iuxta Vetustiores Editiones Cum Criticis Collatas*. 5 vols. Milan: Typis Giuffré, 1964–67.
Novellae Constitutiones Divi Caesaris Iustiniani, Quae Authentica Vulga Appellant. Editio Postrema. Venice: Apud Nicolaum Bevilaqua, 1569.
Ochoa, Xaviero, and Aloisio Diez. *Index Canonum et Legum Totius Corporis Iuris Canonici et Civilis*. Universa Bibliotheca Iuris: subsidia 2. 2 vols. Rome: Institutum iuridicum Claretanum, 1964–65.
Pandectarum Iuris Civilis. Lyon: Apud Hugonem à Porta [Hugues de la Parte], 1560.
Pandectarum, seu Digestorum Iuris Civilis. Editio Postrema. Venice: Apud Nicolaum Bevilaqua, 1569.
Volumen. Lyon: Apud Hugonem à Porta, 1558.

General Bibliography

Alciato, Andrea. *Paradoxorum ad Pratum, Libri Sex*. Milan: Alexander Minutianus, 1518.
Apel, Johann. *Methodica Dialectices Ratio, ad Iurisprudentiam Adcommodata*. Nuremberg: Apud Fridericum Peypus, 1535.
Aquinas, Thomas. *Summa Theologiae of St. Thomas Aquinas: Second and Revised Edition*. Translated by Fathers of the English Dominican Province. London: Burns Oates & Washbourne Ltd., 1921.
Aristotle. *The Complete Works of Aristotle: The Revised Oxford Edition*, edited by Jonathan Barnes. Princeton: Princeton University Press, 1984.
Aristotle. *Nicomachean Ethics*, edited by Jeffrey Henderson. Translated by Horace Rackham. Loeb Classical Library 73. Cambridge: Harvard University Press, 1934.
Aristotle. *Posterior Analytics*. Translated by Hugh Tredennick and E. S. Forster. Loeb Classical Library 391. Cambridge: Harvard University Press, 1960.
Arnaud, André-Jean Arnaud. *Les origines doctrinales du Code civil français*. Bibliothèque du philosophie du droit IX. Paris: Librairie Générale de droit et de jurisprudence, 1969.
Asmis, Elizabeth. "The State as Partnership: Cicero's Definition of 'Res Publica' in His Work, 'On the State'." *History of Political Thought* 25 (2004): 569–98.
Azo. *Azonis ad singulas leges XII librorum Codicis Justinianei commentarius*. Paris: Apud Sebastianum Nivellium sub Ciconiis, via Iacobaea, 1577.
Baldus de Ubaldis. *Commentaria*. Venice, 1599.
Barber, Giles. "Haec a Johanne Bodin Lecta." *Bibliothèque d'Humanisme et Renaissance* 25, no. 2 (1963): 362–65.
Baron, Eguinaire. *Institutionum civilium ab Justiniano Caesare editarum libri IV, bipartita commentario*. Pictavii: ex officina Marnefiorum fratrum, 1546.
Bartolus of Sassoferrato. *Commentaria in II^am^ Digesti Novi Partem*. Lyon: Excudebat Petrus Fradin, 1555.
Bartolus of Sassoferrato. *In I^am^ Digesti Veteri Partem Commentaria*. Lyon, 1544.
Bayle, Pierre. *Dictionnaire historique et critique*, vol. 1. Basel: Jean Louis Brandmuller, 1741.
Bellomo, Manlio. *The Common Legal Past of Europe, 1000–1800*. Washington, DC: The Catholic University of America Press, 1995.
Benöhr, Hans-Peter. *Das sogennante Synallagma in den Konsensualkontrakten des klassischen römischen Rechts*. Hamburg: Cram, De Gruyter, 1965.
Berger, Adolf. *Encyclopedic Dictionary of Roman Law*. Transactions of the American Philosophical Society. Philadelphia: American Philosophical Society, 1953.
Birocchi, Italo. *Causa e categoria generale del contratto: Un problema dogmatico nella cultura privatistica dell'età moderna*. Turin: Giappichelli Editore, 1997.

Black, Jane. *Absolutism in Renaissance Milan: Plenitude of Power under the Visconti and the Sforza*. Oxford: Oxford University Press, 2009.
Bower, Calvin. "The Modes of Boethius." *Journal of Musicology* 3, no. 3 (1984): 252–63.
Bracton. *De Legibus et Consuetudinibus Angliae*, vol. 2, edited by George Woodbine. New Haven, CT: Yale University Press, 1922.
Brown, John L. "The Methodus ad Facilem Historiarum Cognitionem of Jean Bodin: A Critical Study." PhD Diss. Washington, DC: The Catholic University of America Press, 1939.
Bryson, William. *Dictionary of Sigla and Abbreviations to and in Law Books before 1607*. Charlottesville, VA: University Press of Virginia, 1975.
Budé, Guillaume. *Annotationes in Quatuor et Viginti Pandectarum Libros*. Paris: Ab Iodoco Badio Ascensio Impressae, 1508.
Cabos, Alban. *Guy Du Faur de Pibrac: Un Magistrat Poète au XVIe Siècle, 1529–1584*. Paris: Édouard Champion, 1922.
Caesar, Julius. *Gallic War*. Translated by Cynthia Damon. Loeb Classical Library 72. Cambridge: Harvard University Press, 2025.
Calvinus, Johannes. *Lexicon Iuridicum*. Frankfurt: Impensis Johannis Marnii Haeredum, 1610.
Canning, Joseph. *Political Thought of Baldus de Ubaldis*. Cambridge: Cambridge University Press, 1987.
Chauviré, Roger. *Jean Bodin, auteur de la République*. Paris: Librairie Ancienne Honoré Champion, 1914.
Cicero. *De Finibus*. Translated by Horace Rackham. Loeb Classical Library 40. Cambridge: Harvard University Press, 1914.
Cicero. *De Inventione*. In *Cicero: In Twenty-Eight Volumes*, vol. II. *De Inventione*. Cambridge: Harvard University Press, 1968.
Cicero. *De Legibus*. Translated by Clinton Walker Keyes. Loeb Classical Library 213. Cambridge: Harvard University Press, 1928.
Cicero. *De Natura Deorum*. Translated by Horace Rackham. Loeb Classical Library 268. Cambridge: Harvard University Press, 1933.
Cicero. *De Officiis*. Translated by Walter Miller. Loeb Classical Library 30. Cambridge: Harvard University Press, 1913.
Cicero. *De Oratore* I–II. Translated by E. W. Sutton and Harris Rackham. Loeb Classical Library 348. Cambridge: Harvard University Press, 1948.
Cicero. *De Re Publica*. Translated by Clinton Walker Keyes. Loeb Classical Library 213. Cambridge: Harvard University Press, 1928.
Cicero. *Topica*. Translated by H. M. Hubbell. Loeb Classical Library 386. Cambridge: Harvard University Press, 1949.
Connan, François. *Commentariorum Iuris Civilis Libri X*. Basel: Apud N. Episcopium, 1562.
Cujas, Jacques. *Observationum et Emendationum Libri XVII*. Cologne: Apud Ioannem Gymnicum, 1578.
Decock, Wim. "Lessius and the Breakdown of the Scholastic Paradigm." *Journal of the History of Economic Thought* 31, no. 1 (2009): 57–75.
Decock, Wim. *Theologians and Contract Law: The Moral Transformation of the Ius Commune (ca.1500–1650)*. Leiden: Brill, 2013.
Defarrari, Roy, and M. Inviolata Barry. *A Lexicon of St. Thomas Aquinas Based on the* Summa Theologica *and Selected Passages of His Other Works*. Washington, DC: Catholic University of America, 1948.
Deloume. "Tableau des Professeurs de la Faculté de Droit de Toulouse." *Revue des Pyrénées et de la France Méridionale* III (1891): 124–28.
Derrer, Sebastian. *Iurisprudentia* I. Lyon, 1540.
Desan, Philippe. *Naissance de la méthode: Machiavel, La Ramée, Bodin, Montaigne, Descartes*. Paris: Nizet, 1987.
Despotopoulos, Constantin. "La notion de Synallagma chez Aristote." *Archives de philosophie du droit* 13 (1968): 115–27.
Donellus [Doneau], Hugues. *Commentarii de Jure Civili*. Lyon: Antonii Pillehotte, 1619.

Donellus [Doneau], Hugues. *Opera Omnia: Commentariorum de Iure Civili*, vol. 3. Lucca: Typis Joannis Riccomini, 1763.

Du Plessis, Paul J., and John W. Cairns, eds. *Reassessing Legal Humanism and Its Claims: Petere Fontes?* Edinburgh: Edinburgh University Press, 2016.

Ducos, Michèle. "'Le Tableau de droit universel' de Jean Bodin et la tradition romaine." *Bulletin de l'Association Guillaume Budé* 1 (1987): 49–61.

Fasolt, Constantine. *The Limits of History*. Chicago, IL: University of Chicago Press, 2004.

Feenstra, Robert. "La systématique du droit dans l'oeuvre de Grotius." In *La sistematica giuridica: Storia, teoria e problemi attuali*, edited by Luciana Buccellato. Rome: Istituto della Enciclopedia Italiana, 1991.

Ferenczy, Endre. *From the Patrician State to the Patricio-Plebeian State*. Translated by G. Dedinszky. Budapest: Akadémiai Kiadó, 1976.

Fiori, Roberto. "The Roman Conception of Contract." In *Obligations in Roman Law: Past, Present, and Future*, edited by Thomas McGinn. Ann Arbor, MI: University of Michigan Press, 2012.

Fournier, Marcel. *Histoire de la Science du Droit en France*, vol. 3. Paris: Librairie du Recueil Général des Lois et des Arrêts et du Journal du Palais, 1892.

Franklin, Julian. *Jean Bodin and the Sixteenth-Century Revolution in the Methodology of Law and History*. New York: Columbia University Press, 1963.

Freigius, Johann Thomas. *Partitiones Iuris Utriusque*. Basel: Ex Officina Sixti Henricpetri, 1571.

Gaius. *Institutes of Gaius*, edited by Francis de Zulueta. Oxford: Clarendon Press, 1953.

Garnsey, Peter. *Thinking About Property: From Antiquity to the Age of Revolution*. Cambridge: Cambridge University Press, 2009.

Gellius, Aulus. *The Attic Nights of Aulus Gellius*, vol. 3. Translated by John Rolfe. Loeb Classical Library 195. Cambridge: Harvard University Press, 1927.

Gentili, Alberico. *De Iuris Interpretibus Dialogi Sex*. London: Apud Johannem Wolfium, 1582.

Gerbier, Laurent. "Une méthode pour interpreter les histoires: Machiavel et Jean Bodin." *Revue de Métaphysique et de Morale* 2, *Méthode et interprétation à l'âge Classique* 2, no. 62 (2009): 151–66.

Giesey, Ralph. "Medieval Jurisprudence in Bodin's Concept of Sovereignty." In *Jean Bodin: Verhandlung der Internationalen Bodin Tagung in München*, edited by Horst Denzer. Munich: C.H. Beck, 1973.

Gilmore, Myron Piper. *Argument from Roman Law in Political Thought, 1200–1600*. Cambridge: Harvard University Press, 1941.

Girard, P. F. "La jeunesse de Cujas (Toulouse, 1522–1554)." *Nouvelle revue historique de droit* 40 (1916): 429–504.

Göckel, Rudolf. *Lexicon Philosophicum*. Frankfurt: Matthias Becker, 1613.

Gordley, James. "Equality in Exchange." *California Law Review* 69 (1981): 1587–656.

Gordley, James. "Ius Civile: The Roman Jurists." In *The Jurists: A Critical History*. Oxford: Oxford University Press, 2013.

Gordley, James. *The Philosophical Origins of Modern Contract Doctrine*. Oxford: Clarendon Press, 1991.

Gottely, Alexandra, Dario Mantovani, and Xavier Prévost, eds. *Jacques Cujas, la fabrique d'un grand jurist*. Paris: Collège de France, 2024.

Goudy, Henry. *Trichotomy in Roman Law*. Oxford: Clarendon Press, 1912.

Goyard-Fabre, Simone. "Commentaire philosophique de l'Exposé du Droit Universel." In Jean Bodin, *Exposé du droit universel: Juris universi distributio*. Translated by Lucien Jerphangnon. Edited by Simone Goyard-Fabre and René-Marie Rampelberg. Paris: Presses Universitaires de France, 1985.

Grégoire, Pierre. *Syntagma Iuris Universi*. Frankfurt-am-Main: Peter Fischer, 1599.

Grotius, Hugo. *De Iure Praedae Commentarius: Commentary on the Law of Prize and Booty*, vol. 1. Translated by Gwladys Williams and Walter Zeydel. Oxford: Clarendon Press, 1950.

Grotius, Hugo. *De Jure Belli ac Pacis Libri Tres*. Amsterdam: Iohannes Blaeu, 1646.

Grotius, Hugo. *Jurisprudence of Holland*. Translated by R. W. Lee. Oxford: Clarendon Press, 1926.

Hanson, Stephen, and Jeffrey Kopstein. *The Assault on the State: How the Global Attack on Modern Government Endangers Our Future*. Cambridge: Polity, 2024.
Hohfeld, Wesley Newcomb. "Some Fundamental Legal Conceptions as Applied in Judicial Reasoning." *Yale Law Journal* 23, no. 1 (1913): 16–59.
Hotman, François. *Francogallia*. Translated by J. H. M. Salmon, edited by Ralph Giesey. Cambridge: Cambridge University Press, 1972.
Hotman, François. *Partitiones Iuris Civilis Elementariae*. Basel: Apud Nicolaum Episcopium Iuniorem, 1561.
Kelley, Donald. "Civil Science in the Renaissance: Jurisprudence in the French Manner." *History of European Ideas* 2 (1981): 261–76.
Kelley, Donald. "De Origine Feudorum: The Beginnings of an Historical Problem." *Speculum: A Journal of Mediaeval Studies* 39, no. 2 (1964): 207–28.
Kelley, Donald. *Foundations of Modern Historical Scholarship: Language, Law, and History in the French Renaissance*. New York: Columbia University Press, 1970.
Kelley, Donald. "Gaius Noster: Substructures of Western Social Thought." *American Historical Review* 84, no. 3 (1979): 619–48.
Kelley, Donald. "The Rise of Legal History in the Renaissance." *History and Theory* 9, no. 2 (1970): 174–94.
Kelsen, Hans. "What Is a Legal Act?" *American Journal of Jurisprudence* 29, no. 1 (1984): 199–212.
Kepler, Johannes. *The Harmony of the World*. Translated by E. J. Aiton, A. M. Duncan, and J. V. Field. Philadelphia: American Philosophical Society, 1997.
Kim, Keechang. "L'étranger chez Jean Bodin." *Revue historique de droit français et étranger* 76, no. 1 (1998): 75–92.
Kim, Marie Seong-Hak. "Civil Law and Civil War: Michel de l'Hôpital and the Ideals of Legal Unification in Sixteenth-Century France." *Law and History Review* 28, no. 3 (2010): 791–826.
Kuhn, Thomas. *The Structure of Scientific Revolution*. Chicago, IL: University of Chicago Press, 1962.
Kuntz, Marion Daniels. "Harmony and the Heptaplomeres of Jean Bodin." *Journal of the History of Philosophy* 12, no. 1 (1974): 31–41.
Kuttner, Stephan. "Notes on the Presentation of Text and Apparatus in Editing Works of the Decretists and Decretalists." *Traditio* 15 (1959): 452–64.
Latournerie, Roger. "L'humanisme juridique et l'acte de volonté." *Revue du droit public et de la science politique en France et à l'étranger* 64 (1948).
Lee, Daniel. "Citizenship, Subjection, and the Civil Law: Jean Bodin on Roman Citizenship and the Theory of Consensual Subjection." In *Citizenship and Empire in Europe 200–1900: The Antonine Constitution after 1800 Years*, edited by Clifford Ando. Stuttgart: Franz Steiner Verlag, 2016.
Lee, Daniel. "Office Is a Thing Borrowed: Jean Bodin on Offices and Seigneurial Government." *Political Theory* 41, no. 3 (2013): 409–40.
Lee, Daniel. *Popular Sovereignty in Early Modern Constitutional Thought*. Oxford: Oxford University Press, 2016.
Lee, Daniel. *The Right of Sovereignty: Jean Bodin on the Sovereign State and the Law of Nations*. Oxford: Oxford University Press, 2021.
Lesaffer, Randall. *European Legal History: A Cultural and Political Perspective*. Cambridge: Cambridge University Press, 2009.
Levack, Brian. *The Civil Lawyers in England, 1603–1641: A Political Study*. Oxford: Clarendon Press, 1973.
Livy. *History of Rome, Books VIII–X*, vol. 4, edited by Benjamin Foster. Loeb Classical Library 191. Cambridge: Harvard University Press, 1926.
Lloyd, Howell. *Jean Bodin, This Pre-eminent Man of France: An Intellectual Biography*. Oxford: Oxford University Press, 2017.
Long, Alex. "Seneca on Human Rights in *De Beneficiis* 3." *Apeiron* 54, no. 2 (2021): 189–201.
Loughlin, Martin. *Foundations of Public Law*. Oxford: Oxford University Press, 2010.

Maclean, Ian. *Interpretation and Meaning in the Renaissance: The Case of Law.* Cambridge: Cambridge University Press, 1992.

MacPhail, Eric. "Jean Bodin's First Reading of Machiavelli." *Jus Cogens* 7, no. 1 (2025): 131–44.

Maffei, Domenico. *Gli inizi dell'umanesimo giuridico.* Milan: Giuffré, 1956.

Maffi, Alberto, and Joe Jackson. "Sparta." In *Oxford International Encyclopedia of Legal History,* edited by Stanley Katz. Oxford: Oxford University Press, 2009.

Maitland, Frederic. *The Collected Papers of Frederic William Maitland,* edited by Herbert Fisher. 3 vols. Cambridge: Cambridge University Press, 1911.

McRae, Kenneth. "Ramist Tendencies in the Thought of Jean Bodin." *Journal of the History of Ideas* 16, no. 1/4 (1955): 306–23.

Ménage, Gilles. *Vitae Petri Aerodii, quaesitoris andegavensis, et Guillelmi Menagii, advocati regii andegavensis.* Paris: Apud Christophorum Journel, 1675.

Merille, E. *Dissertatio in libros tres ex Cujacio* in *Cujacii Opera Omnia,* vol. 3, edited by C. J. Fabroto. Naples, 1758.

Mesnard, Pierre. "Introduction a la méthode de l'histoire de Jean Bodin." *Bibliothèque d'Humanisme et Renaissance* 12, no. 3 (1950): 318–23.

Mesnard, Pierre. "Jean Bodin à Toulouse." *Bibliothèque d'Humanisme et Renaissance* 12 (1950): 31–59.

Mesnard, Pierre. "La Place de Cujas dans la querelle de l'humanisme juridique." *Revue historique de droit français et étranger* 27 (1950): 521–37.

Mesnard, Pierre, ed. *Oeuvres philosophiques de Jean Bodin.* Paris: Presses Universitaires de France, 1951.

Mesnard, Pierre. "Un rival heureux de Cujas et de Bodin: Étienne Forcadel." *Zeitschrift der Savigny-Stiftung für Rechtsgeschichte: Romantische Abteilung* 67 (1950): 440–58.

Metzger, Ernest, ed. *A Companion to Justinian's Institutes.* Ithaca, NY: Cornell University Press, 1998.

Moreau-Reibel, Jean. *Jean Bodin et le droit public comparé dans ses rapports avec la philosophie de l'histoire.* Paris: Librairie Philosophique J. Vrin, 1933.

Nicholas, Barry. *An Introduction to Roman Law.* Oxford: Clarendon Press, 1962.

Odofredus. *Lectura Super Digesto Veteri.* Lyon, 1550.

Ong, Walter. *Ramus, Method, and the Decay of Dialogue: From the Art of Discourse to the Art of Reason.* Chicago, IL: University of Chicago Press, 2004.

Palazzini Finetti, L. *Storia della ricercar delle interpolazione nel corpus iuris giustinianeo.* Milan: Giuffrè, 1953.

Pedrazza Gorlero, Cecilia. *La Iuris Universi Distributio di Jean Bodin.* Rovereto, Italy: Edizioni Osiride, 1999.

Pennington, Kenneth. "The Big Bang: Roman Law in the Early Twelfth Century." *Rivista internazionale di diritto commune* 18 (2007): 43–70.

Pennington, Kenneth. *The Prince and the Law, 1200–1600: Sovereignty and Rights in the Western Legal Tradition.* Berkeley: University of California Press, 1993.

Pennington, Kenneth. "Roman and Secular Law." In *Medieval Latin: An Introduction and Bibliographical Guide,* edited by F. A. C. Mantello and A. G. Rigg. Washington, DC: Catholic University of America, 1996.

Pennington, Kenneth, Charles Donahue, Jr., Atria Larson, and Brandon Parlopiano. *Bio-Bibliographical Guide to Medieval and Early Modern Jurists.* Online: Harvard University and the Ames Foundation, 2011–17.

Piano Mortari, V. "La scienza del diritto in François Baudouin." *Diritto, logica, metodo nel secolo XVI* (1978): 407–28.

Piano Mortari, V. "La sistematica come ideale umanistico dell'opera di Francesco Connano." In *La storia del diritto nel quandro della scienza storiche.* Florence: L.S. Olschki, 1966.

Plato. *Euthyphro, Apology, Crito, Phaedo, Phaedrus.* Translated by Harold North Fowler. Loeb Classical Library 36. Cambridge: Harvard University Press, 1914.

Plato. *Timaeus, Critias, Cleitophon, Menexenus, Epistles.* Translated by R. G. Bury. Loeb Classical Library 234. Cambridge: Harvard University Press, 1929.

Pothier, Robert Joseph. *A Treatise on the Law of Obligations, or Contracts*, vol. 1. Translated by William David Evans. London: A. Strahan, 1806.

Powell, J. G. F. "Cicero's Style." In *The Cambridge Companion to Cicero*, edited by Catherine Steel. Cambridge: Cambridge University Press, 2013.

Prévost, Xavier. "Jacques Cujas (1522–1590)." In *Great Christian Jurists in French History*, edited by Olivier Descamps and Rafael Domingo. Cambridge: Cambridge University Press, 2019.

Prümmer, Dominic. *Handbook of Moral Theology*. Translated by Gerald Shelton. New York: P.J. Kenedy and Sons, 1957.

Pufendorf, Samuel. *De Jure Naturae et Gentium Libro Octo*. Amsterdam: Apud Joannem Wolters, 1698.

Quaglioni, Diego. *À une déesse inconnue: La conception pré-moderne de la justice*. Translated by Marie-Dominique Couzinet. Paris: Éditions de la Sorbonne, 2019.

Quaglioni, Diego. "L'Éducation du juriste face au pouvoir: la 'methodus' de Matteo Gribaldi Mofa." In *Science politique et droit publique dans les facultés européennes, XIIIe–XVIIIe siècles*, edited by J. Krynen and Michael Stolleis. Frankfurt am Main: Klostermann, 2007.

Quaglioni, Diego. "Una fonte del Bodin: André Tiraqueau (1488–1558), giureconsulto: Appunti su *De Republica* III, 8." *Il Pensiero Politico* 14 (1981): 113–27.

Quintilian. *The Orator's Education: Institutio Oratoria*, vol. 3. Translated by Donald A. Russell. Loeb Classical Library 126. Cambridge: Harvard University Press, 2001.

Ribeiro de Barros, Alberto. "Bodin et la Projet d'Une Science du Droit: La *Juris Universi Distributio*." *Nouvelle Revue du XVIe Siècle* 21, no. 2 (2003): 57–70.

Riccobono, S., J. Baviera, and C. Ferrini, eds. *Fontes Iuris Romani Antejustiniani, in usum scholarum*. Florence: Apud G. Barbera, 1909.

Riley, Patrick. *Leibniz's Universal Jurisprudence: Justice as the Charity of the Wise*. Cambridge, MA: Harvard University Press, 1996.

Rolker, Christoph. "The Two Laws and the Three Sexes: Ambiguous Bodies in Canon Law and Roman Law (12th to 16th Centuries)." *Zeitschrift der Savigny-Stiftung für Rechtsgeschichte: Kanonistische Abteilung* 100 (2014): 178–222.

Rose, Paul Lawrence. *Bodin and the Great God of Nature: The Moral and Religious Universe of a Judaiser*. Geneva: Droz, 1980.

Rossi, Guido. "Deconstructing *Iurisdictio*: The Adventures of a Legal Category in the Hands of the Humanist Jurists." In *Reassessing Legal Humanism and Its Claims: Petere Fontes?*, edited by Paul J. du Plessis and John W. Cairns. Edinburgh: Edinburgh University Press, 2016.

Rousseau, Jean-Jacques. *The Basic Political Writings*. Translated and edited by Donald Cress. Indianapolis: Hackett, 2012.

Ryan, Magnus. "Bartolus of Sassoferrato and the Free Cities." *Transactions of the Royal Historical Society*. Sixth Series 10 (2000): 65–89.

Santoro, Raimondo. "Il contratto nel pensiero di Labeone." *Annali del Seminario Giuridico dell'Università di Palermo* 37 (1983): 5–304.

Schmitt, Carl. *Political Theology: Four Chapters on the Concept of Sovereignty*. Translated by George Schwab. Chicago, IL: University of Chicago Press, 1985.

Schulz, Fritz. *History of Roman Legal Science*. Oxford: Oxford University Press, 1953.

Scott, Alexander. "*Tractatus de Controversis Jacobi Cujacii Sententiis et Singularibus Contra J. Bodinum*." In Dominicus Albanensis. *Promptuarium Universorum Operum Jacobi Cujacii*, vol. 2. Naples, 1763.

Seneca. *Moral Essays* III: *De Beneficiis*. Translated by John Basore. Loeb Classical Library 310. Cambridge: Harvard University Press, 1935.

Skinner, Quentin. *Forensic Shakespeare*. Oxford: Oxford University Press, 2014.

Skinner, Quentin. *The Foundations of Modern Political Thought*, vol. 1. *The Renaissance*. Cambridge: Cambridge University Press, 1978.

Smith, David Baird. "Roman Law and Political Theory." *Scottish Historical Review* 22 (1925): 249–77.

Smith, T. B. "*Pollicitatio*—Promise and Offer: Stair v. Grotius." *Acta Juridica* 41 (1958): 141–52.

Sourvinou-Inwood, Christiane. "Themis." In *Oxford Classical Dictionary*, 4th ed., edited by Simon Hornblower, Antony Spawforth, and Esther Eidinow. Oxford: Oxford University Press, 2012.
Spiegel, Jacobus. *Lexicon Iuris Civilis*. Lyon: Apud Sebastianum Gryphium, 1548.
Spiegel, Jacobus. *Lexicon Iuris Civilis*. Basel: Apud Ioan. Heruagium, 1554.
Stacey, Peter. *The State in Machiavelli*. Cambridge: Cambridge University Press, 2025.
Stein, Peter. *Roman Law in European History*. Cambridge: Cambridge University Press, 1999.
Stevens, Linton. "The Contribution of French Jurists to the Humanism of the Renaissance." *Studies in the Renaissance* 1 (1954): 92–105.
Stintzing, Roderich von. *Geschichte der Deutschen Rechtswissenschaft*. Vol. 1. Munich: Drud und Berlag von R. Didenbourg, 1880.
Thomas, J. A. C. *A Textbook of Roman Law*. Amsterdam: North Holland, 1976.
Tierney, Brian. *Liberty and Law: The Idea of Permissive Natural Law, 1100–1800*. Washington, DC: The Catholic University of America Press, 2014.
Tierney, Brian. "The Prince Is Not Bound By The Law: Accursius and the Origins of the Modern State." *Comparative Studies in Society and History* 5 (1963): 378–400.
Tolomei, Claudio. *De Corruptis Verbis Iuris Civilis Dialogus*. Siena: Simone Nardi, 1517.
Tunberg, Terence. "Humanistic Latin." In *Medieval Latin: An Introduction and Bibliographical Guide*, edited by F. A. C. Mantello and A. G. Rigg. Washington, DC: Catholic University of America, 1996.
Van Orden, Kate. *Music, Discipline, and Arms in Early Modern France*. Chicago, IL: The University of Chicago Press, 2005.
Vasoli, Cesare. *Armonia e giustizia: studi sulle idee filosofiche di Jean Bodin*. Florence: L.S. Olschki, 2008.
Viard, Paul-Émile. *André Alciato, 1492–1550*. Paris: Société anonyme du Recueil Sirey, 1926.
Vile, M. J. C. *Constitutionalism and the Separation of Powers*. Oxford: Oxford University Press, 1967.
Villey, Michel. "La Justice Harmonique selon Bodin." In *Verhandlungen der Internationalen Bodin Tagung in München*, edited by Horst Denzer. Munich: Verlag C.H. Beck, 1973.
Von Savigny, Friedrich Karl. *Das Recht des Besitzes: Eine Civilistische Abhandlung*. Vienna: Druck und Verlag von Carl Gerolds Sohn, 1865.
Warren, Christopher. "Gentili, the Poets, and the Laws of War." In *The Roman Foundations of the Law of Nations: Alberico Gentili and the Justice of Empire*, edited by Benedict Kingsbury and Benjamin Straumann. Oxford: Oxford University Press, 2010.
Watson, Alan. "The Evolution of Law: The Roman System of Contracts." *Law and History Review* 2, no. 1 (1984): 1–20.
Winkel, Laurens. "Rights II." In *Cambridge Companion to Hugo Grotius*, edited by Randall Lesaffer and Janne Nijman. Cambridge: Cambridge University Press, 2021.
Woolf, C. N. S. *Bartolus of Sassoferrato: His Position in the History of Medieval Political Thought*. Cambridge: Cambridge University Press, 1913.
Xenophon. *Cyropaedia*, vol. 1. Translated by Walter Miller. Loeb Classical Library 51. Cambridge: Harvard University Press, 1914.
Zarlino, Gioseffo. *Le Istitvtioni Harmoniche*. Venice, 1558.
Zimmermann, Reinhard. *The Law of Obligations: Roman Foundations of the Civilian Tradition*. Oxford: Clarendon Press, 1996.

Index

For the benefit of digital users, indexed terms that span two pages (e.g., 52–53) may, on occasion, appear on only one of those pages.

Figures are indicated by an italic *f* following the page number.

The manufacturer's authorised representative in the EU for product safety is Oxford University Press España S.A. of el Parque Empresarial San Fernando de Henares, Avenida de Castilla, 2 – 28830 Madrid (www.oup.es/en or product.safety@oup.com). OUP España S.A. also acts as importer into Spain of products made by the manufacturer.

www.ingramcontent.com/pod-product-compliance
Ingram Content Group UK Ltd.
Pitfield, Milton Keynes, MK11 3LW, UK
UKHW021137160926
475595UK00025B/194/J

9780198810483